A Guide to Hiking in Israel

with

Forty selected one-day Hikes

Joel Roskin

The Jerusalem Post

Safety precautions are a necessary concern regarding all outdoor activi- ties. No guidebook can alert you to every possible danger. Nor can a guidebook aim to adapt itself to the individual limitations of the reader. The routes described in this book are not representations that any particular hike is safe for you or your party. When you engage in an outdoor activity, you assume responsibility for your own safety. All of the outings in this book require the appropriate supply of water. You must leave the details of your route with at least two people, either a friend or an official. Awareness of particular hazards will be required due to changing topographical and/or seasonal factors. Keeping informed on current conditions and exercising common sense are the keys to a safe, enjoyable trip.

ISBN: 965-356-018-2

© Copyright 1991
Joel Roskin

Photographs: Joel Roskin,
except photographs on pages 164 and 181, taken by Orit Pasternak
Cover photograph: Richard Nowitz
Maps/cartoons: Ziv Fuchs
Editing: Shira Twersky-Cassel
Design and layout: Judith Fattal/Yael Tal
Cover design: Yael Tal

Printed in Israel 1991

I am deeply indebted to my parents, Dr. Michael and Lessa Roskin who taught me to appreciate nature and brought me to our home, Israel. Their warm support and assistance constantly accompanied all the stages of creation and work on this book. Special thanks go to Shira Twersky-Cassel, not only for her conscientious editing but also for her patience and helpful comments. I would like to acknowledge the cooperation of Ziv Fuchs who drew the fine maps and cartoons which are an invaluable addition to the book. I also note with appreciation the constructive comments of Yael Chaver, editor of *Land and Nature*, whose door at the SPNI offices was always open to me. Last but not least, this book could not have taken shape without the companionship of all my friends who accompanied me and shared my pace throughout all the trips and trails.

Joel Roskin
Jerusalem, 1991

Table of Contents

Judea

Judean Desert

Eilat Mountains

Foreword

This guidebook is intended for those who understand that seeing Israel on foot is the best way to enjoy getting to know the country.

Witnessing a sudden flash flood of torrential rain become a hundred meter waterfall flowing into a parched abyss; gazing out at the Galilee vista stretching from the Mediterranean Sea to Lake Kinneret; or bathing in a pool formed by a waterfall, after a challenging trek — all these are both exhilarating and special experiences.

There are many ways to tour our country and its natural treasures — by bus, car, jeep, plane, camel or donkey. A Guide to Hiking in Israel offers you another option.

Walking provides the leisure to experience the sights and sounds at your own pace. Tackling a tough ascent, thousands of years old, leaves you with the singular satisfaction of a goal achieved. Listening to the 'sounds of silence' in the desert or on a mountain top, is an ideal means of communing with nature, a sorely lacking element in the pressured and hectic daily city life.

Hiking in Israel is incomparable — we invite you to experience it.

Gideon Patt
Minister of Tourism
State of Israel

March 1991

Introduction

Hiking in Israel

Hiking in Israel is unique. The changing landscapes, seasons, and views of the local flora and fauna can be viewed in a global context. However, the rewards of walking the length and breadth of the 'promised land' are all this and more.

Along the mountains and deserts of Israel, wherever you walk, a rich tableau of human history has preceded you. A considerable proportion of Israel's water sources and landscape have been shaped and reshaped by the different peoples and cultures that lived in, ruled and trampled over this land. On many sites, bits of ancient pottery are scattered about.

In Judea, for example, most of the hills are terraced, a supreme example of land utilization and preservation. In the desert the bare hills are lined with goat and sheep paths. When the Children of Israel first scouted out the Land of Israel they described it as a, 'Land of Milk and Honey.' However, during the 19th century, travelers wrote of what was then Palestine as a poverty stricken and barren land. Compare these accounts to the landscapes you see today when you travel through Israel.

On these hikes you enjoy the natural elements against a backdrop of rich and varied history of each region. You are offered a comprehensive picture which usually the English-speaker in Israel does not enjoy since most English language guidebooks concentrate on the religious-historical background of Israel.

Here, the three continents of the old world meet — Asia, Africa and Europe. Not only man, expanding territorial boundaries, has been here and left his mark. Plant and animal life as well have always been alternatively extending and limiting their habitat throughout Israel. Modern Israel's flora and fauna are a blend of many regions, from the savannahs of Africa to the reaches of Asia. The great Syrian-African rift runs from the Red Sea, through the Dead Sea region and to Lake Kinneret, the Hula Valley and further north. This area has been the geographical doorway for many species on the move north or south. In addition, the many nationalities which came to settle and control the Land of Israel, each in turn uprooted native species and introduced various plants and animals which were native to their home regions; several are common today and others are now extinct.

Twice a year, huge bird migrations traverse our skies — towards Africa in the fall and returning to Europe in the spring. Israel is the land-bridge east of the Mediterranean Sea.

This narrow strip of land is blessed with a disproportionate blend of unique and differing geographical regions. Often the only element which these regions have in common is the short distance between them. Indeed, you can travel the length of Israel in *one day's time* and the width in a lot less.

Human diversity has had a dominating influence here. Jerusalem has been the focal point of Judaism for many thousands of years, as well as the birthplace of Christianity and the third holiest Moslem city. Smaller ethnic groups have also settled or been settled here, such as the Druze, Circassians, Samarians, Bedouins, and others.

Hiking is a relatively new sport and leisure activity. It seems mainly to be a product of the urbanization and industrialization of western society. People tiring of city noise and grime yearn for the outdoors and a return to their roots. After the first modern wave of Jewish settlements in the Land of Israel during the late 19th century, several teachers began to take their classes on field excursions. In the years before the State was established, small groups explored the vast areas reaching Transjordan. Youth groups initiated the tradition of long endurance hikes, still current today, to sites such as Masada. However, at that time the main emphasis was on exploration and the links to the revitalized Jewish homeland being rebuilt. Nature preservation per se was not the prevailing goal.

The past twenty years have witnessed a positive change in the attitude of all the communities of Israel to nature and nature preservation. Today, hiking in Israel is a subject included in the curriculum of Israel's public school system.

The Society for the Protection of Nature in Israel (SPNI) was officially formed in 1953. Today, it conducts over twenty field study centers (FSC) and maintains many other wonderful projects. Hundreds of thousands of men, women and children of all ages have enjoyed SPNI hikes. They have succeeded in awakening public and private awareness to nature preservation, and they serve as loyal watchdogs of planned and mis-planned development. A division of the SPNI is responsible for trail-marking. Currently, there is an 'Israel trail' project stretching from Mount Hermon in the north to Eilat in the south, which will cover 1000 km. of territory. Thanks to the SPNI, influenced by the current global efforts to preserve the very fragile and wonderful environment which we inhabit, nature preservation awareness and outdoor related activities are on the rise throughout Israel.

Before you go . . .

To maximize your trip's success, I wish to stress several important points. Please take the time to read the following before hitting the trail.

Before choosing a suitable route for your party, read all the information, both the area introduction — most important being the 'Hiking in . . . .' section — and the specific hike outline. It is also recommended to read through the hike description carefully so that you will not be caught unprepared in the middle of the hike.

The 'hiking time' listed is an estimate. Each person and party move at a different pace. 'Length of hike' does not always correlate with the difficulty ('Suitable for'). When the hike is suitable for 'All' this means that the route poses no specific hardship, such as an especially long distance, high ascents, steep declines or the necessity to clamber up ropes. 'Experienced hikers' will know how to measure themselves against the terrain. Families must pay close attention to 'Length of hike,' taking into account the ages of children participating and their physical stamina.

Before starting off, make sure that you understand the exact route 'Starting & ending point.' If the hike is a loop trip you will finish in the vicinity of your starting point. Naturally you can decide to hike a loop trip in the opposite direction.

Regarding 'one-way' routes, if you plan to leave your car at the starting point, I suggest that you leave a second vehicle parked at the ending point. Otherwise take into account that you will either have to hitchhike, catch a bus, or return on foot to the starting point. If you use the latter alternative, don't forget to double the length of the hike and estimated hiking time. In general, all the one-way hikes include access by public transportation to locations near the starting and ending points, although you may have to walk a distance on the road to close the gap.

Some of the loop trips which are inaccessible to public transportation are geared for hikers with a vehicle. This is especially applicable in the Golan Heights where buses do not run as often as in the center of the country.

Trails are not always clearly marked and since, like many other things in Israel, routes are undergoing constant change, up to date and official trail maps are a necessity for all hikes. The best maps are the marked hiking trail maps with a 1:50,000 scale which are in Hebrew. There are marked hiking trail maps for nearly all hikes, and these are indicated. Other maps available are the 1:50,000 scale topographical maps. There are several English language 1:100,000 scale maps.

It is best to hike during the recommended 'Preferred season.' Remember that in the summer it is hot and dry everywhere. During the rainy season, between October and April, there can be flashfloods and some trails are very slippery. To avoid problems and to enjoy your hike to the maximum don't forget the 'Special preparation.'

Nature Preservation

Israel is a very small country which holds dear every square meter of its land. Many of the hikes in this book enter nature reserves which require even more considera- tion on the part of hikers. Trails strewn with garbage will infringe both on your own enjoyment and the enjoyment of others, and will eventually harm the flora and fauna as well.

Here are several guidelines:

1. Refrain from littering; burying litter does not solve the problem since wild animals will dig it up and scatter it about. Carry extra plastic bags and whatever you bring in, take out.
2. Cover human excrement and burn soiled toilet paper.
3. Leave loud instruments at home.
4. Disturbing and feeding wild animals can be harmful for both parties.
5. Fires and camping are prohibited within the nature reserves.
6. Several hikes pass habitats of locals who have value systems and customs different from your own. Don't fiddle with sites or articles in that vicinity. Behave with respect and you will be treated with respect.
7. Dress modestly, wearing long slacks and head coverings when visiting religious sites belonging to any religion.
8. When trails traverse orchards and agricultural fields do not pick the produce if you don't wish to be picked on in turn.

Trails

The trail mark in Israel is the 'sandwich'; a painted mark consisting of two white lines about 20 cm. long with a colored line — red, blue, black and green — of the same length sandwiched in between them. Each color signifies a specific trail. There is no connection between color and difficulty of the trail. These trailmarks are painted on signs, stones, posts, barrels and various structures, as well as on paved roads such as at a trailhead. Sometimes trailheads have specific signs.

Many of the routes in this book follow these trailmarks, which can be found on trails, dirt roads, and gravel roads. When the trail is unclear, there is usually eye contact with the next trail mark. On clear trails and dirt roads, trailmarks appear less often but that should not cause you any concern. The marked hiking trail maps, which are in Hebrew, cover many parts of the country and have been produced on the basis of these marked trails at a scale of 1:50,000.

Some of the starting and ending points of hikes described in this book follow paved roads. Some of the typography covers unmarked trails and dirt roads and occasionally there is no trail at all. In this case, follow the book's instructions and route map. Certain landmarks are denoted by numbers within the text, in coordination with the specific hike maps.

Remember, exact route details cannot appear on the maps. If for some reason, you feel you have departed from the prescribed route, calmly retrace your steps until you recognize your previous surroundings.

Clothing and Equipment

The correct shoes are extremely important for all hiking. Sandals should not be worn. Sturdy hiking boots are best, but good gym shoes will usually do. The 'Paladi'im' kind of denim and rubberized hiking boots are excellent, not expensive and can be purchased at many stores in Israel. Do not go hiking in a 'new' pair of shoes, no matter how suited to hiking they eventually may be. Break in all shoes first!

The hot summer sun can burn your skin very quickly and in desert areas can cause sunstroke. No one is immune. A light weight hat which is suitable for sun protection is a must. The evenings are usually cool in all of the hilly regions of Israel even in summer, so it is a good idea to take a light weight, long sleeved sweater or jacket and a pair of slacks for all hikes. During the day, short sleeves and shorts will make hiking easier. In winter it is best to dress in warm, light layers which can be peeled off as the sun heats up during the day and then rewrapped as the day grows cool. During rainy months, one should have a change of clothing, especially socks.

To be adequately prepared, the following should be included in your backpack on every hike: food which does not easily spoil, pocket knife, compass, suntan cream, flashlight, matches in waterproof container, first aid kit, guidebook, toilet paper, phone tokens, maps, and plastic garbage bags. Don't forget the 'Special preparation' noted in each hike. Sufficient water is a must. It is also suggested that you take along: binoculars, compass, small gas stove and accessories, several books about the area which are not too heavy in weight, water purification tablets and mosquito repellent.

Water

The importance of this vital issue cannot be over-exaggerated. There is usually no drinking water along the routes. Any available water sources are unreliable, being dependent on conditions of drought or seasonal change and many may be partially contaminated. Drinking fresh spring water can be harmful but any doubt can be dispelled by utilization of water purification tablets.

Before starting out on any hike, drink a substantial amount of water. The quantity suitable for each hike is noted in the 'Hiking in. . .' section of each specific region. Calculate your water cache with water to spare at the conclusion of the hike.

The sun can cause dehydration suddenly and without warning. Take rest breaks in shady spots. Drink constantly, even when you do not feel thirsty. Make sure that all of your party does the same.

Carbonated drinks are not recommended.

Dangers — Precautions

The following should be taken into account before starting out on your hike:
1. The strong sun can be hazardous, wear a hat and use suntan cream. When resting, find a place in the shade.
2. Take care to drink plenty of water (from your own supply). *Drinking natural sources of water is risky.*
3. Look out for scorpions and snakes before sitting down, putting on your shoes in the morning or poking hands into dark and unseen places.
4. Don't befriend wild animals. You may misunderstand each other.
5. There are leopards living in the desert; although they have never attacked any humans in Israel yet. If you meet one, retreat posthaste.
6. If darkness falls on the trail, it is best to wait where you are until morning.
7. If you feel you are lost: at night stay put and light a fire; if it is day, retrace your steps to an area that you recognize.
8. Some of the hikes pass close to live minefields. The minefields are fenced-in and are posted with small yellow signs with black writing on the barbed wire fences. You will also see small red triangles on the poles.
9. Remnants of Israel's heavy military activity are common in many places. Therefore, don't touch any unfamiliar item. Keep yourself and curious children strictly away.
10. Do not enter a military zone without official permit.
11. Hiking alone is risky and not recommended.
12. Lock your car and do not leave valuables inside.
13. Walk alongside paved roads, off the pavement and against the direction of traffic.
14. Don't hike in foggy conditions.
15. Check trails and rocks for slippery conditions.
16. On damp days, try to stay dry.
17. Beware of flashfloods. On rainy days abstain from hiking in riverbeds.
18. In the Judean Desert, the large wadis collect their flashflood water from the distant hills. Clear desert skies do not mean that further up the wadi the sun is shining. Even on sunny days, clarify the general weather forecast.

Most important, before going on any hike, check into a field study center to learn up-to-date news about the area. Leave your names, the number of members in your party, particular medical instructions for individuals of your party, if any, and your chosen route with the field study center. Don't forget to also leave your route with someone you know personally, as well as on the windshield of your car.

Chronological Table — Regional

B.C.E.

Paleolithic (Old stone age)	250,000-10000
Mesolithic (Middle stone age)	10,000-7500
Neolithic (New stone age)	7500-4000
Chalcolithic	4000-3150
Early Bronze	3150-2200
Middle Bronze	2200-1500
Late Bronze	1500-1200
Iron Age (Israelite)	1200-587
Persian	587-332
Hellenistic	332-152
Hasmonean Kingdom	152-37
Early Roman I	37-70 (C.E.)

C.E.

Roman II	70-180
Late Roman III	180-324
Byzantine	324-640
Early Arab	640-1099
Crusader	1099-1291
Mameluke	1291-1517
Turkish	1517-1917
British	1917-1948
Israeli	1948

Glossary

A number of Hebrew words and terms appear frequently throughout this book. These describe a site by its original name.

Hebrew/Arabic	English
beit, bet	house
berekhat	pool of water of . . .
emek, bika'a	valley
en, enot	spring, springs
gesher	bridge
giva, givat	hill, hill of
har	mountain
hirbeh, hirbet	ruined building, settlement
kefar	village
kibbutz	cooperative settlement
ma'ale	ascent, steep trail/way that ascends
mapal	fall, waterfall
mitzpe	viewpoint, look out point
moshav	agricultural (part co-op) settlement
mtzad	fort
nahal	dry riverbed, stream
tel	artificial hill formed of ruins from many periods
tzuk, tzukei	cliff, cliffs
wadi	dry riverbed

Map Key

Trail of specific hike	▬ ▬ ▬ ▬ ▬ ▬ ▬ ▬ ▬ ▬ ▬
Marked trail	▬ - ▬ - ▬ - ▬ - ▬ - ▬
Trail	....
Dirt road	≡≡≡≡≡≡≡≡≡≡≡≡≡≡≡
Unpaved road	══════════════
Secondary road	▬▬ ▭ ▬▬ ▭ ▬▬
Main road	▬▬▬▬▬▬▬▬▬
Dual lane road (highway)	▰▰▰▰▰▰▰▰▰
Railway	───────────
Spot height in meters, trig. point	.⁵⁶⁹ △¹⁶⁹
North pointer	←─z──▶
Border	·+ + + + + + + + +
Minefield	𝔚
Cliffs	⊓⊓⊓⊓⊓⊓⊓⊓⊓⊓⊓
Steep slope	⊓⊓⊓⊓⊓⊓⊓⊓⊓⊓
Wadi (dry riverbed)	~~~~~~~~~~~
Perennial stream	≈~~~~~~~~~
Water cistern	o
Spring, (water) fall	· I
Ruins (hirbeh)	⊛
Buildings	·:
Cave	∩
Observation point	⏚
Pool	▢
Bridge	⋉
Kilometer stone	▬▬▬▬ ⸙¹⁹ ▬▬▬▬
Cable car wire	o─────────o

Golan

The Golan Heights are part of a considerably larger range — 35,000 square km. — of volcanic basalt fields which stretch eastward into the Druze mountains of Syria; 11,200 km. of this range is known as the Bashan and the western region of the Bashan is the Golan. The Hebrew word 'golah' means exile and is related to the tribe of Menashe's shelter city 'Golan in Bashan' (Dt. 4:43) where accidental or unintentional murderers were permitted to exile themselves in order to hide from the victim's avenging relatives. Similarly, Golan in Arabic means 'area of wandering.' During the Second Temple period, the name Gaulanitis referred to the western Bashan.

1070 sq. km. of the Golan Heights has been under Israel's jurisdiction since 1967 when it was captured during the last two days of the Six Day War. The Golan rises high above the Syrian-African rift where there are many Jewish settlements. Control of the Golan ensures the security of these settlements along Lake Kinneret and the Hula Valley. The Hermon mountain range, which is a separate geographic entity, rises high above the Golan to the north and was also captured in 1967. Only 7% of the Hermon today is under Israeli control. Unlike the Golan, the Hermon consists of limestone rather than volcanic residue.

Geography

The Golan's geographical borders are quite distinct. Nahal Sa'ar cuts between the basalt of the Golan and the limestone of the Hermon range to the north, creating an impressive canyon. To the west is the Syrian-African rift which contains the Hula Valley, the Jordan River Canyon and the Lake Kinneret Valley.

To the south runs the Yarmuk River, and south of this rises the Gilead which is located within the boundaries of the monarchy of Jordan. The eastern border of the Golan is less distinct, the basalt plateau continuing eastward. The Rukad River which begins under the southern slopes of the Hermon arcs eastward, heads south and merges into the Yarmuk River at the site of a spectacular canyon. The current Israel-Syria border extends just west of the Golan's geographical border, which is the Rukad, however the Israeli Golan also maintains an arc shape to the east. At its widest point, the Golan is 29 km. and its maximum length is 62 km. The full extent of the Golan is 1222 sq. km., with 88% of it under Israeli jurisdiction. The Golan is divided into 3 sections: north, central and south.

The northern Golan falls north of the Benot Ya'akov Bridge on the Jordan River, the dividing line between north and central Golan running along Nahal Gilabon. The northern Golan includes the peaks of the Golan, Har Avital, Har Bental, and Har Hermonit and its elevation is over 700 meters. Harsh weather conditions prevail in winter, and the summers are cool. The valleys are utilized for agriculture and the more difficult terrain for pasture.

The central Golan is located north of Nahal Daliyot near Gamla. Not suitable for agriculture, the area today is utilized by the Israel Defense Forces (I.D.F.). for

9

maneuvers and by the settlements for pasture. The famous canyons of the Golan which flow with water all year round are located here and it is here that the Golan makes its most gradual descent to the Syrian-African rift.

The bulk of settlement is concentrated in the southern Golan — a very flat plain made of fertile basalt soil which is suitable for various grains and other kinds of agriculture. Unlike the other parts of the Golan, much of the rock in the south is sedimentary rock. From the southern Golan there is a sharp drop to Lake Kinneret.

The Golan differs geologically from the rest of Israel; it is layered with lava flows stemming from several local volcanic mountains. These lava flows are quite young geologically — only several tens of thousands of years old.

There are three main types of volcanic rock in the Golan: basalt, scoriae and tuffs. The ridges of the Golan are actually basalt flows. Common basalt is a hard, heavy black rock. Magma at 1200°c-1400°c is heated up underground and bursts forth to the earth's surface. Hot gases are released in the slowly cooling magma flow, and result in a solid heavy rock which contains very few air pockets. These pockets are called vesicles.

The scoriae is a pyroclast, meaning parts of five. The light black or red scoriae is formed by magma quickly released to the earth's surface under great pressure. The gases are trapped in the magma which has cooled very quickly. During its release, the magma is blown to small pieces. Usually scoriae will be found near volcanic mountains.

Tuffs are also pyroclasts. During strong eruptions, often the volcanic release is torn to tiny bits, powder and ashes disperse and eventually accumulate on the ground in layers in the form of tiny loose volcanic particles. This is tuff. The thickness of the tuff is a direct function of the proximity to its volcanic sources.

Throughout the Golan are many interesting volcanic sites. The most famous is the hexagon pool (meshushim). Hexagons form during a certain variation of magma cooling.

Climate

Sharp climatic contrasts differentiate the regions of the Golan. The northern Golan, which rises at many places to an altitude of over 1000 meters, is only 50 km. from the Mediterranean Sea; the southern Golan, only a few hundred meters above sea level, is 65 km. from the Mediterranean Sea.

Nearly the whole of the Golan declines to the west, with its eastern border running just east of its watershed. The result is a mild Mediterranean climate with moderate temperature contrasts. Humidity is even higher than in the Galilee.

The northern Golan enjoys the heaviest annual rainfall, more than any other location of western Israel. Precipitation which is influenced by the Hermon range to the north is often as high as 1200 mm. The annual average rainfall in the southern Golan is 600 mm. whereas just 40 km. to the north the precipitation is 100% higher.

Snow is common in the upper Golan. The annual average temperature in the northern Golan is only 8.5°c and in the south 19.5°c, similar to Beer Sheba in the northern Negev.

Strong winds whip over the flat, mainly unforested, plains of the Golan, especially in the south. To the east in the Bashan, the air heats up early in the morning, creating a vacuum which causes the air to be drawn in from the areas nearby in the north and the Golan to the west. The annual average dewfall is 80 nights in the southern Golan, compared to 170 nights in the north.

Vegetation

Vegetation is typical of the Mediterranean zone, with a scattering of vegetation native to the Irano-Turanian zone. Desert plants, such as the white broom, grow along the scarps of the southern Golan dropping to the Yarmuk River and Lake Kinneret.

Today the Golan consists mainly of young grasslands and bulbous plants; the previous natural foliage was destroyed by man through misuse such as over-grazing, timber-felling and agriculture.

Throughout history, the Golan has been a source of timber. Initially the Phoenicians utilized the wood to build their famous sea vessels. The prophet Ezekiel says of Tyre on the coast north of Haifa, "of the oaks of Bashan they made thine oars." (27:6) The oak was commonly used for building and heating and it served the charcoal industry for the markets of Damascus.

The Circassians arrived in the Golan in the 1870's. They then proceeded to cut down the last forest — growing on 18% of Golan land — for their agricultural needs, to free land for settlement, to construct tools, and for building and fuel.

Between 1948 and 1967 the Syrian army prohibited logging. They made use of the small remaining forest to camouflage their bases.

The Golan forest was once a natural Mediterranean forest. Today only 3% of the Golan is covered by trees including the Odem Forest in the north, a remnant of the past, and forests in the east along the border on the Bashanit ridge and on Har Avital situated approximately 1000 meters above sea level.

In the lower central part of the Golan is the Yehudiya Forest, consisting of large, 150-year-old Tabor oaks; the individual trees grow at spaced distances. Encouraged by the warm climate along the western slopes below 300 meters, many jujube trees thrive.

A large variety of flowers adorn the grassy fields of the Golan in the spring. Rare flowers bloom in the canyons and the forest of the northern Golan: several species of iris, crocus and, in the Odem Forest, the round-leaved cyclamen.

Intense military use causes brush-fires in the dry fields in May and June, thus the fields perpetually maintain only one-year growths.

Wildlife

The geographical variations of the several Golan regions have allowed for a variety of fauna and species of various origins to find their home in the Golan — from the tropic to the Iro-Siberian. Since the 19th century many species have become extinct. When Israel took control of this area, a large number of nature reserves were established and today the wildlife is making a strong comeback. Ibex and 400 gazelles were brought to the Golan by the Nature Reserves Authority. Today, a herd of 50 ibex roam the scarps of the Yehudiya Forest. The gazelles have even over-populated themselves. Today, half of Israel's mammal species are found here.

The largest mammal of Israel, the wild boar, is found in the Golan which is also the habitat of twelve different species of rodents. Also common are predators, such as the badger, the common red fox, the jackal and African wildcat; more rare are the striped hyena and wolves. The common otter is rare, but can be spotted in the streams. A bird unique to the Golan is the rare night predator — the fish owl, who lives along the streams. Many other predators live here; for example, Gamla is the main habitat of the griffon vulture which today feeds mainly on carcasses of dead cattle.

All seven of Israel's amphibians are found only in the Golan. The fire salamander and the newt inhabit the cooler areas of the northern Golan. Fifteen types of fish swim in the streams, half of the number of freshwater species in Israel. The largest is the catfish, reaching 30 kg. and $1^{1}/_{2}$ meters long. A number of cichlids and members of the carp family are common.

Half of Israel's reptile species are natural to the Golan. The only poisonous snake, the Palestinian viper, feeds on the large population of field rodents. Starred lizards are a usual sight, often sunbathing on the dark basalt rocks.

Human Involvement

Several small prehistoric sites have been discovered in the area of the Golan. Judging by the many relics unearthed, it appears that during the Chalcolithic period nomads partially settled the central and southern Golan alongside the streams. During the Bronze period, the Megalithic culture developed. Several structures remain of this strange culture, the most noticeable being the dolmen. The dolmen is most likely a burial spot consisting usually of two upright flat rocks balancing a third. The dolmens are sometimes inserted in the ground or covered by heaps of small rocks known as tumulus.

The Golan has few remnants dating from the mid-Bronze period and the following 1000 years; the reason for this is unknown. The Israelite tribe of Menashe did not succeed in gaining control of the area in the 12-14th century B.C.E. King David's empire reached Damascus and the shelter city of Golan was established. King Solomon lost control of the Golan and for 500 years it became an area of dispute between Israel and Aram.

Many remnants have been unearthed from the Herodian period. King Herod settled Edomites from southern Israel in military colonies together with Babylonian Jews in the Golan. Josephus Flavius fortified three cities of the Golan against the Romans during the great revolt of 66-70 A.D.; Gamla was the only city that refused to surrender. Following the destruction of the Second Temple, Jewish settlement in the central and southern Golan flourished. Over 20 Jewish and many more mixed population settlements thrived on cattle raising, cultivation of olives, fruits and field crops. Rich architectural relics from this period are strewn amongst the ruins in this area. The most unique have been relocated to the Golan museum in Katzrin.

The building elements of the typical two story Byzantine building were long basalt pieces, arches and a stone floor. These remnants can be seen clearly today. There was a brief and temporary halt to settlement during the 4th century.

In 636 the famous Yakutza battle took place in the southern Golan in which the Moslems defeated the Byzantines and took control of Palestine. Following this period, nomads inhabited the Golan. The connecting road to the Damascus region from the Galilee ran through the Golan and a number of traveller khans (Inns) were established along the main roads.

Being mainly uninhabited, a large variety of ethnic groups settled in the Golan. In the 15-16th century, Druze settled the northern Golan and during the Egyptian rule of the 1840's, Sudanese were settled there along with refugees from Samaria. Bedouins usually harassed the new settlers, and were often successful in uprooting them.

In 1840 not only Algerians settled this area but Kurds also purchased large amounts of property. In the 1870's the Turks brought Circassians to stabilize the frontier of the Ottoman empire on the mountainous area of the Golan. Withstanding Bedouin tactics, they managed to expand toward the central Golan.

There were a few unsuccessful attempts at Jewish settlement in the late 19th century; at Rumtaniya, Bnei Yehuda and in the Bashan east of the Rukad River. Many of the various settlements made use of the foundations and stones of the Byzantine settlements.

In 1948, the Syrian army took control of the Golan, building roads and constructing water systems, military camps and fortifications, thus supplying an important source of employment for the locals.

In the 1960's, the Syrians initiated a multi-national Arab project to divert the sources of the Jordan River southward to a channel running along the western slopes of the Golan. Their intention was to cut off Israel's water sources. One of Israel's few main water reservoirs is Lake Kinneret, and the Jordan River is the Kinneret's main source. Israel clarified to the Syrians that it considered this project a belligerent act and that the price of Syria continuing this project would be costly. The short military encounters which ensued are known as 'the battle over the water.' Today, in different parts of the western Golan, you can see signs of this planned diversion channel.

Until 1967 when Israel captured the Golan following the Syrian attack, the Syrians took advantage of their topographical superiority and shelled Israeli farms, fishermen and kibbutzim. Of the nearly 300 Syrian villages of pre-1967, only the occupants of five villages did not flee during the Six Day War. On the 9th and 10th of June 1967, the Israel Defense Forces, responding to Syrian shelling, took control of the entire Golan and part of the Hermon range.

During the Arab initiated Yom Kippur War in 1973, Israel almost lost the Golan to the Syrians. Although Israel suffered many casualties, the I.D.F. held on to this area.

Today in the Golan there are approximately 40 Jewish settlements which cultivate wheat, myrtle, apples and cherries and who raise cattle. Grapes grown for the world renown Golan winery in Katzrin are also a booming business. Katzrin, named after the Talmudic town, is the regional center of the Golan with a population of 700 families and is still growing. A national consensus, regarding the unquestionable strategic importance of the Golan for the State of Israel, lead the Knesset to officially annex the Golan in 1981.

The Golan is the only part of the State of Israel which lies east of the Jordan. A number of ancient Roman roads cross the southern Golan, not far from Gamla. The main road today from Rosh Pina across the Ben'ot Ya'akov Bridge is based on an ancient road. Another main road follows the line of the eastern, arc shaped border.

Following the Six Day War a number of roads were constructed throughout the Golan. The waterfall road (HaMapalim) runs along the edge of many canyons leading from Katzrin to the southern Golan settlements, thus its name. From this road, several additional roads descend to Lake Kinneret, the main ones are from the southern settlements to Kursi and from nearby Katzrin through the Yehudiya Forest to the northern top of Lake Kinneret.

Difficult weather conditions and heavy military use have bruised and battered the Golan roads.

Water

The watershed of the Golan is unique. Almost all waters of the plateau flow into Lake Kinneret. The far eastern Golan drains into the Rukad River which flows south to the Yarmuk. The Yarmuk River drains off areas of the southern Golan, flowing into the Jordan River just south of Lake Kinneret.

The large amount of precipitation and the unique geology have combined to form a large number of springs, which drain off marl and shards between basalt flows or over their surface. The heated basalt flow has also cooked parts of the earth into an impermeable layer, as you can observe springs along the steep banks of various canyons.

The springs in the eastern Golan which drain over the basalt flows are unstable due to the small reservoir area. Following a rainy winter, water runs everywhere in the Golan. The springs in the flat areas create swamps, which attract unique water flora and fauna.

The small swamps drain into narrow channels known as 'masils' in Arabic. Mesilah in Hebrew means track or path. As the 'masils' drain westward, several meet and become a stream. When the stream reaches a geological fault, or a crack in a basalt flow, a waterfall and a canyon are formed. Most of your hikes will run along this type of canyon. A few natural pools are found in the Golan, mainly in the north, the most famous of which is Berekhat Ram.

Today a large number of reservoirs drain the masils of most of the Golan's main streams. One of the essential environmental problems of these dams is that they reduce the vigor of the strong flashfloods that tear down the canyons in winter. What may eventually occur is an accumulation of debris at the base of the canyon, causing severe damage to these lovely waterscapes. Prior to the damming of these streams, water had to be transported by truck to various locations on the Golan. This is a good illustration of the eternal conflict between the environment and population's needs.

Israel's bottled mineral water is taken from several Golan springs.

The Golan is one of the few places in modern Israel were streams flow all year round. Rich greenery surrounding flowing water in a deep canyon offers the hiker a great contrast to the flat rocky plateau above, adding another dimension to the unique qualities of the Golan's streams.

Hiking in the Golan

The Golan is actually a small area which serves many purposes: settlement, agricultural and pastoral lands, nature reserves, military maneuvers and infrastructure, the latter mainly along the border. These uses sometimes overlap: cows grazing between the bullets; tanks that have to cease maneuvers in order to close fences. Many sites in the Golan are accessible only with special permission from the I.D.F. or on Saturdays when there are no maneuvers. Some of the hikes run close to firing zones so *it is vital that you stick to the trail.*

Minefields are strewn throughout the Golan, all of these are fenced in and indicated by yellow and black warning signs. Small red triangles, both on the signs and appearing separately, also warn that you have come upon a minefield.

Stick to the trails and check at least twice before crossing any fence. Please close gates. A moment of careless negligence can cost a rancher who must herd up his strayed cattle an entire day's work.

The summer is very hot in the central and southern Golan; four litres of water is necessary per person daily. In the winter you need 2 litres. *Do not drink the stream water!* On some of the hikes you can walk through the stream, a refreshing experience. In Nahal Yehudiya, you have to swim and negotiate deep waters.

In the winter, the trails are very slippery. Please take care.

Important phone numbers:

(Area code: 069)

Hermon Field Study		Border Police Moshav Aniam	61776
Center (Senir)	41091	Katzrin Police	61444
Katzrin Field Study Center	61234	Katzrin Magen David Adom	
Keshet Field Study Center	61702	(First Aid)	61333

Early morning at Mitzpe Ofir (hike 2)

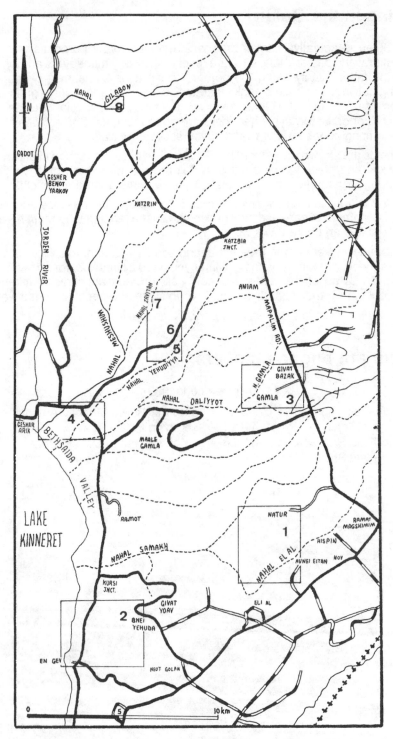

Central and southern Golan. Numbers represent hike numbers.

Nahal El Al

Points of interest: Ancient synagogue, views, waterscape, swimming.
Length of hike: 14 km. loop trip.
Hiking time: 8 hours.
Preferred season: All year.
Suitable for: Experienced hikers.
Maps: Golan marked hiking trail map.
Special preparation: Swimsuit.
Starting & ending point: Kibbutz Natur.

To begin hike:

By car: Drive to Kibbutz Natur off the Mapalim Road in the southern Golan. Ask permission to park in the kibbutz. Two hundred meters before the entrance to the kibbutz, a blue trail mark on a stone on the paved road takes you onto a trail heading around and along the fence of the small kibbutz to the southwest. (1)

The narrow trail heads through open fields. Pass through gate and follow blue trail mark onto dirt road passing the sewage pool of the kibbutz on the left. After 1 km., near a grove of trees, the blue-marked road leaves the dirt road to the right, re-crosses dirt road and passes through gate. Please close the gate.

Descend on dirt road, enjoying view of Nahal Samakh and Um El Kanatir. Note the white chalk bare slopes. Many caper bushes and great fennel grow here. The road curves to the right and then left. Turn right on clear trail to the spring of Um El Kanatir near the large Byzantine arcs. (2) Um El Kanatir means 'mother of the arcs.' Head into the deserted village where a sign indicates a large building, the ruins of an ancient synagogue. Note the different architectural remnants and remaining section of a lion carved out of the rock to the left of the entrance. Several interesting artifacts have been taken from here, some to the Golan Museum in Katzrin. This synagogue was most likely a two-story building, dating from the 1st or 2nd century.

Return to and continue down dirt road, turning left along base of small cliff heading south.

You are walking now on part of the diversion route that the Syrians began constructing during the 1960's along the western slopes of the Golan. Their plan was to divert the sources of the Jordan River from the northern Hula Valley to the Yarmuk River south of the Golan and thus cut off Israel from one of its few main water sources. Lebanon and Jordan also

See map on page 19

17

cooperated in this plan. Israel's quick military response served its purpose and the Syrians quickly canceled this project. The whole episode is known as *'the battle over the water.'*

The trail passes a spring and before the next one, near an almond tree and a jujube tree, the blue-marked trail heads back up to the plateau to a dirt road following it to the right. Look out for gazelles here. After two easy kilometers, the trail reaches the southwest border of the plateau, with the canyon of Nahal El Al stretching to the south.

Here you will find a huge pile of rocks. This is the Bardawil complex (3) known as the Bardawil fort to the people of the area, named for the Crusader king, Baldwin; however, there are no Crusader relics in the area. The triangular shaped site is from the Bronze period. Two aspects are bordered by an abyss and to the north there is a 120 meter long huge stone wall, 8 meters high and 30-40 wide. Look for the moat north of the wall. Enjoy view before descending on blue-marked trail to the south.

On the slope the trail swerves northeast, slowly descending to the stream bed of Nahal El Al. A lot of round symmetrical blue thorns bloom here in the early summer. This perfectly shaped plant is called kipodan in Hebrew, meaning 'the hedgehog plant' due to its shape. In English, it is called the globe thistle and grows in areas where there is a lot of grazing.

Note how the vegetation changes as you enter the white sedimentary rock of Nahal El Al. Soon you will see the white waterfall of Nahal El Al ahead of you, dropping onto the white limestone. Follow trail to the bottom of the waterfall to the pool, a great place for a dip. (4)

Head up clear trail on southern bank and take left onto red-marked trail heading across the stream above the waterfall. The trail heads up Nahal El Al on its northern bank. Nahal El Al in Arabic is Wadi Dufayle, meaning 'oleander.' This plant blooms in pinkish colors along the streams of Israel in the early summer. The aroma of these flowers is very pleasant, and especially no-ticeable toward evening. The name oleander comes from the word olea in Latin meaning 'olive,' due to a similarity in the leaves. The tree-like bush grows up to 4 meters high and the leaves and stems contain a toxic milky substance. A certain poison is prepared from the bark. The oleander is most popular in the Golan, being the most common tree growing along the stream bed. The oleander also grows in Judea and Samaria and throughout northern Israel.

The trail continues, passing through small olive groves. Less than 2 km. from the white waterfall arrive at the black waterfall falling on dark basalt rock near the tall plane trees. Head around the fall on your right, continuing on red-marked trail. The red-marked trail soon recrosses the wadi to the southern bank and reaches Moshav Avnei Eitan.

Where the red-marked trail crosses the stream, continue straight along northern bank on narrow unmarked trail heading northeast. One hundred and fifty meters after a group of tall eucalyptus and poplar trees growing across the stream, head up northern bank on small trail to the plateau to the right (northeast) of some old houses and to the left of a lone tree.(5)

Reach dirt road that loops through two gates in a fence. Enter left gate and head northwest along fence running southeast on dirt road toward a cattle enclosure, 500 meters from gate. Cross through complex on the right side and connect with clear gravel road that reaches it from the north. Head north on gravel road. Far off to your right is the volcanic Har Peres which is also the site of a volcanic scoriae and tuffs quarry. Soon you will see Givat Natur ahead of you. Less than 2 km. along the gravel road brings you just to the east of the starting point on the road leading to Natur. (1)

Hike 1, Nahal El Al

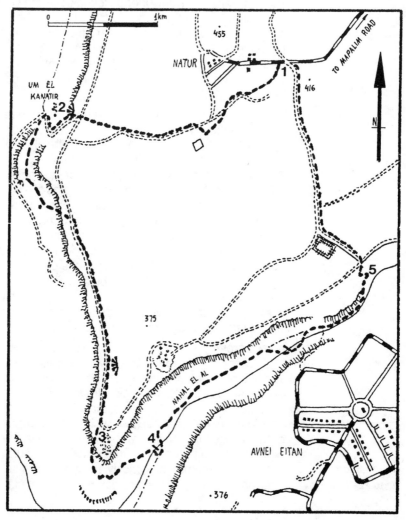

Mitzpe Ofir to En Gev

2

Points of interest: Views, spring.
Length of hike: 7 km. one-way.
Hiking time: 4 hours.
Preferred season: All year.
Suitable for: All.
Maps: Golan marked hiking trail map.
Special preparation: None.
Starting point: Bus stop by Golan Israel Aircraft Industry before Moshav Bnei Yehuda.
Ending point: Entrance to Kibbutz En Gev.

To begin hike:

By bus: Take bus from Tiberias to the southern settlements of the Golan on road leading up from Kursi Junction. $1\frac{1}{2}$ km. before Moshav Bnei Yehuda get off at Golan Israel Aircraft Industries. Walk down the road 250 meters and take left to the west onto blue-marked gravel road at km. stone 9 (1) near wooden sign, 'Mitzpe Ofir.' Head along dirt road for 1 km. to Mitzpe Ofir. (2)

Enjoy the great view of Lake Kinneret from here; 'kinor' in modern Hebrew means 'violin,' but the original word meant the ancient harp, similar in shape to the outline of this lake. Follow the clear blue-marked trail to the south along escarpment. A lot of germander grow here. The trail leaves the dirt road, continuing along the cliffs and passing remains of a Syrian outpost that was taken in 1967. From here it is easy to understand the significance of the Golan Heights for Israel's security. The pre-1967 border ran along the base of the 400 meter drop to Lake Kinneret. Israel had control of only a narrow strip of land curving around the eastern shore of the Lake. Until 1967, the Syrians consistently shelled Kibbutz En Gev and other Jewish farm settlements. In the spring, the Haynes Iris blooms here. *Stick to the trail and don't cross unnecessary fences as the area to the left (east) may still hold some leftover mines!*

Near a grove of small olive trees, the trail descends to the right and reaches a dirt road. The olive (zayit) is one of the seven species of Israel, a native of this region, which has been cultivated and is a prominent typical feature of Israel's landscape. Reaching a height of 8 meters, the olive tree trunk twists with age into unique shapes and, while outwardly expanding in girth, can become hollow with time. The olive tree trunk has been known to reach a circumference of up to 6 meters. The branches are sometimes prickly and the underside of the small oval dark green leaves are covered with miniature whitish

See map on page 22

scales. The small white-yellow flowers grow in clusters and bloom in the spring. The olive fruit ripens from a green color to a black-brown-purple in the fall. The evergreen olive tree grows wild in the mountains of Israel. It is cultivated in this area as well as in the valleys, foothills and semi-desert areas. Today it is grown commercially both for its fruit and its oil which is one of the unsaturated oils. The oil of the olive was very important for the Hebrews in Biblical times. It was used to light the menorah in the Temple and was the main oil used for cooking. Today the Arab sector still commonly uses the oil every day. Mentioned numerous times in the Bible, the olive tree is considered a tree of beauty and symbolizes light, fertility and prosperity and peace, "And the dove came to him in the evening and lo' in her mouth was an olive leaf." (Gen. 8:11) During the Roman and Byzantine period, olives were an important industry.

The globe thistle blooms in late spring

Turn left on dirt road, following trail mark, 100 meters down this road take right and reach curve in wadi. Here is the small spring of Bir e Shikum (3) trapped in an arched structure. This spring supplied small quantities of water for the people of the village and is a layer spring.

It was here that a relatively unknown organization of Jews, known as 'Bnei Yehuda' from the Old Yishuv in Tiberias and Safed, made several attempts to settle the Golan and Bashan over a period of 30 years. They chose this remote place since the land was cheap and seemed promising. There were many historical Jewish connections to the Golan which is just across from Tiberias and Safed. In 1885, 'Bnei Yehuda' was established as a society of 52 families.

In 1891, after an earlier failure, 3000 dunams of Bir e Shikum were purchased. The settlers went through many hardships until the end of World War I when only one family remained. In 1920 a settler named Moshe Bernstein was murdered while working in the field, bringing the original Bnei Yehuda episode to an end. In 1971, the Bnei Yehuda regional center was re-established 2 km. east of Bir e Shikum.

Large jujube trees grow around the spring and around the bend to the left grows a large white broom bush, a visitor from the desert.

Four hundred meters along the ridge, the blue-marked trail breaks off to the right from the dirt road and begins a descent toward En Gev point. The trail hits white sedimentary rocks and the vegetation changes a bit. Ascend up to En Gev point. (4) Enjoy view. Note Susita to your south with the zigzag road leading toward its summit; this was one of the I.D.F.'s most elevated guard posts along the pre-1967 border with Syria.

Below is En Gev. One km. directly to the south lie ruins of the Arab village of E Nukayeb which the Beduins called 'E Ngaib' (meaning 'the passageway' or 'ascent'). The Jews who came to the area in 1937 named their kibbutz En Gev, which means 'spring of the water hollow.' Jerusalem's mayor Teddy Kollek was one of the founders.

From En Gev point descend on the steep trail. *Take care as on wet days the going is slippery!* Link onto dirt road following blue mark through grazing area. Follow dirt road around curve and continue on blue-marked trail into small wadi (not as marked on Golan marked hiking trail map).

The trail passes to the left of the cemetery and passes between farm structures out to the main road. (5) Take left for 200 meters to bus stop and finish your hike at the entrance to Kibbutz En Gev.

Hike 2, Mitzpe Ofir to En Gev

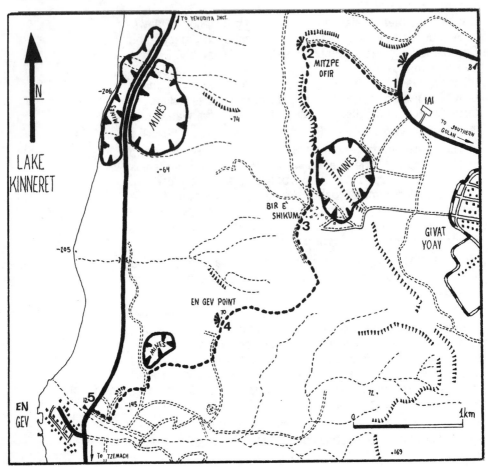

Gamla

Points of interest: View, highest waterfall in Israel, interesting relics, vultures.
Length of hike: 11 km. loop trip.
Hiking time: 8 hours.
Preferred season: All year.
Suitable for: Experienced hikers.
Maps: Golan marked hiking trail map.
Special preparation: swimsuit, binoculars.
Starting & ending point: Gravel road to Gamla beneath Givat Bazak

This hike covers practically all the sights of the reserve. To get a clear picture of Gamla it is advised to separately spend a trip to the historical site by itself. Entrance costs a small fee.

To begin hike:

By car: Turn off Mapalim Road between Ramat Magshimim and Katzrin near orange sign 'Gamla.' Begin your hike near gravel road leading up to the hill to your right, 1 km. off the Mapalim Road just before passing through stone gateway. (1)

Head up wide gravel road to the left (western) peak of Givat Bazak. (2) Enjoy view of most of the Golan Heights topped by the Hermon Mountain range in the north which peaks at 2807 meters. To the north and the east, note the line of volcanic mountains. Not far to the east lie two reservoirs just across the Mapalim Road that collect the waters of the masils of upper Nahal Gamla and Nahal Daliyot. To the south are the settlements of the southern Golan and Syria and to the west, Lake Kinneret and the Galilee. From here you get a vista of the Golan, as it rises slowly to the north and east.

Proceed on your hiking route, descending to the northwest and crossing large boulders and barbed wire fence until you arrive at the wide dirt road at the bottom of the hill. Head northwest on dirt road which suddenly ends 200 meters before Nahal Gamla. Head along fence until you arrive above the stream lined with green vegetation. Turn left here and follow stream from above, along the animal trails. The going is rough but after only 400 meters you receive your due reward — with a 51 meter waterfall, the highest in Israel, whose stream empties into a magnificent canyon. (3) *Be careful not to get too close!* There is no negotiable descent to the bottom of the canyon.

Just before the waterfall a clear red-marked trail crosses the stream. Follow it along the northern bank 200 meters to the waterfall lookout point. From here you also have a view of

See map on page 25

Gamla. Further along the white-marked trail on the northern cliff is a good point to observe vultures. Return to waterfall and continue on trail toward the main entrance to the Gamla reserve.

Along this trail you pass dolmens, Megalithic structures from the mid-Bronze period, 4000 years ago; 'dol' means table and 'men' means rock in the ancient Keltic language. The dolmens here are trilithons as they consist of 3 main rocks. There are about 150-200 of these in the vicinity. A few metal and pottery artifacts have been found near the bones of the deceased buried under the dolmens.

The trail reaches the village of Dir Krookh. (4) 'Dir' in Arabic means monastery and this village has many such remnants from the Byzantine period. Visit the Byzantine house. Take right at signs on dirt road and as the road curves to the right, approach the building directly ahead, a handsome structure with several arches and other fine architectural elements, for instance an inscription and a cross on the left (the western) part of the building near some bushes, one of them a caper.

Further down the dirt road is a building that was a church, and near the cliff — close to the new vulture observation point — are the remnants of an oil press. Head beyond Dir Krookh to the entrance to the site. There are facilities, kiosk, information and tables. Here at the booth of the Nature Reserves Authority on the gravel road you pay admission to Gamla.

Atop the cliff, just south of the parking lot, is a memorial for the first settlers of the Golan Heights who fell in the defense of Israel. The names of the people appear and above the inscription attached to the rock is the legend: "As you stand here, you face toward the city Gamla beyond Lake Kinneret, across from Tarichaea, (Tarichaea is the town of Migdal north of Tiberias on the western shore of Lake Kinneret) where the first settlers of the Golan who renewed Jewish settlement gave their lives for the peace of Israel."

From this memorial you enjoy a wonderful view of Gamla and Nahal Daliyot, and in the distance Lake Kinneret and the Galilee. This special spot serves the State for memorial day ceremonies and also I.D.F. army units for graduation of basic training courses. Exactly 1900 years passed from the year 67 when Gamla fell and 1967 when the Golan returned to Israel and Jewish settlement was renewed.

Return to parking lot and take the clear trail west that descends to Gamla. Along the trail you will find signs which display printed excerpts from the book of Yoseph ben Matityahu (Josephus Flavius), *War of the Jews* relating the battle of Gamla.

The peak of Har Gamla is 330 meters above sea level 540 meters above Lake Kinneret. 'Gamal' in Hebrew means camel, a picturesque description of the shape of this mountain. The ancient inhabitants of Gamla hewed waterholes out of the mountain which is composed mainly of impermeable marl and you can see such hollows along the lower path that leads to the city.

A short loop trail brings you to the entrance of one of the 3 openings in the wall made by the Romans led by Vespasian and his 3 elite legions, no. 5, 10, and 15, consisting of 6000 soldiers.

Immediately as you enter on your right, is a room piled with catapult stones. From the area of Dir Krookh the Romans shelled Gamla unceasingly. Archaeologists estimate that on average, the Romans succeeded in striking each square meter of Gamla with these catapult stones. The trail leads to a large public building above these rooms, passing a mikveh ritual bath on the left, before the entrance to what most believe to be one of the oldest synagogues unearthed to date. This synagogue was built before the destruction of the Second Temple in the year 70.

You can head west on trail from synagogue, passing 2 olive presses and another ritual bath. Remnants from the early Bronze period were found here. Below the mountain peak excavations have uncovered the wealthy section of the ancient town. Climb to the top of the mountain, (6) here you can enjoy a lovely panoramic view.

Many refugees fled to the fortified city of Gamla which was the last city to resist the Romans in the region. A total of 9000 Jews fell there, 4000 killed by the Romans and 5000 who, toward the end of the battle, leaped off the northern cliff to the abyss to

Hike 3, Gamla

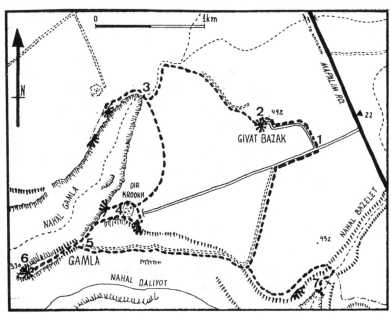

avoid being captured by the enemy. Only 2 women survived. It is easy to surmise why Gamla is known as the Masada of the Golan.

Exit the upper opening in the wall. Pass archaeological camp and as trail ascends, veer to the right onto dirt road (5) that gradually continues the ascent of the northern bank of Nahal Daliyot. Pass spring embellished by rich vegetation, including many reeds signifying the presence of water. Many springs of Israel can be recognized at a distance by the tall plants. Reeds, reaching 3 meters in height, grow adjacent to underground water which is close to the surface of the ground.

Reeds have been used for huts, mats, and sun shades and are also a base for paper. The young sprouts and roots are edible. The reed is mentioned a number of times in the Bible. "And the Lord shall smite Israel as a reed is shaken in the water," Kings I, 14:15.

This spring was one of the water sources of Gamla. The water of the springs that emerge along the slopes of the canyon runs along a layer of claylike earth that has been roasted a red color by the hot basalt which formed an impermeable layer. Where exposed, the water escapes to the surface, and these are the springs you will view along the cliff canyons of the Golan.

Reach plateau at gate and turn right onto red-marked trail for 1 km. down to Nahal Bazelet, meaning basalt, the northern tributary of Nahal Daliyot. Right before wadi take clear unmarked trail along northern bank. *During the winter the trail is very slippery and dangerous!*

The trail drops to the stream bed, lined with oleander and willow. Just up to the left is a 10 meter waterfall and a large pool below. (7) To your right 50 meters down the wadi is the crest of a 25 meter waterfall. *Take care as there is no approach to the bottom of this waterfall!* During the summer when there are no rains this stream may dry up. The Honey Reservoir, 2 km. to the east, collects all water residue.

Nahal Daliyot is fed by 32 springs and at one time had the largest water flow of all the streams of the Golan. The stream drains into the northeastern part of Lake Kinneret at the southern section of the Bethsaida Valley.

Retrace your steps, returning to the dirt road. The red-marked trail continues to the southern tributary of Nahal Daliyot and reaches the Daliyot Junction on the Mapalim Road.

Take right on dirt road which is used to transport heavy equipment and to remove heavy finds from the archaeological excavations. A 1 km. walk toward the volcanic Givat Bazak takes you to the gravel road leading to Gamla. Take right, back to starting point. (1)

Za'aki

4

Points of interest: Interesting waterscape.
Length of hike: 3 km. loop trip.
Hiking time: 5 hours.
Preferred season: April-November.
Suitable for: Rated difficult but suitable for all — *must be swimmers!*
Maps: Golan marked hiking trail map.
Special preparation: Clothing for constant walking in water, waterproof gear.
Starting & ending point: End of green-marked gravel road 1¹/₂ km. off eastern Kinneret Road.

It is best to read the hike description before starting out.

To begin hike:

At the northeastern section of the road that hugs the eastern shore of Lake Kinneret, 1¹/₂ km. south of the Yehudiya Junction between km. stone 25 and 24, a gravel road with a green trail mark turns off to the west. (1) From here a dirt road also leads to the east. Head west on clear road into Bik'at Bethsaida. After 800 meters, the road turns to the right (north); 700 meters later a good dirt road turns to the left. Continue straight ahead for 200 meters until dirt road narrows to a wide path. Park near eucalyptus tree (2) and begin hike, walking in the same direction.

After 100 meters, cross stream which is Nahal Yehudiya and take left toward olive grove. (3) Here, after 100 meters, there is a trailmark leading you on a clear trail of 5 meters into the stream amongst thick vegetation overhead. From this point on, you will be walking in water.

Hike 4, Za'aki

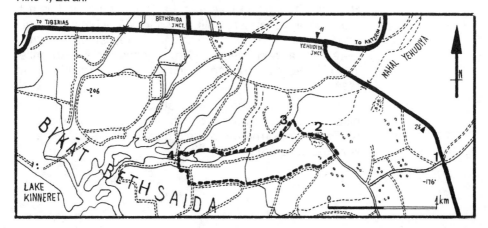

27

Follow the stream which alternately opens and narrows into pool formations, adhering to the stream course all the time. In the stream there are no trail marks and at certain spots the water is deep so you have to swim. *Try not to drink the water!* Like many of the Golan streams, the vegetation here is composed of much oleander, willow and bramble. The bramble blooms in late spring, the fruit ripening in mid to late summer similar to the fig, grape and date, all of which grow here.

The entire region is unique. This low flat area was formed by the many streams which carried great quantities of alluvium. The Jordan River, Meshushim, Yehudiya, Daliyot and Shfamnun streams all flow into Lake Kinneret along only 4 kilometers of shore line. Bik'at Bethsaida is part of the Kinnrot Valley region which includes Lake Kinneret.

The valley has two large lagoons and five small ones in the south; today these are closed to the public for nature preservation. Fifteen tributaries flow in the valley before merging. This hike is along one of these tributaries. During years with heavy rainfall the lagoons 'crawl up' the tributaries. At the time of writing, the waters have receded considerably, due to two straight years of drought on the Golan Heights — 1988-89, 1989-90.

The lagoons contain 23 different types of fish, and are a breeding place for cichlids. Some of these fish are mouth breeders (the parents carry their young in their mouths). The famous St. Peters fish belong to this family. Large catfish roam the deep and dark parts of the lagoon.

Many types of migrating birds spend the winter here. Desert birds reach their most northern habitat here, having gradually extended their habitat up the Syrian-African rift. Other types of animal life are also abundant here.

Historical evidence of Jewish presence in this area is recorded in the Talmud as well as other texts. Rabbi Joshua ben Hanina brought pheasants from Za'aidan (Kohelet Raba 2:8) to Caesar Hadrian. Throughout time man has had interest in this rich area, mostly fishermen. Until 1967, the border between Israel and Syria ran 10 meters from Lake Kinneret. Israeli fishermen were shot at and even killed by Syrians more than once. Today, there is a lot of illegal hunting and fishing in this nature reserve.

After $1\frac{1}{2}$ km. of walking in the water, the stream opens up a bit and is blocked by a sort of dam with a path that crosses it. (4) There is a sign here which informs you that the continuation is a closed nature reserve.

Exit water and take left for 100 meters towards eucalyptus trees and you will arrive at dirt road. Take left again, heading east parallel to the stream you hiked in. The road takes a few turns between the citrus and banana plantations. Stick to the north. After 1$^1/_2$ km. reach turn in dirt road by starting point. (2)

Petals of oleander floating in a Golan stream

Nahal Yehudiya

2 Options

5

Points of interest: Rich waterscape, huge pools of water, waterfalls, swimming, ancient village.

Length of hike: a) $3^1/_2$ km. loop trip; b) longer option 5 km. & $1^1/_2$ km. on Yehudiya Road to make the hike a loop trip.

Hiking time: a) 3 hours; b) longer option 6 hours. A large group can result in considerable extension of hike.

Preferred season: April-November.

Suitable for: Experienced hikers; *swimmers only!*

Maps: Golan marked hiking trail map.

Special preparation: Clothes for swimming in water, waterproof everything you take. The hike has parts that cross long deep pools of water; air mattress, life preserver suggested.

Starting & ending point: Yehudiya parking lot.

To begin hike:

By car: The Yehudiya parking lot (1) just north off the Yehudiya Road heading toward Katzrin between km. stone 18 and 19. Here you can get drinking water and there is a kiosk and information center.

See map on page 33

Follow red-marked trail from behind the kiosk across the main road toward the left side of the ancient village of Yehudiya. (2) Arrive at red/green-marked trail divergence.

Yehudiya, from the word 'Yehud' meaning Jew, is the name of a village that was deserted in the 4th century. The buildings you see are of more recent construction, built onto the earlier foundations. Explore village, noting contrasts between old and new. The new actually seems more crude than the sophisticated architectural designs of the Roman and Byzantine periods. This village is identified as Sogana which Yoseph ben Matityahu (Josephus Flavius) fortified along with Gamla and Seleucia. The villages of Yehudiya and Seleucia made a pact with Agrippas at the beginning of the Jewish revolt. A menorah with 5 branches carved in rock was found here.

During the 19th century, the Turkomans — a nomadic people originating in central Asia — settled here. After 1948 the Syrians changed the name of the village to 'Arabia' to disclaim Jewish identification with the place.

From Yehudiya, enjoy a fine view of Nahal Yehudiya. Take wide red-marked trail to the northeast along the top of the canyon for 1 km. Here the trail descends to the foot of the large waterfall of Nahal Yehudiya. Not far from the beginning of this descent, the trail passes through a large clump of myrtle. The myrtle is one of the 4 species important to the festival of the Tabernacles (Succot). The leaves have a most wonderful aroma. The myrtle is grown commercially around Safed and at Nov, one of the settlements in the southern Golan.

Enjoy a swim at pool. Continue down the marked trail. After 450 meters reach the famous 8 meter waterfall (3) which you can descend on the ladder installed to the left. From the ladder drop to the water and swim across pool. *Make sure that all your important gear is secured in waterproof containers!* Remember, the more clothes you wear, the more difficult it will be for you to negotiate the pool. Until recently there was no ladder here and a necessary element of the hike was to jump 8 meters into the very deep pool.

Continue through another small pool and a large pool. The trail lines the southern bank and crosses to the right and then back to left. One km. from the series of pools the green-marked trail departs to the right, (4) near some white writing on a rock. To follow hike (a) take trail which crosses the stream, heading up a rocky slope. The trail turns to the left and ascends back to the western part of the Yehudiya village. Follow the marked trail through the village and onto the trail leading back to the starting point. (1)

b) For longer hike, continue on red-marked trail along stream bed of willows and oleander. Soon reach another canyon as the stream drops in a series of waterfalls that you pass on your left.

Along Nahal Yehudiya, you may notice the grape vine. The grape vine (gefen) is one of the seven Biblical species of Israel.

Its products are predominant among the agricultural products mentioned in the Bible and Talmudic literature. The wild vine does not grow today in Israel, although in various spots, such as along streams and springs, vines once cultivated clamber and grow wild. Grapes ripen in the summer, the specific month depending on the elevation where they grow. The grapes of the Druze village of Bet Jan near Har Meron, for instance, are known to ripen late in the season due to Bet Jan's elevation. The grape, like the fig, is one of the most ancient fruits of Israel. During Biblical times the grape was a common produce for the average farms, and served as a symbol of the Children of Israel's fundamental ideals and their hope for future peace, "They shall sit every man under his vine and under his fig tree and none shall make them afraid," (Micah 4:4). During the time of Israel's wandering in the desert, the men sent out to spy the Land of Israel returned with a giant cluster of grapes, "They came to the brook of Eshkol and cut down from there a branch with one cluster of grapes." (Numbers 8:23) Many private Arab and Jewish rural homes have vine trellises growing along patio beams which offer both shade and the welcome harvest of their fruit. Grapes are grown commercially today throughout Israel not only for wine but for grape juice, raisins, and of course for eating fresh. The Druze make a certain honey called, 'dibes' from grapes.

250 meters later along the trail, the stream drops another short fall. You can slide down into the long deep pool which you have to swim across. This is the last pool of the hike. Continue nearly 1 additional km. down the stream. Be careful not to miss the red-marked trail that ascends to the right, heading out where there is a steep pile of rocks. (5) Follow red-marked trail to the plateau on the top. Say farewell to Nahal Yehudiya which continues into the northeastern part of Lake Kinneret after widening into the Za'aki Lagoon.

The red-marked trail is not very clear at the top, but you will be able to follow path to the northwest for 800 meters through the sparse Tabor oak forest to the Yehudiya Road which you intersect at km. stone 17. (6) On road head right for $1^1/_2$ km. back to starting point. (1)

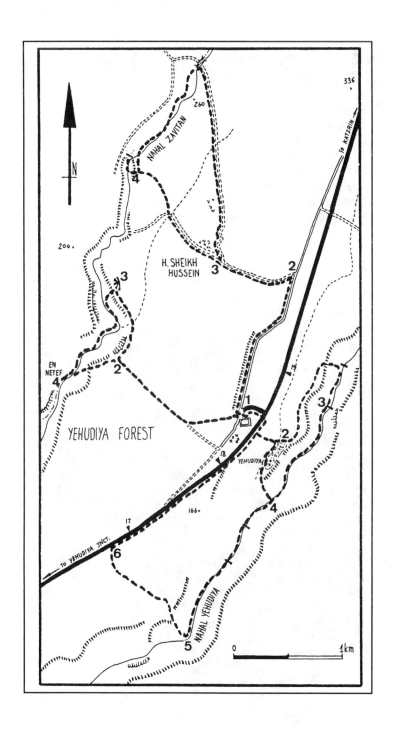

Hikes 5, 6, and 7
Nahal Yehudiya, Nahal Zavitan

Nahal Zavitan – Lower

6

Points of interest: Waterscape, showerspring.
Length of hike: 6 km. loop trip.
Hiking time: 4 hours.
Preferred season: All year.
Suitable for: All.
Maps: Golan marked hiking trail map.
Special preparation: Clothing for water, swimsuit.
Starting & ending point: Yehudiya parking lot.

To begin hike:

By car: Turn off into Yehudiya parking lot on Yehudiya Road that leads toward the town of Katzrin. Park in the parking lot. (1) Here you will find drinking water, a snack-bar and an information center which is not always open.

Pool in Lower Nahal Zavitan. See map on page 33

Take the green-marked trail indicated by sign in Hebrew to Nahal Meshushim. The trail crosses the cattle grazing area of the sparse Tabor oak forest. The Tabor oak grows up to elevations of 600 meters and sheds its leaves in the fall. The Turks cut down the large Tabor oak forests which grew along the coastal plain about 100 years ago. After $1^1/_2$ km. you arrive at a precipice overhanging Nahal Zavitan and to a red-marked trail. (2) Take a right, and continue your walk above the canyon. Cross Masil Sheikh Hussein, follow black-marked trail that you intersect and descend to the left on clear stepped path to Lower Nahal Zavitan. (3)

Observe the many caper bushes which abound in the Golan, usually blooming in June. The thorny caper (tzalaf), is one of the few plants to be found throughout all of Israel. Its large silvery green leaves do not shed even in the desert climate, the lovely white flowers and purple pollened stems give the caper a unique aspect. The flowers open up toward evening and stay open throughout the night until morning. The caper grows in stony areas such as high niches of the Kotel (the Western Wall) and along the cliffs of wadis. It is mentioned in the Talmud, where it is called the "most tough of trees" most likely due to the fact that it takes quite an effort to truly uproot it. The caper fruit is also mentioned in Ecclesiastes 12:5 as a symbol of shortness of a man's life because shortly after it blossoms the fruit scatters its seeds and the plant's outer leaves wither but the plant does not die, ". . . the almond tree shall blossom . . . and the caperberry shall fail." The caper's flowerbuds and fruit can be pickled in salt or vinegar and eaten. The caper is a useful medicinal plant, the Arabs of Israel using it for hearing problems, rheumatism, male and female infertility, breathing problems and diabetes. The fig caper grows in the Eilat region. This is a different, larger type of caper. The whole fruit is edible raw. Bedouins in the Sinai make a liquid curative for the bones and joints from a combination of the salted fruit and dates. The dried ground ripe fruit can be used as a condiment.

Turn left in the stream bed, following trail mark. You can walk in the stream where you will be able to closely observe the bramble, oleander and willow trees. The trail passes a lovely pool on the right and then crosses over to the left side of the wadi, where soon you arrive at the last and most beautiful pool of this hike. This circular pool is quite deep, notice the fig and maidenhair fern growing beneath the overhang. Enjoy the swim.

The small maidenhair fern is the most common fern of Israel. In Hebrew its name is 'Sa'arot Shulamit,' 'the tresses of Shulamit,' in reference to the lovely and beloved 'Shulamit' of the Song of Songs, as well as to its lush green tumble down cave and cistern walls, so like a women's tresses. The maidenhair grows in many locations adjacent to springs, streams and even in slightly damp spots such as waterholes and cisterns, cliffs and caves, even in the desert. Generally, the other ferns of Israel grow only in the truly wet and cooler northern locations.

In Israel all ferns are protected plants. The dried leaves are suitable for tea while fresh ones can be eaten raw. The maidenhair grows in many locations in the world. In southern Europe it is combined with orange blossoms to distil a cough syrup. In Roman tradition, the powder of this fern offers beauty and love. The leaves are reputed to strengthen hair roots and fortify heart and lungs.

Continue from pool downstream. Reach green and red-marked trail intersection. (2) Continue in stream following the red-marked trail to En Netef on the right side of the stream. By a large willow tree, En Netef descends in a spray of drops from above. (4) Netef means 'drop' and is also the Hebrew word for the substance travertine that composes the cone from which the water is dripping. Travertine nearby water sources is a deposit of mainly limestone compounds.

The red-marked trail continues up and over to Nahal Meshushim as Nahal Zavitan runs dry. From En Netef head back up stream again and continue up on red-marked trail to meet with green-marked trail. (2) Return the same way you came, taking right on wide green-marked trail.

Note how most trees here grow out of rock piles called tumulus dating from the mid-Bronze period. These may be ancient burial sites like the dolmens that are also found nearby and are sometimes covered by smaller rocks. Trees thrive in this cool moist ground layered with rock piles, more so than in the open fields where they are more vulnerable to forest fires and can often serve as lunch for the local fauna.

As you walk back observe the edge of the ridge high ahead of you known as Vultures' Summit. A bit below this, note the diversion route that the Syrians planned in order to divert the sources of the Jordan River along the Golan Heights. After the Syrians shot at an Israeli tractor, Israel retaliated with tank fire destroying the Syrian construction equipment.

Take care to note the left turn in the green-marked trail, 1 km. from above Nahal Zavitan. Soon you return to starting point. (1)

Nahal Zavitan - Middle

7

Points of interest: Waterfall, pools, hexagons.
Length of hike: 6 km. loop trip.
Hiking time: 4 hours.
Preferred season: All year.
Suitable for: All.
Maps: Golan marked hiking trail map.
Special preparation: Swimsuit.
Starting & ending point: Yehudiya parking lot.

To begin hike:

By car: Turn off into Yehudiya parking lot (1) on Yehudiya Road heading toward the town of Katzrin. Turn right (north) before the parking lot onto blue-marked semi-paved road. Cross through gate, close it and head north for $1^1/_2$ km. Park car at the foot of a lava flow to your left, near electricity pole with blue trail mark. (2) Take left onto blue-marked dirt road heading to the west. Jujube trees grow along the trail. After less than 1 km. reach division in dirt road. Here begins your loop trip. (3)

Follow black-marked trail to the right, for $1^1/_2$ km to the north. To your right is a slope and end point of a lava flow. The trail passes a couple of masils and crosses Nahal Zavitan. The trail begins on the western bank of Nahal Zavitan and descends into the stream bed surrounded by oleander. Note along the stream an aqueduct built by inhabitants of the nearby villages. In the spring several beautiful wild flowers bloom here, such as the Hermon iris and anemones of several colors.

Flower and buds of the thorny caper (hike 6). See map on page 33

The anemone (kalanit) is one of the most popular flowers in Israel. The name anemone is based on the Greek 'anemos,' meaning wind, most likely because the flower grows in wind-blown fields. The traditional anemone is a bright red flower

which grows to about 10-40 cm. high, but in northern Israel, there are anemone varieties in many shades; white, purple, pink and lavender. After generations of being picked extensively it almost reached extinction. However, two decades ago this beautiful flower was declared a protected wildflower and today red carpets of anemones grace the early spring fields of Israel once again, except in the extreme deserts. Blooming in January, the anemone is the first red flower of the spring, opening to the morning light and closing at dusk. Some researchers surmise that the verse, "his lips like lilies," (5:13) in the Song of Songs refers to this flower which is the color of lips — the anemone.

A $\frac{1}{2}$ km. down the stream you come to two large pools with unique hexagon formations in the basalt. Three million years ago lava flowed here and in the spots where it cooled quickly, the basalt cracked into formation of hexagons, pillars and other similar shapes. These formations can be found in different places throughout the world. During the California goldrush prospectors in the 19th century found a 3 km. stretch of these formations in the Sierra Nevada Mountains. They called them 'devil postpiles.'

Nahal Zavitan runs into Nahal Meshushim in which Berekhat Hameshushim (hexagon pool) exposes a gallery of the most impressive hexagons in Israel. The trail crosses Nahal Zavitan to the southeast bank passing some myrtle trees and following the ruined aqueduct. $\frac{1}{2}$ km. from the hexagon pools reach the top of Mapal Zavitan where there is another pool with hexagonal 'tiles' at the bottom. From this point there is no descent to the bottom of the waterfall!

Continue on red-marked trail overlooking the 25 meter waterfall. Descend to the right on clear blue-marked trail (4) to Nahal Zavitan. *The trail is very slippery in the winter.*

Cross the stream, and head to the huge pool beneath the waterfall. Head back up the same blue-marked trail to the top. (4) Continuing along the wadi, you arrive at the treacherous but lovely black canyon that has taken several lives. *Unauthorized access to the canyon is against the law.*

The red-marked trail heads along the western bank, by-passing the black canyon to Lower Nahal Zavitan. To combine hikes, see Lower Nahal Zavitan hike.

Follow wide blue-marked trail past the memorial site. Your route now merges with dirt road that crosses Masil Sheikh Hussein and you reach Hirbet Sheikh Hussein, with small huts and eucalyptus trees. Note the roofs of the homes formed from layers of mud and leaves with railroad beams or branches. This Arab village was deserted in 1967. Continue on dirt road to intersection (3) and return to starting point. (2)

Nahal Gilabon

8

Points of interest: Pools, waterfalls, interesting relics.
Length of hike: 4$^1/_2$ km. loop trip.
Hiking time: 4 hours.
Preferred season: All year.
Suitable for: All.
Maps: Golan marked hiking trail map.
Special preparation: Clothes for walking in water (optional), swimsuit.
Starting & ending point: 2$^1/_2$ km. off Gesher Benot Ya'akov-Nafah Road at Nahal Gilabon trailhead.

To begin hike:

By car: From a point 3 km. north of Rosh Pina in the eastern Galilee, a main road leads down to the Jordan River and crosses Gesher Benot Ya'akov (bridge of the daughters of Jacob) heading up to the Golan Heights. At km. stone 16., before orange and black walls of an army base, take north onto wide dirt road. There you will see a Nature Reserves Authority sign in Hebrew.

This dirt road is red trail-marked. The old, now deserted, houses built of basalt along the way once belonged to the Bedouins; the cement structures were occupied by the Syrian army which was defeated in 1967.

After 1$^1/_2$ km. the dirt road takes a left in a clump of trees and descends to the west reaching a turnoff to the right by the trail mark signs. (1) Take right 400 meters to the trailhead just south of Nahal Gilabon. **Along the way on the left of the dirt road note a minefield fenced in with yellow warning signs and red triangles!!**

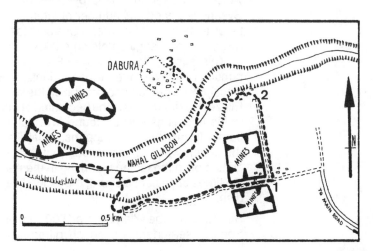

Hike 8,
Nahal Gilabon

The red-marked trail begins (2) among the eucalyptus trees and several ruins. Off to the north in the distance you can see the Hermon Mountain range, usually snow-capped from January to April. To your right observe the slow rise of plateau and in the distance a few peaks of volcanic mountains which reach an altitude of around 1000 meters above sea level; there the tributaries of Nahal Gilabon begin to draw their water down the masils.

Pass Nature Reserves Authority sign and descend. To your left is the canyon. In the distance is Har Kna'an where the city of Safed graces the eastern Galilee, and Upper Galilee summit of Har Meron.

Before crossing Nahal Gilabon, you can veer off to the left and stand a moment above the 15 meter high Dvora Waterfall. Enjoy the view. Cross stream near bushes of sweet smelling myrtle on your right and follow trail to the left under Sabra cactuses to where trail meets blue-marked trail. Take this route, heading up to the ruins of the village Dabura. The blue-marked trail enters courtyard and on your left is a long building (3) with several openings.

Between two doorways there is a very interesting large stone set in the wall and to the right of the second doorway from the raptor with the fish is another stone, most likely a framehead, with two different carvings, one like a ladder and the other a set of connected swastikas. Note the carved stone with the fish. Most likely, the ancient Jewish villagers fished in the Hula Lake in the west and in Nahal Gilabon. Engraved in the upper left part of the rock are two words in Aramaic, 'Avad Tara'ah' meaning 'did the gate,' probably part of a dedication to the person who donated the gate which was most likely part of a public structure like a synagogue.

Dabura is a Bedouin village built with remnants of a village which had been inhabited by Jews during the Roman and Byzantine periods. A number of interesting relics have been taken to museums from here. One of these is a framehead with two short-toed eagles holding snakes in their beaks. Written is "This is the house of study of Rabbi Eliezer Hakapar." This famous rabbi was one of the students of Rabbi Yehuda Ha-Nassi who collected and organized the written oral law. Rabbi Eliezer Hakapar lived in the beginning of the 3rd century. A few of his teachings can be found in a number of texts. Kapar comes from the Greek 'kapparis,' most likely what we know as the caper, which grows throughout Israel and can be found quite a bit in the Golan blooming in the early summer. During the times of ancient Dabura, the pickled caper was a common dish.

Stroll through the village. Note 1500 year old arches still intact. Some researchers, based on different commentators and

Josephus Flavius, believe that this village was the shelter-city Golan of the Bashan. A German archaeologist who was here in 1884 writes of an attempt by Jews to settle here.

Descend, retracing your steps back to Nahal Gilabon onto red-marked trail to the bottom of the Dvora Waterfall. Faults which run north-south are connected to the whole Syrian-African rift. Water flowing into cracked basalt wears down the basalt and creates canyons.

The waterfall gets its Hebrew name from the village that you came from. After enjoying the cool pool below the waterfall, continue down the marked trail. You can choose to hike in the stream bed and enjoy the oleander and willow. Nahal Gilabon is one of the most popular hiking routes in Israel.

One of the few flowers in Israel that blooms in late summer before the first rains, standing out among the pale, dry vegetation, is the white squill. The bulb stores sugars which enable it to produce a leafless stem which flowers around late August, without the help of photosynthesis. This stem can reach the height of 1 meter and at the crest bloom a large vertical cluster of small white-yellow flowers. Each day a row of fresh blossoms opens above the row of the previous day. About one hundred blossoms flower in this way during a 7 to 10 day period. The thick green leaves appear with the first rains and begin to wilt with the onset of a new summer. The squill grows throughout Israel, except in the extreme deserts (southern Negev, Arava). The large 10-20 cm. squill bulb stores a poison which is utilized in some countries to kill rodents. The white squill has a special place in Arab folklore which maintains that the white squill flowers begin to emerge on 'olive day,' when the olives begin to be saturated with oil. They say, "take an olive between your fingers on the day the white squill blossoms and you will be able to squeeze oil from it. Before that day there will be no oil." The stem or stalk of the white squill is also called 'the dew stalk' or 'moisture stalk' since after their appearance the rainy season begins. Whereas in the culture of the west the 'autumn leaves' express the nostalgia of the fall season in the songwriter's lexicon, for modern Israelis the 'hatzav,' the white squill, is one of the poetic symbols of the approaching rainy and cold season. Many songs and poems utilize this theme.

The trail crosses and recrosses the stream and on the southern bank passes a cave, which is not common in the basalt. After the cave reach sign by blue-marked trail leading up to the left, south. (4) But first continue on a bit to the 41 meter Gilabon waterfall, the second highest in Israel after Gamla (51 meters). To the right of the trail by the stream is a small observation point. Look for rainbows in the spray.

Do not get too close to the edge of the cliff!! On wet days the ground can be very slippery!!

Continue on trail past the waterfall and follow red-marked trail to the stream bed. Take right and reach the large pool beneath the falls. If you have hiked in other streams in the Golan, you will note how the waters of Nahal Gilabon are cooler than the streams of central and southern Golan. Nahal Gilabon is the dividing line between northern and central Golan. The red-marked trail continues to Gálbina, a ruined village which gave the stream its name. From Gálbina the trail drops to the Jordan River.

Return by retracing your steps, up the blue-marked trail intersection (4) and head up bare slope to small parking lot. Take left on clear dirt road, heading gradually up to the east between minefields! After 1 km. reach turnoff previously passed (1) by you in your car, take left back to starting point. (2)

Blooming oleander below the Gilabon Waterfall

Galilee

The name Galil was first mentioned by Pharoah Thutmose III of the Egyptian empire during the 16th century B.C.E. The Galilee is mentioned in the Bible only once, in Isaiah 8:23, "and afterward he afflicted her more grievously by the way of the sea beyond Jordan in Galilee of the nations." Josephus Flavius wrote about the Galilee, where he helped fortify a number of towns during the great revolt of 66-70. The Galil is mentioned in the Mishnah (the Jewish oral law) and by Arab historians.

Today the Galilee, covering 2260 sq. km., is a clearly defined geographical entity. The Litani River which today is part of Lebanon, is known in Arabic as the Kasamia — the divider — being Upper Galilee's northern border. The Mediterranean coast in the west, the Jezreel and Harod Valley in the south are clear boundaries; in the east the Galilee drops in a series of scarps to the Syrian-African rift where the Jordan River complex forms the eastern boundary.

The Galilee is clearly divided into the upper and lower regions. Har Meron at an altitude of 1208 meters is the peak of Upper Galilee, while the summit of Har Kamon in Lower Galilee is 602 meters, less than half the height of Har Meron. Rainfall and temperature differ as well; no snow falls in Lower Galilee. Because of uncomfortable weather conditions and wilder terrain in Upper Galilee, Lower Galilee is more densely populated; the Bet Hakerem Valley runs between the two, at the feet of Upper Galilee's sharp escarpments. The Mishnah outlined ancient Israel's border-line between the two Galilees, (Shvi'it 9:3). "All that does not grow sycamore is Upper Galilee, and from Kefar Haninia down all that grows sycamore is Lower Galilee."

Upper Galilee

Geography

Upper Galilee is divided into three sub-regions: west, east and, at the highest elevation, Merom (upper) Galil. The western region is relatively flat with a large number of parallel wadis which flow into the Mediterranean Sea. Nahal Keziv is the central wadi draining a large portion of Upper Galilee. The decline to the west is very gradual with a gradient of only 5°. The plateau-like ridge shape, divided by the wadis, offers a nice view from almost every spot along the ridge as your view is rarely blocked.

A large proportion of the eastern region of the western Galilee is the Peki'in Valley. Western Galilee descends from a maximum elevation of 800 meters to sea level.

Upper Galilee (Merom Galil) is the Meron block consisting of the Har Meron range of chalk and limestone, and the Har Peki'in range to the west, consisting mainly of dolomite. The geographical makeup and terrain of this area has always proven an obstacle to human settlement with its many peaks of over 1000 meters covered with dense vegetation. For this reason, this area has never been well populated nor are there any main roads crossing through here.

Today most of the Merom Galil area of Upper Galilee is a nature reserve. The area boasts few springs. Eastern Upper Galilee includes a number of different sub-regions. The basic terrain of the eastern Galilee is plateau cleft by several wadis. Here, similar to other sites throughout the Galilee, we find evidence of karstic process. Karst is an area in Yugoslavia where this process is common. We find karst weathering usually in an area which consists of rock soluble to acids, i.e., limestone and dolomite, sedimentary rocks from seas which existed millions of years ago; these are made up mainly of carbon calcium sensitive to carbonic acid. When this type of area enjoys considerable rainfall, the rainwater containing carbonic acid penetrates these cracked rocks and causes them to deteriorate, thereby creating varying formations such as caves, sink holes and sculpted rock, known as 'lapies formation.' Basalt covers some of the eastern Galilee. The Safed block or the Canaan Mountain range peaking at 955 meters is a separate region.

Interestingly, the eastern Galilee is split by two large wadis which run in opposite and unusual directions. Nahal Ammud runs north-south to Lake Kinneret and Wadi Dibbe in the Lebanon runs south-north into the Litani River.

Climate

The Galilee enjoys a typically moist Mediterranean climate. In Safed, the annual average temperature is 16°c, one degree less than Jerusalem — where there is only a partially moist Mediterranean climate. Humidity is similar at 60% as well as the amount of hot *sharavs* — a barometric high developing over the country which compresses the subsiding air and heats it.

On Har Meron the annual rainfall exceeds 1000 mm., the only place in Israel west of the Jordan that receives over 1000 mm. Throughout Upper Galilee, the annual rainfall averages over 600 mm. In winter, there are 60-70 days of rain on average, mainly in January and February, and in the summer there is no rain, a typical Mediterranean climate. Snow falls approximately five days in the higher areas of the Galilee, mainly in Upper Galilee and parts of the eastern regions. Droughts are relatively rare. Winter winds can be strong in high spots. Gales of 120 km./h. have been recorded at Mount Canaan.

Vegetation

The high amount of precipitation in the Galilee and the relatively sparse human involvement have allowed the Galilee to remain one of the richest areas in plant life in Israel; the abundant rainfall also encourages burnt out vegetation to rejuvenate quickly. The quality of the earth has also had a considerable influence on the kinds of vegetation, especially in the western and Upper Galilee: Mediterranean forest growing on limestone and dolomite based earth are richer in quantity and variety of plant life. Many Israeli species can be found only in Upper Galilee, such as the forest peony and certain types of ferns.

The Mediterranean forest of the Galilee is also rich in species of trees. In the Har Meron range, cyprus, oak, bear plum and thorny hawthorn grace the local flora. In the western Galilee, maple and laurel are common. Laurel for example needs a lot of precipitation and moderate temperatures. Aleppo pine grows wild at several locations in the western Galilee. The only juniper trees in Israel grow at Hirbet

Shefanim east of the village of Bet Jan. Another tree growing along the stream banks is the tall plane tree which grows in the Golan as well; rarely does this tree grow in the rest of the country. The open fields in the Galilee are unused agricultural lands, many deserted in 1948 and today the natural forest here is making a comeback. It is estimated that a period of 200 years is needed for decimated forest to return to its original growth level in this region.

In the spring, the fields are carpeted with lavishly colored wild flowers. Many rare orchids can be seen alongside multicolored anemones and many other protected and rare wild flowers.

Wildlife

The Galilee's rich variation in wildlife has been diminished. Human settlement, agricultural development and expansion of the minority villages has limited the Galilee's wilderness. Today in Upper Galilee you cannot find an area within a radius of 3 km. without human settlement.

Until the turn of the century, brown bears, leopards, row deer, fallow deer and many raptors such as vultures, bearded vultures and kestrels were common. Many of the mammals are of Mediterranean and Iro-Siberian origin and several are tropical species such as the honey badger and the hyrax. Few desert species live here, whereas along the Mediterranean coast to the west, and in the Hula Valley to the east in the Syrian-African rift quite a few animal species have extended their habitats north.

The open fields of the eastern Galilee is the habitat of the graceful gazelles, which farmers consider a nuisance because they strip bark off trees. A large variety of rodents also live here, the largest is the Indian crested porcupine. Three types of northern field mice inhabit the forests of Upper Galilee. The common otter which used to thrive in the streams is a rare specimen today. Wild boars are a favorite hunted animal by kibbutzniks of the area. At twilight, many bats can be observed, among them the European fruit bat.

Although the waterscapes have been severely damaged, six kinds of amphibians can still be found in the Galilee. Among these, the edible frog and green toad are common, while the fire salamander and newt are usually found at higher altitudes. The spade foot toad is rarer while the lemon tree frog can be found throughout the Galilee although not as common as the edible frog; the latter found in nearly every body of water.

The Palestinian viper is the only poisonous snake in the Galilee and it is sometimes mistaken for the coin-marked snake. As in many places in Israel, the starred lizard can often be caught sunbathing on rocks and the smooth lizard making a racket in the underbrush. Often you can catch sight of a chameleon. During the warm months, many other lizards and snakes emerge from their hiding places. There are fresh water crabs in the waters. The fish of this area are mainly members of the carp family and cichlid (St. Peter's Fish).

Human Involvement

The major settlements of the Galilee region are concentrated in the lower areas. Due to weather, transportation and agricultural conditions, groups which were considered outsiders often gravitated from the centers of population along the Syrian-African rift and the coast to the Galilee.

Water sources are abundant, but are not conveniently situated. The best land for farming is on the chalk and basalt soil of eastern Galilee. Many villages have been established on lands of limestone and dolomite with adjacent chalk or basalt soil suitable for agricultural use.

We find remnants of cities from the early bronze period in the hilly parts of Upper Galilee, such as Kedesh, Gat, and Yanuah. But even these cities were not established in the upper region of Upper Galilee. From that era, the relatively large population of Upper Galilee diminished.

The tribe of Asher settled the west and the tribe of Naftali settled the eastern region of the Galilee. The coastal region, however, was not taken over by the tribes of Israel and remained under the control of the Cana'anites.

In 723 B.C.E., the Assyrian Tiglath Pilesar exiled the Israelites and not until the beginning of the Second Temple period was the Galilee resettled by Jews, who slowly began to extend their presence there. During the Great Revolt of 66-70 that led to the destruction of the Second Temple, Josephus Flavius fortified three cities in Upper Galilee: Safed, Akhbara and Meron.

After the destruction of the Second Temple, the center of Jewish life gravitated to the Galilee and many synagogues from this period have been found.

During the Byzantine period, many people settled in Upper Galilee, evidenced by the churches and mosaics of that period discovered here, and settlement extended to previously uninhabited areas of the Meron range.

The Crusaders were in the Galilee for about 150 years, during which time they built impressive forts and farms. They exported oil, fruit, sugar cane and other goods to Europe.

When the Mamelukes came on the scene, they made use of the Templer fort of Safed for their administrative center and destroyed Acre.

The Turks rebuilt Acre, which they considered an important port town, and encouraged its development. From the 17th century onward, the central Turkish role deteriorated and local influences were felt.

In 1799, Acre withstood Napoleon's siege. At that time, Jewish communities shared villages with Arabs. Today in the Druze village of Peki'in only a Miss Zinati remains, claiming to be the ancestor of the Jewish community which thrived there 2000 years ago.

The Druze presence is first mentioned in the Galilee in the 14th century. They have always suffered the tribulations of a minority, therefore, Upper Galilee was an ideal locale for the Druze to establish settlements. Today most of the 18 Druze villages of Israel are located in the Galilee. The Druze faith originates from 10th century Egypt, at which time this sect broke off from mainstream Islam. They suffered much persecution throughout the ages, settling mainly in Lebanon and Syria where an entire mountain range is named after this religious sect. Their faith is a secret one, the details of which are unknown to most Druze, who only keep the outward customs. In each community several are chosen to become the priests and are known as 'the initiated.' The Druze have no homeland and are renowned for their loyalty and bravery in battle, related to their concept of fate. Since 1948 the Druze of Israel have taken their stand on the Jewish side of the Israeli-Arab conflict and today many of them serve and work in different security positions in Israel. However, the Druze of the Golan seem to have developed loyalties to Syria.

In the 16th century Safed became the pulsating heart of the Jews of Palestine. Many famous rabbis, several of whom were forced to leave Spain at the time of the great Jewish expulsion, wrote great tomes of Kabalistic learning here, investing the very cobblestones with an aura of the secrets of God's universe. To this day, its mystical tradition lends Safed an air of other-wordliness; the sunrise and sunset hours become an unforgettable experience.

The Lebanese border was decided by a French-British resolution after World War I. In the 1930's and 1940's the first modern Jewish settlements began to sprout in the hills of the Galilee. Hanita and Yehiam in the west are famous. Biryah near Safed, which is not occupied today, is another historic settlement site.

During the War of Independence, many Arabs fled and are refugees until this day. Those who remained occupy a number of villages mainly in Lower Galilee. Being an Arab minority in a Jewish state has complicated their own self-definition, and the pressures placed on them by the surrounding Arab states have exacerbated their status and led to many problems.

After the establishment of the State of Israel in 1948, there was a great immigration wave in the early 50's. A large number of moshavs were established here close to the Lebanese border to absorb these immigrants and offer them a new way of life.

The Safed-Acre Road, a main thoroughfare and axis from west to east, runs between Upper and Lower Galilee. Another road runs from Nahariya to Safed through the development town of Ma'alot. There is a good north road from Rosh Hanikra, heading west-east just south of the Lebanese border to the Hula Valley. There is no main road crossing the upper Galilee from north to south. The roads in Upper Galilee, unlike many places in Israel, are not based on ancient ways.

Water

As a rule, water is abundant in Upper Galilee. The main springs are located in some of the wadis east and west of the central upper part of Upper Galilee (Merom Galil). These wadis were once lengthy perennial streams but today, due to intense utilization of water sources, only brief sections of Nahal Keziv, Nahal Betzet, Nahal Ammud and Nahal Dishon still flow with water. Along these streams are flour mills which utilized the running water for activating the wheels. These have not been in use since 1948.

Although wells are not common, water cisterns are found near most ruins. Several of the wadis carry water for several weeks during the winter.

Springs are usually layer springs. In Upper Nahal Ammud there is a karstic spring (En Po'em) similar to the Gihon Spring in Jerusalem. Unfortunately, today a number of wadis drain sewage, i.e., Nahal Akhbara near Safed which runs into Central Nahal Ammud.

Hiking in the Galilee

The hikes in this book are centered around Har Meron. In the western Galilee, public transportation usually begins at Nahariya's Central Bus Station where you can also board a bus from Haifa that crosses the Galilee to Safed. In the eastern Galilee buses run from Haifa to Safed and down to Rosh Pina. In addition there are a few buses from Safed which travel to other areas of the northeast Galilee.

The roads in the Galilee are scenic and winding, but often weather-beaten and negotiating them in your car in winter can be hazardous, especially on foggy, snowy or rainy days.

There are many marked trails in the Galilee and most of the hikes follow them.

The summer days are not too hot but are quite sunny. Four litres of water per person are needed for a full day of hiking. In the winter, two litres is sufficient. No matter where you hike, you are never far from a village or road. Spring water can be drunk but it is not recommended.

Important phone numbers:

(Area code 069)

Mt. Meron Field Study Center	89072
Hermon Field Study Center (Senir)	41091
Nature Reserves Authority — Safed	71918
Police — Safed	30444
First Aid (Magen David Adom) — Safed	30333/463

(Area code 04)

Western Galilee Field Study Center	922762
Police — Nahariya	920344
First Aid (Magen David Adom) — Nahariya	82333

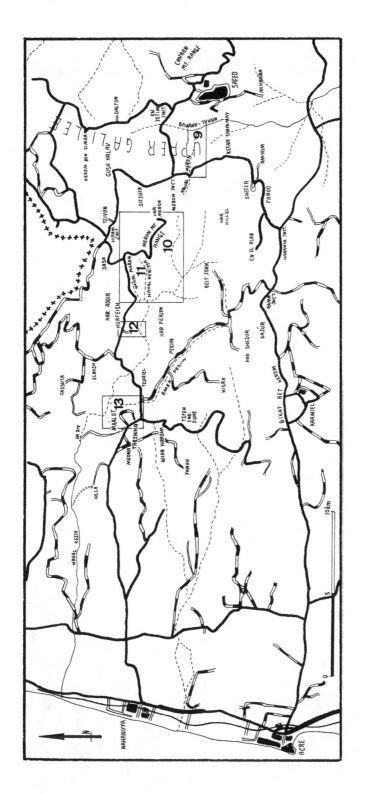

Upper Galilee.
Numbers represent
hike numbers.

Nahal Ammud · Upper

9

Points of interest: Rich waterscape.
Length of hike: 4 km. loop trip.
Hiking time: 4 hours.
Preferred season: All year.
Suitable for: All.
Maps: Upper Galilee marked hiking trail map.
Special preparation: Swimsuit (in spring and summer).
Starting & ending point: Parking lot 1$\frac{1}{2}$ km. off of Safed-Carmiel Road.

To begin hike:

By car: Take gravel road 2$\frac{1}{2}$ km. south of Moshav Meron on Safed-Carmiel Road, near orange colored sign, 'Nahal Ammud' that heads eastward. (1) This road crosses a cattle barrier near a large carob tree and continues through the sweet smelling planted Aleppo pine forest, descending to large parking lot. Park here.

Follow wide red-marked trail along water pipe for $\frac{1}{2}$ km. to deserted structure.(2) For a nice view, climb to the top. Observe your position between the Meron range to your west and the Har Kna'an range including the town of Safed to your east. This building served as a British police station which guarded the water pumping station below at En Yakim from Arab attacks during the famous Arab uprisings of 1936-1939 which were finally suppressed by the British.

Upper Nahal Ammud looking north. See map on page 52

The structure is deteriorating so watch out!!

Follow good trail, with hand-railings, down to the north to En Yakim. There is an information center here which is most likely

closed. Yakim was the 12th of the 24 priestly rotations who served the Temple, and they are mentioned in Chronicles I 24:12. They lived in Safed.

The Arabs call this spring, which yields 800 cubic meters per hour, the fig spring (En a Tina) since many fig trees grow here along with walnut and many other kinds of trees. Follow trail along water carrier on southern bank of Nahal Meron past sign. The wadi drains the eastern slopes of the Meron range. One hundred meters along your route, drop to the left and cross stream over bridge, following trail down with tall plane trees down to wadi. The stream is also named Dilbai after the plane tree called Dolev in Hebrew, as the Jews of Safed named the wadi after this impressive tree.

This carrier brought water to many of the 12 flour mills of Nahal Ammud; the last ones were worked until 1948 when many of the local Arabs fled as their brethren from surrounding countries attempted an invasion of the fledgling State of Israel.

The water also irrigates deserted orchards of lemon, pomegranate and other fruits that were raised here, which gave the stream its other name, 'Wadi Limon.'

The pomegranate (rimon) is one of the seven species of the Land of Israel. This tree blooms between April and June, has large, orange-red flowers with bright yellow pollen at the heart. The pomegranate fruit ripens toward the end of the summer with some fruits maintaining a red color and others turning yellow. Although not natural to Israel, the pomegranate is found throughout the country, except for the desert. Today the fruit is not a big commercial item though rural Arabs still grow them, usually for home use and trees are frequently found near Arab homes. The pomegranate's colorful flower and fruit, along with its delicate taste, has been used to symbolize beauty and fertility. The Song of Songs mentions the pomegranate six times, "I will cause thee to drink of spiced wine of the juice of the pomegranate." (8:2) In Israel, fresh pomegranate fruits symbolize hope for the New Year at the Rosh HaShannah table, platefuls of the juicy seeds handed around to everyone for the 'Sheheheyanu' blessing over newly harvested fruits. The whole fruits are also hung as colorful Succa decorations during the Festival of the Tabernacles. The kernels can be eaten fresh or pressed into juice. Dried kernels are a sort of raisin. The peel is quite bitter and contains a dark brown dye that was used in Talmudic times not only for dying but also in order to reveal texts written in invisible ink. It is said that the juice fortifies hair roots.

Nahal Ammud is also known as the wadi of the flour mills. Ammud in Hebrew is pillar. At the base of the stream and at the end of a canyon not far from Lake Kinneret stands a pillar, giving the stream its name. In the past, Nahal Ammud was very rich in wildlife; bears, wolves and leopards roamed the stream which flowed all year round.

Nahal Ammud continues down a 22 km. course where it empties into Lake Kinneret. Today an average of one million cubic meters of water passes through Nahal Ammud annually.

The trail crosses a bridge to return to the southern bank where it comes to meet the other main tributary coming in from the north. Here there is a sign. (3) Head straight down to stream bed to blue-marked trail. Take right following stream on eastern bank. Reach trail intersection by bridge over stream. Continue straight on now black-marked trail and soon drop to the pools of Sekhvee by a deserted flour mill. Here Nahal Sekhvee comes in from the east from Safed.

From the pools return on black-marked trail to blue-marked trail. Continue on black-marked trail across Nahal Ammud to flour mill. Follow trail along water channel until reaching another building known by the Arabic name of Tahunet el Batan. (5) Here the Jews of Safed, who were expelled from Spain, returned to reside in Eretz Israel and set up a wool textile industry. The running water was used to turn the grooved wooden mallets which pounded and flattened the wool. In the 16th century the wool of Safed was renowned throughout the Middle East.

From here a green-marked trail heads up through open area, overlooking Safed and Nahal Ammud to the police station along the way. A white-marked trail leads back to En Yakim.

Hike 9, Upper Nahal Ammud

The green-marked trail reaches the deserted building (2) where you can take a last glimpse of your route. Follow the same wide red-marked trail to starting point. (1)

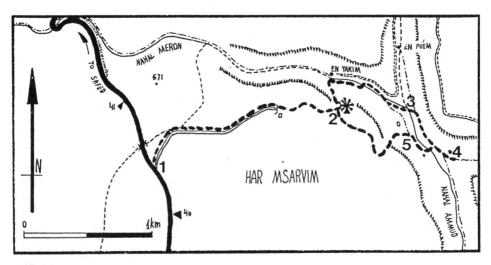

Har Meron Range

10

Points of interest: Views, karstic sink holes, relics, varied vegetation.
Length of hike: 18 km. loop trip.
Hiking time: 9 hours.
Preferred season: All year.
Suitable for: Experienced hikers.
Maps: Upper Galilee marked hiking trail map.
Special preparation: None.
Starting & ending point: Mt. Meron Field Study Center.

To begin hike:

By bus and car: Reach Mt. Meron Field Study Center 1 km. off the main Nahariya-Safed Road. (See hike # 11 Nahal Moran — Nahal Neriyya)

A hundred and fifty meters past the Mt. Meron Field Study Center there is a parking lot and picnic area. (1) The old building here is Hirbet el Humema and its arches are typical of Arab architecture. Nearby are a number of remnants from the Bronze period; pottery, house foundations, a water cistern and a cavity used for plaster manufacture. Here you will see the beginning of the black-marked trail that reaches the summit of Har Meron. Take it.

Har Meron, looking southwest from Lake Dalton. See map on page 57

Work is being completed on a 900-1000 km. trail which will cross Israel from north to south, from Mt. Hermon to Eilat and this trail forms part of it, as indicated by the additional trail mark. The trail passes En Humema, a layer spring which emerges from a man-made cave; observe the yellowish marl around the spring that holds back the water from seeping through. Here you may find small yellow dotted fire salamanders.

Aleppo pine trees have been planted alongside the trail here to enrich the natural forest. Note how the pine needles have neutralized vegetation around the base of the trees. A lot of asparagus bushes grow just past the trees and a bit further on you can see some small planted cedars of Lebanon. Most of those planted trees did not survive while further north in the cooler climate of Lebanon these cedars have flourished since Biblical times.

Reach the Har Neriyya lookout point to the north and east with a grove of oak trees in the center of the circular patio. From here you can see parts of Lebanon and the antenna of Har Adir, the most northern mountain of the Har Meron range. To the east you can easily see Lake Dalton on Dalton plateau.

Just beyond the lookout point at the beginning of the forest, a small trail leads off to the right reaching some fort remnants, most likely remnants from the Iron Age. Since no sign of ancient settlement turned up in this area, it is assumed that this was a lookout and guard outpost.

Less than 1 km. from Har Neriyya reach the loop 'summit trail' of Har Meron. (2) The red-marked 1$\frac{1}{2}$ km. trail leading around the summit of Har Meron passes many interesting sites. The actual summit area is a closed military area and this is the purpose of the well-paved road which climbs Har Meron.

Along the trail many rare flowers bloom, each typical of a different season of the year. In the early winter, round-leaved cyclamens grace the sides of the trail. Many of these bulb-based plants were unearthed and relocated from the summit when construction of the I.D.F. army base began, but unfortunately most of the delicate plants did not survive the move.

Turn left on trail. After 400 meters of open area, pass wine press hewn in the rock, most likely from the Roman and Byzantine period. The Romans built many roads and aqueducts throughout the country and their settlement expanded to outlying areas such as Har Meron and the northern Negev. Most relics in the Meron Mountains are from this period.

The trail passes the Lebanon lookout and following that the Safed lookout. Here in the fall the large bright yellow sternbergia flower blossoms.

Har Meron is 1208 meters above sea level, and is the highest mountain west of the Syrian-African rift between the Sinai Peninsula and Lebanon. The trail drops to a paved road near a camp ground with tables and water. Take left on paved road that leads to Har Bar Yochai. Just beyond the camp ground a blue-marked dirt road veers off to the right near a wooden sign. Take it. After $\frac{1}{2}$ km. a green-marked dirt road leads to left to the south and reaches the Druze village Beit Jan. Continue along blue-marked trail.

As the road drops to its lowest point, the blue-marked trail heads off to the left through Hirbet Bek. (3) This was the site of a Druze village called Germak which is also the Arabic name for Har Meron. Here Yisrael Bek, a Jewish printer from Safed, led a number of families to settle after their homes were destroyed in the famous 1837 earthquake in Safed. The tough conditions there took a heavy toll and this attempt failed four years later. Today, the Arabs call the place 'ruins of the Jews,' Hirbet Yahud. You can see flourishing walnut trees, often heavy with fruit. The trail passes a well and an olive press basin. Soon the trail passes a water cistern in a cave that is usually filled with water.

The clear blue-marked trail heads west on the southern slope of the ridge. A little more than 1 km. after you have passed Hirbet Bek the trail reaches a small wadi and a small dirt road crosses the trail. Follow the dirt road on its descent to the left; at the end on your left you will see a hole in the ground (4) which was created by the karst phenomenon: carbonic acid eats away at the limestone sculpting caves, rock formations and sink holes. There are many of these deep sink holes in the Har Meron area. Some reach 100 meters deep. This one is about 70 meters deep. The villagers have a number of folktales about the 'mysterious' openings. They tell of a shepherd who dropped his flute here. Many months later he met another shepherd from the village of Peki'in, 9 km. to the west, and he was carrying the first shepherd's flute. The second shepherd claimed that he had found the flute in the village spring. This story actually illustrates the area's underground water routes. The large amount of rainfall that drops here seeps through the ground of cracked dolomite and limestone only to resurface at lower points to the west and east. These holes are also known as 'huta,' meaning whale, as they equal the dimensions of a whale's mouth. This particular one is known as 'huta Germak.' It is said that the Druze of Germak threw different teams of Turkish tax collectors into the hole again and again until the Turks found out and sent a brigade of soldiers who destroyed the village. When this huta was checked out, no remnants of anyone turned up, just a football covered with mud.

Return to blue-marked trail, take left. As the trail rounds another small wadi you come to an open area, head off to the right side of the ridge. Here are two pools that have been hewn into the rock, one of them containing stairs that lead to the bottom. (5) These are most likely from the Roman-Byzantine period.

Return to blue-marked trail and continue through brush and forest down the ridge. A lot of marjoram can be found growing along the way. The trail crosses the perfect remains of an ancient wine press, evidence of extensive vineyards in the area, most likely also Roman-Byzantine. The workers extracted the grape juice by treading the grapes with their bare feet. Perhaps they also shouted as they worked, as mentioned in Jeremiah 25:30 "he shall give a shout as they that tread the grapes against all the inhabitants of the earth." The wine press is usually composed of 3 sections: the trampling area, the hole which collected the grape seeds, flesh and peel and the collection aperture where the clean juice was drained off.

The trail begins to descend toward upper Nahal Keziv, passing some plum trees and joining a dirt road which leads to the wadi of Nahal Zeved. At Nahal Zeved, take right 150 meters to the wadi bed of Nahal Keziv. Cross Nahal Keziv by black and blue trail mark intersection and head up path on western bank. The trail becomes a newer, wider dirt road. Take left at top to En Sartava, (6) the largest spring in the area. The Har Meron reserve consists of two main sections. The Peki'in ridge and the Meron ridge in the east separated by upper Nahal Keziv and its many tributaries. You are now on the Peki'in ridge.

From En Sartava return to dirt road and continue straight, gradually descending to Nahal Keziv. Follow the black-marked trail along the wadi, crossing to both sides. Follow the river bed, passing fruit orchards and garlic fields. After 2 km. the trail reaches a forest and heads along the eastern bank as the wadi becomes a bit canyon-like.

Reach tobacco field and the Nahal Keziv-Moran-Neriyya intersection. (7) Take right onto green-marked trail heading between fields. At bottom of ridge (3) between Nahal Moran and Nahal Neriyya take right onto dirt road with red trail mark into Nahal Neriyya. Nahal Neriyya begins on the watershed by Hirbet el Humema. Follow clear trail into forest along wadi for 3 km. back to starting point. (1)

Nahal Moran‑Nahal Neriyya

11

Points of interest: Mediterranean forest, springs.
Length of hike: 8 km. loop trip.
Hiking time: 4 hours.
Preferred season: All year.
Suitable for: All.
Maps: Upper Galilee marked hiking trail map.
Special preparation: None.
Starting & ending point: Mt. Meron Field Study Center.

To begin hike:

By bus: Take Haifa-Safed bus which passes through Nahariya. At turn-off to Har Meron between km. stone 32 and 33 get off and walk down paved road 1 km. to Mt. Meron Field Study Center.

Hike 10, Har Meron and hike 11, Nahal Moran

By car: On Nahariya-Safed Road between km. stone 32 and 33 west of Kibbutz Sa'sa turn right onto road leading to the top of Har Meron. One km. up this road the Mt. Meron Field Study Center will be on your right. You can park there. (The Field Study Center guides will be happy to give you up-to-date information.)

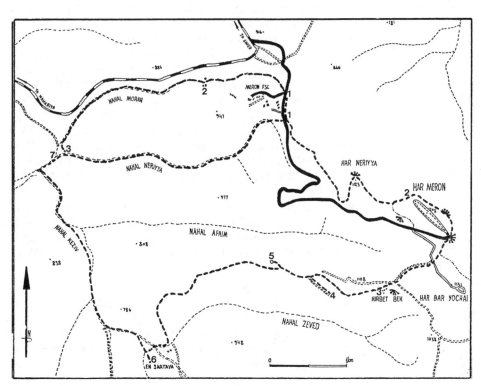

57

Your hike begins at road turn-off to the Field Study Center. (1) There is a green trail mark on electricity pole near open area. There is also a trail mark by the side of the main road.

Follow clearly marked trail into forest. The trail descends to the bottom of Nahal Moran's southern bank. The moran in Hebrew is the laurestinus tree which grows in Israel only in the upper Galilee and Carmel. It is a small tree that blooms in a cluster of small white flowers in the spring and is related to the honey-suckle. The trail passes plum orchards growing in the wide wadi bed of Nahal Moran, beginning more or less near the road leading to Har Meron, on the watershed of Israel. One km. from the trailhead reach Enot Neriyya.

The few springs that flow in the Meron Mountains are meagre. The water sinks deeper into the cracked limestone ground and emerges along the outer extent of mountain mass. Nahal Keziv, Nahal Ammud, and Nahal Dishon, have large numbers of springs. Nahal Moran is a tributary of Nahal Keziv. The two largest springs, one of them En Sartava, are near the Druze village of Bet Jan, and are layer springs as are most of the springs in the Har Meron region.

In the open areas along the trail you can find marjoram, the 'eizov' called za'atar in Arabic, which is perhaps the most popular wild herb growing in Israel. The small, 30-50 cm., shrub is made of green-grey leaves that are covered with small hairs that produce an aromatic oil. Its small white flowers grow in round clusters and bloom between April and September. Marjoram grows in open fields throughout the hills of Israel and in the high areas of the Negev. Mentioned in the Bible, and usually translated as 'hyssop' it symbolized simplicity and humbleness. The Children of Israel used marjoram to put the lamb's blood on their doorposts as a sign in Egypt before their great exodus from slavery (Ex. 12:23). Marjoram was also used for purification in the Temple. King David in Psalms 51:9 beseeches the Lord, "Purge me with hyssop and I shall be clean." Marjoram tea can be made with leaves and sugar. This is reputed to be a cure for colds, toothaches, to clear the mind and improve memory. Fried marjoram leaves are added to bread, soup and meat and the fresh leaves are added to salads. To make za'atar, grind dry marjoram leaves and add sesame seeds, salt and ground fruit of the sumac. Za'atar is used daily by many Arabs, together with olive oil, as a spread for pitta-bread.

Due to the tremendous popularity of this plant, Arabs in Israel have over-picked the wild marjoram commercially, in order to ship tons of the herb via Jordan to other lands of the Middle East. The only solution was for the authorities to declare this small plant a protected plant. Today one is only permitted to pick a small amount for personal use.

Head above wadi bed on small cliff. Here in the late spring one of the species of wild garlic blooms in a sphere of pink flowers. Garlic is grown in many places in Upper Galilee by locals, including in Nahal Moran.

Follow trail into dark wadi bed in forest which opens up into garlic fields. A dirt road crosses the wadi by a lone olive tree. Continue on trail toward the left and 100 meters farther on reach red-marked trail. Take left and begin to climb up Nahal Neriyya. (3) Here are tobacco fields. Hyacinth squill bloom in the wild fields in the spring. Nahal Neriyya is surrounded by dense Mediterranean forest, which here consists mainly of the kermes oak. Creepers grow along the trail beneath the leaf filigree of light and shade.

Three km. up the wadi, reach the watershed by Hirbet el Humema (1) on road leading to Har Meron just south of the starting point. Take left to starting point. (1)

Blooming garlic fields in Nahal Moran

Har Zvul

12

Points of interest: Druze religious site, view, springs, waterscape.
Length of hike: 5 km. loop trip.
Hiking time: 4 hours.
Preferred season: All year.
Suitable for: All.
Maps: Upper Galilee marked hiking trail map.
Special preparation: Bathing suit.
Starting & ending point: Main square in the village of Hurfeish.

To begin hike:

Take bus or drive to the Druze village of Hurfeish on the Nahariya-Safed Road. The trailhead begins at the main square on the main road intersecting the village. Just to the west of two small grocery stores the road leads up to Nebi Sabalan where there is a sign and a black trail mark on a light post. (1)

Head up the street. Just past the pastoral looking oak and Aleppo pine landscaped cemetery, the trail parts from the main street. Ascend steep black-marked trail to the left through Hurfeish's residential area on the outer fringe of this friendly village of around 3000 inhabitants, about 90% of which are Druze; the remainder are Moslem and Christian. Many of the Druze serve in the different security forces of Israel. A number have fallen in the defense of the State of Israel and there is a memorial in the town.

The trail passes a dirt road which curves to the right. Continue the straight ascent, toward the top, the trail cuts through a small grove of large oak trees 'decorated' with hanging rags. Nebi Sabalan is where the Moslem and Druze believe that the

En Hotam in upper Nahal Keziv. See map on page 61

60

prophet Zevulun is buried. No one knows exactly who this prophet was and some say that he was the son of Jacob. These trees are now a holy site since the Druze believe that Zevulun used to sit and study beneath them. They are known as 'mother of the rags' and believers come here to make their vows and bring gifts. Continue through fig planted open fields till you reach the top of Har Zvul. (2) Take left and enter site, *taking care to behave in a manner suitable to a holy site.* This is the second most holy religious site of the Druze in Israel, the most important being Nebi Shueb, west of Tiberias. They took control of it in 1948 when it was deserted by the Moslems. Being outside of any village jurisdiction, Nebi Sabalan is a public place for all where Druze come to pray and petition Allah. If a person's petition is fulfilled, he will invite friends and family to a feast here.

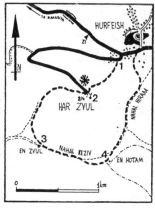

Every year on September 10th all the Druze come to this site for a celebration. Every prophet has a feast day and this is the holiday of Zevulun. The Druze believe that when he was escaping the Moslems, Zevulun crossed Nahal Keziv and climbed the 814 meter mountain where he hid in a cave and studied religion. The Moslems did not find him until the day they saw him leaving the cave. Zevulun prayed to Allah for help and a dam formed in Nahal Keziv. The waters rose until they reached the entrance to Zevulun's cave, and this saved him from the Moslems since their approach was blocked, but Zevulun did not drown. Therefore this hill is called Nebi (prophet) Sabalan, and the section of Nahal Keziv beneath you is called Wadi Hubeiz, meaning dam.

Hike 12, Har Zvul

The site is undergoing development. The cave is in the large building; *remember to take off your shoes and cover your head if you enter.* The interior is quite colorful, the ground covered with rugs and there are many hued pieces of clothing which the Druze usually leave here. There are facilities on the spot.

From Har Zvul enjoy view of the peaks of the Har Meron reserve. Looking from the northeast to southeast, is Har Adir which is 1008 meters high, Har Hiram — 996 meters, Mt. Meron Field Study Center — 900 meters, Har Meron — 1208 meters, Har Hillel — 1071 meters and to the south you can see the village of Bet Jan, the highest village in the Galilee.

Just before the entrance to the complex, there is a wooden sign in Hebrew, 'Upper Nahal Keziv,' and a black trail mark. Follow trail mark down to the west. Pass water cistern and continue through open fields. The trail reaches the beginning of a wadi and begins a steep descent just to the right of the gully and through an oak forest.

Here and there grow sage, a greenish-grey bush growing up to $1^1/_2$ meters. Quite a few species of the sage, also known as the moriah, are found in Israel. A large plant, it is covered with small porous hairs which emit a strong but pleasant odor. The bluish white flowers bloom late into the spring, usually in late April and May. This species grows on the dark-brown terra-rossa soil in the mountainous parts of Israel. The sage herb is a well-known curative; among other things, sage tea is used for stomach aches, colds, sore throat and more. To make the tea, boil a few leaves with water and add sugar. You can also add a leaf or two to a cup of hot water or tea. The leaves are also used as a spice for meat and to give taste to liqueur. Small amounts of the leaves are sometimes eaten raw. This plant was once commercially shipped to the Persian Gulf. Some researchers point to the striking resemblance of certain sage plants to the Jewish Temple's menorah.

Farther down, the trail crosses to the left side of the gully and the oak forest begins to thin out. Pistachio trees now appear, more sage and the thorny calycotome.

The trail drops to Nahal Keziv where En Zvul emerges in a picturesque pool. (3) The springs in Nahal Keziv are layer springs, the deep wadi having cut through the many strata until reaching a water impermeable marl layer, thus releasing the water flow. Head up Nahal Keziv on green-marked trail alongside some miniature pools — several of these are large enough for a nice dip.

Here you will see the rush bush with sharp $1/_2$ meter long leaves emerging from the base growing near the water. One km. from En Zvul the trail rises on the southern bank and reaches En Hotam (4) emerging from an arched structure into a large trough above some tall cottonwoods. 100 meters east is another spring in the rock. Here you may find fire salamanders.

From En Hotam, take blue-marked trail descending down to Nahal Keziv and heading up Nahal Hiram which enters from the north. (King Hiram of Lebanon supplied King Solomon with cedars of Lebanon for building the First Temple.)

The clear trail crosses to the eastern side of Nahal Hiram that flows down from Har Hiram, the round-shaped mountain 3 km. east of Hurfeish. One km. from Nahal Keziv you reach the outskirts of Hurfeish. In the first building to your left is an oil press. Note piles of pressed olives on the side of the dirt road. Fall is the season for pressing olives.

The trail then becomes a paved street which links with the main road crossing the village. Take left on main road to starting point. (1)

Nahal Peki'in

13

Points of interest: Mediterranean forest, Crusader fort, cliff.
Length of hike: 9 km. loop trip.
Hiking time: 5 hours.
Preferred season: All year.
Suitable for: All.
Maps: Upper Galilee marked hiking trail map.
Special preparation: None.
Starting & ending point: Town of Ma'alot.

To begin hike:

By bus: Take bus from Nahariya Central Bus Station. Get off at first stop after bus has turned off to Ma'alot at the eastern approach. Head down road and after passing large concrete Ort school complex to your left you will come to a wide street, Rakefet Street, which curves right. (1) Begin your hike here.

By car: Enter Ma'alot eastern entrance. Head straight for 1 km., pass below large concrete Ort school complex to your left. Park near wide street that curves right, Rakefet Street. (1) Begin your hike here.

Goat Cliff. Note the clear notches at its base. See map on page 67

Head right down Rakefet St. between 'buy your own home' community and an unspoiled field of original Galilee landscape; shepherds bring their flocks into Ma'alot to graze here. Note the strong karstic rock weathering formations.

The development town of Ma'alot was established in 1957, its population is made up of immigrants from North Africa who originally were housed in temporary structure camps, 'ma'abarot,' near the neighboring Arab village of Tarshiha.

Early in the morning of May 15, 1974, Arab terrorists infiltrating from Lebanon broke into a Ma'alot home and murdered a couple and their child. They then seized the Ntiv Meir school where over 100 Safed children enjoying a school outing were spending the night. The pupils and their teachers were held hostage for many nightmare-filled hours. The terrorists demanded immediate release of 26 terrorists jailed in Israel, threatening to blow up the school, thereby killing all the children and their teachers if their demands were not met by 6:00 p.m. The population of Israel watched in horror and pain as the hours ticked by. Then, shortly before the deadline, I.D.F. troops stormed the school in a last-minute attempt to save the innocent lives. The terrorists opened fire and tossed grenades on the children, killing 21 and wounding 70. This tragic incident put the forgotten development town of Ma'alot on the map of national consciousness.

In the last 15 years, the northern town has developed considerably. The industrial zone now includes several highly advanced technological industries. The green Rakefet (cyclamen) Hill on which Ma'alot stands has its own Hesder Yeshiva; here young men combine Jewish studies with their army service. There is an art center, a Nature Community Center of the Society for the Protection of Nature and a resort across the main road. The town includes several 'Build your own home' communities which you can see nearby. Arabs call the site of Ma'alot, 'the gate of winds'; being 591 meters above sea level at the summit and only 20 km. from the Mediterranean Sea.

At the end of Rakefet St. cross Yakinton (hyacinth) Street and descend on dirt road. Take right at intersection, walking along the western slope of Nahal Peki'in which is below you. Before curve to the right take unmarked trail down left to the wadi.

Most of the streams in the upper western Galilee flow along an east-west gradient to the Mediterranean Sea. Nahal Peki'in drains the Peki'in Valley from south to north, flowing into central Nahal Keziv at a point below Ma'alot.

Peki'in is a minorities village, mainly Druze, at the foot of the Peki'in range's western slopes. There is one Jewish lady residing in Peki'in, who takes care of the synagogue there. She claims to be an ancestor of a Jewish family which has lived in Peki'in continually since the time of the Second Temple. Her claim has never been disproved.

After a rainy period, Nahal Peki'in may return to life for a couple of weeks.

The trail passes through a cattle gate on the right of the river bed, recrossing to the left. A hidden wadi (4) enters from the left and the trail crosses Nahal Peki'in to the right bank near some large oaks. The trail again crosses to the left and $1/_2$ km. later reaches an abandoned quarry, (2) right before the intersection with Nahal Keziv. This quarry once served the villages of Tarshiha and Suhmata. The now narrow trail was once a well used dirt road.

Cross Nahal Peki'in and head up stream along wide path that soon merges with the river bed. Twenty meters along your way there is a pile of rocks on the left signifying a trail leading up to Mtzad Karha. Ascend, through marjoram and thorny calycotome. If you have chosen to make this climb in late winter you can also enjoy their fragrant blossoms.

A short steep climb brings you to an open area. At ridge head enter brush to the left, heading up several terraces. As you negotiate this vegetation, you will enjoy the surprise of a view of Mtzad Karha, (3) a Crusader tower and part of a fortified Crusader farm. One hundred meters south of the fort is a dry water cistern. Enjoy view of Ma'alot and Nahal Keziv.

One of the most important flowers on the landscape of these hills is the crocus which blooms after the first rains, during the fall. Every year the bulb produces a small stem with a couple of tiny leaves with a thin white line down the center. Atop the stem blooms an aromatic white flower tracing several purple 2-3 cm. long lines. The crocus bulb is edible by March and April; it can be cooked, fried or roasted. In Arabic, the crocus bulb is called the poor man's potato. From the stigma a yellow-orange colored seasoning is prepared called saffron; the saffron is an important element of certain curry blends. The crocus appears in Talmudic literature, and is mentioned once in the Bible, Song of Songs, (4:13), as one of the perfumes growing in the garden of King Solomon.

Retrace your route back down to Nahal Peki'in. Take left up the nahal, walking through the wadi bed itself. In the spring the flowers of Ma'alot's street names bloom along Nahal Peki'in.

As trail crosses the wadi at curve, return to trail on eastern bank. When the trail recrosses the stream bed to the west bank, look for that hidden ravine under the trees. Here a steep dark wadi descends from Ma'alot to Nahal Peki'in, known as the Garden of Eden. (4) Ascend here, do not leave the gully.

Note dug up roots — a wild boar was here. Be careful not to trip on the green briers strewn through this miniature jungle.

As the trail exits the forest, the incline becomes less steep and soon you arrive at a small pit. This was once the site of Ma'alot's shooting range. Take right onto red-marked trail. This is the Alon ben Shahar trail.

The trail gradually rises to the northeastern corner of the Rakefet (cyclamen) Hill. Here a marked trail leads 100 meters to the right. You arrive at an open area of karstic shaped stone above the Nahal Peki'in-Nahal Keziv intersection. From here you have a nice view of the Peki'in range, the bare top of Har Zvul (Hike 12) and Har Meron in the distance.

Return to main trail, head down and then along the southern bank of mid-Nahal Keziv. The large cliff ahead of you on the southern bank is Goat Cliff which you will come to later on. The trail passes by Mitzpe Alon, here are a few wooden benches and a monument (5) for Alon ben Shahar who was a member of a Nahal group which came to Ma'alot. Nahal is the fighting pioneer youth program which combines military service with national service, usually at a kibbutz or a development town. Alon was a nature lover and a bird watcher who would walk the lovely countryside around Ma'alot daily. Alon's life ended abruptly when he was killed in a battle with terrorists during his military service in Lebanon in 1985.

The trees surrounding the monument are Kermes oaks, Alon in Hebrew. This is one of the three species of oak trees growing in Israel and one of the main components of Israel's Mediterranean forest. Kermes oaks usually grow in a circular bush shape and reach about 4 meters high, though they can reach a height of 15 meters. The Kermes oak is an evergreen, unlike the two other species which grow in Israel, the Tabor and the Cyprus. The jagged leaves are small 2-4 cm. and the acorn 1.5-3 cm. The tree blooms in the spring, its roots are deep and this sturdy tree is able to withstand fire, drought and disease. The oak is mentioned often in the Bible. It has also been a common tree in pagan worship. Many large oak trees can be found around tombs of important Jews and Arab Sheikhs. Abraham "dwelt between the oaks of Mamre." (Gen. 13:10) The oak also symbolizes strength; the prophet Amos, 2:9, says about the Amorite, "and he was strong as the oaks." The strong wood of the oak is excellent both for utensils and charcoal, which is still manufactured today, especially by Arabs in Samaria and Lower Galilee. The roasted acorns can be eaten or used as a substitute for coffee, though the resultant beverage will have an unpleasant bitter aftertaste. The roasted shelled acorns are reputedly a good remedy for stomach aches.

As you continue on trail, pass small wadi and reach trail intersection. Take right descending down to the impressive Goat Cliff, (6) a favorite grazing hangout for the shepherds from the Tarshiha and Ma'ileya region as the quantities of sheep and goat dung underfoot will testify. This cliff is actually a number of notches.

From here you will find a trail leading down to Nahal Keziv. Return, retracing your hike to the trail intersection. Follow red-marked trail, a gradual climb through terraced fields, which lead to the northwest edge of Ma'alot's industrial zone. The trail hits a dirt road, follows it for 150 meters, and continues up as road curves to the right. Pass animal farmyard and reach piles of debris where you turn right, ascending to industrial zone until you come to garage. (7) Turn left onto clear road back to Ma'alot.

At intersection, (8) to bus stop, head straight to Ma'alot town center. Here there are also cooperative 'sherut' cabs. To return to car take left along outer road back to starting point. (1)

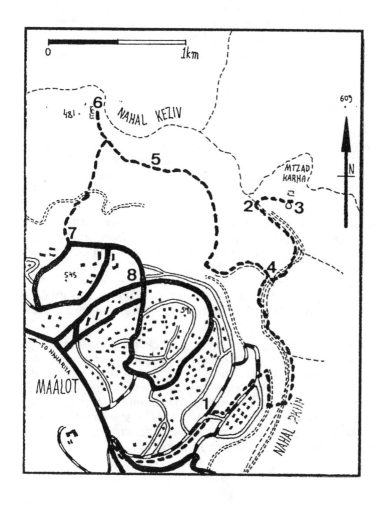

Hike 13,
Nahal Peki'in

Carmel

The Carmel Mountain range is the northwestern part of the Samarian hills. It is the only mountain range in Israel, except for Rosh Hanikra on Israel's border with Lebanon, that borders directly on the sea. The name Carmel has several meanings in Hebrew and is mentioned numerously in the Bible: it was the name of a village in the southern Hebron Hills; the word means roasted wheat; and 'kerem el' also means 'God's vineyard.' In Jeremiah, 2:7, the word 'carmel' refers to a fertile place, "And I brought you into a plentiful (carmel) country to eat the fruit thereof." And in Isaiah,10:18, 'carmel' was an area covered with vegetation such as the Carmel range of modern Israel, "And shall consume the glory of his forest and of his fruitful field (carmel)."

Today the Carmel Mountain range is graced by the city of Haifa and at its heart is a large national park.

Geography

The Carmel range, 700 sq. km., is divided into three regions: the Amir Mountains; the Menashe Plateau; and the Carmel where you are going to hike. The Carmel is a peninsula of 232 sq. km. To the south stretches the Menashe Plateau and to the northeast and east, the Acre Plains and Jezreel Valley; to the west extends the Carmel coast.

The Carmel anticline is not part of the national watershed, as both sides of the range, the sharp drop to the east and the more moderate decline to the west, drain into the Mediterranean Sea. The Carmel divides into four sections: 1) upper Carmel spanning the Haifa-Usifiya Road on the spine of the mountain, is approximately 500 meters above sea level. The Carmel peak is 546 meters above sea level; 2) central Carmel, with Har Shokef prominent; 3) lower Carmel, south of Daliyat el Carmel on the southwestern part of the range; 4) the Carmel coast to the west, 24 km. long and 0-4 km. wide.

The Carmel is a block of several strata of sedimentary rock. As a result of a large number of sub-marine volcanic explosions in the area, tuffs are found at a few sites on the Carmel. Tuff is a volcanic rock that cooled very quickly in tiny drops, unlike the basalt which is more common on the Golan Heights. The latter is volcanic lava which cooled slowly on earth's surface. Throughout the Carmel we find examples of karst weathering caused by carbonic acid dissolving the limestone and dolomite. The soil is mostly red-brown terra rossa which is made of dolomite and limestone and grey rendzina soil consisting of marl and chalk stone.

Climate

Because of its proximity to the Mediterranean Sea, the Carmel is one of the most rainy regions of Israel; lower elevations, such as the Etzba Ridge, receive 600 mm. precipitation annually, while higher up nearly 900 mm. falls annually. The Carmel's annual average daily temperature is 18.8°c, more than Upper Galilee at 16.1°c and the Judean Hills at 17.1c. Tel Aviv's annual daily average is not much higher — 19.1c. Temperature on the Carmel is similar to that of the coastal plain.

The Mediterranean Sea conditions dominate the climate, keeping the humidity of the Carmel at 69%, in contrast to 58% in Safed and 52% in Jerusalem. The Carmel has more cloudy days and fewer *sharavs* than other hilly areas, a *sharav* being a barometric high developing over the country where the subsiding air is compressed and heated. Snow does not fall on the Carmel and dew fall occurs most nights of the year.

Vegetation

The vegetation on the Carmel is relatively rich compared to other parts of Israel. The sharp escarpments to the east and the many cliffs on the west have made the Carmel a difficult place to farm, and the large amount of precipitation helps to quickly restore local vegetation. The Carmel is covered with the typical Mediterranean forest, the dominant trees being Kermes oak and Palestinian pistachio. The Aleppo pine and St. John's wart is another leading component in certain parts of the Carmel, the only region in Israel where large sections of the natural forest consist mainly of Aleppo pine. Today, most of Israel's Aleppo pine forests are planted by the Jewish National Fund. The Aleppo pine thrives on light rendzina soil due to its ability to withstand more arid conditions than the oak. Rendzina soil also stores water in its upper layer, a good condition for the shallow rooted pine. The oak is deep rooted, searching out small water reservoirs submerged in the rock.

Mastic and carob trees grow in the lower, warmer areas of the Carmel near the sea; these trees suit the warmer climate conditions and are able to withstand the Mediterranean Sea spray. Carobs are useful trees and were usually never cut down except to make room for other planting. The mastic tree of the pistachio family seems to be a survivor as well, making a good comeback after being cut down compared to other species. On the cooler and northern slopes of the Carmel you can find laurel, cyprus oak and buckthorn trees.

Rare wildflowers such as the Madonna Lily and different orchids grow on the Carmel. The Carmel also hosts a few plants which grow only on its slopes, i.e., the yellow flowering thorny broom, which is similar to the soft hairy calycotome. The thorny broom grows on rendzina soil and blooms in the spring.

Wildlife

The Carmel is the habitat for a large variety of mammals, amphibians and bird life. For several, the Carmel is the southern most point of their dispersion, such as the green lizard and a number of birds. The fallow deer and the roedeer were hunted and became extinct at the beginning of the century. Leopards also used to be observed here on the mountain. Today the hyrax and the wild boar thrive. Gazelles, which prefer open areas, are not common in the upper Carmel. Many species of bats and raptors have been decimated by civilization's misuse of different pesticides, however, night raptors are common.

There were crocodiles in Nahal Taninim west of the lower Carmel until the end of the 19th century. With the drop in the raptor population, the reptiles increased, especially snakes; among them the Palestinian viper.

Today several species of mammal are being raised in an open park zoo known as the Hai-Bar (meaning wildlife) Reserve. This reserve, along with another in the Arava near Kibbutz Yotvata, has imported several species from other parts of the world which had become extinct in Israel. Under constant observation in a fenced-in area, the animals are gradually becoming accustomed to the natural surroundings. The hope is that they can be released to roam free following this acclimation period.

During several of the hikes, you will enter a gate into this reserve which was damaged by the large fire, set by Arab political arsonists, that raged in the Carmel in the summer of 1989. In the Hai-Bar you may see the fallow deer, roedeer, wild goat and wild ram. This reserve is under the control of the Nature Reserves Authority.

Human Involvement

Due to the Carmel's moderate temperature, high precipitation and proximity to the sea which in the past reached the very foot of these mountains, the Carmel has been a convenient habitat for both man and animal.

The remains of the most early civilizations in Israel have been found here, and in Nahal Hama'arot, now a national park, human relics dating 12,000 years ago were unearthed on the Carmel.

It was most likely the Carmel, which Pharoah Pepi the 1st of 2,300 B.C.E. called 'Deerpoint,' and indicated as a navigating point for the ships of Egypt on one of their conquering quests. During the First Temple period when the coast was under Philistine control, the Carmel was part of the land parcel of the Israelite tribe of Menashe.

The slopes, coast and valleys near the mountain were preferred sites for settlement. The higher mountain areas were settled more reluctantly by those who had no other options, such as the Jews during the Byzantine period and the Druze in the 18th century, the latter establishing 16 villages, most of which were destroyed by the Moslems. Today two still stand, one the home of the Israeli Druze's spiritual leader. Few Arabs settled in the Carmel area.

Several of the first Jewish settlements from the First Aliya period were established on the lower Carmel with the help of Baron Rothschild, whose father's name is commemorated in the name of the town Zikhron Ya'akov.

During the British mandate, Arab gangs from the city of Haifa carried out raids on the local Jews. During the same period, the Jewish fighter movements practised their military maneuvers in the Carmel Mountains. Prior to the British mandate, Jewish spies living below the Etzba Ridge, known as the 'Nili' group, conducted undercover activity aiming to remove the Turkish regime from power in Palestine. Today on the upper Carmel are two small Druze towns and Kibbutz Bet Oren.

Water

The Carmel receives a lot of precipitation in the mountains but does not release it. The mountains contain a few small layer springs and these do not flow with much water. Some of the layer springs are not typical as the water impermeable rock is made of volcanic tuff and not the more common marl. At the bottom of the Carmel some larger springs flow, such as the source of Nahal Taninim.

The small amount of rainwater is probably another reason that the Carmel has never been intensely cultivated. In the Carmel Mountains there are no running streams, but a few streams can be found in the Menashe Plateau.

Hiking on the Carmel

Hiking is relatively easy on the Carmel where the trails are generally clear and well-marked. Buses run from Haifa up to the Haifa University and one bus line continues south to the Druze towns and Kibbutz Bet Oren. Other lines run from Haifa along the old road to Tel Aviv at the foot of the western slopes. This road reaches the town of Hadera.

There are numerous camp grounds throughout the upper Carmel, though the bathroom facilities and water may be disconnected. The Hebrew language Carmel 1:50,000 marked hiking trail map is a great asset, even if your Hebrew is limited.

There are many rainy days during the winter when trails will be quite slippery. Two litres of water per person is enough for a winter hike, 4 litres of water will suffice in the summer.

Important phone numbers:

(Area code: 04)

Carmel Field Study Center	664159
Haifa office of the Society for the Protection of Nature	664135
Carmel National Park	228983
Police	100; 571044
Magen David Adom, First Aid	101

(Area code: 06)

Carmel Coast Field Study Center	390800; 399655

Almond blossoms in the winter throughout the hills of Israel.

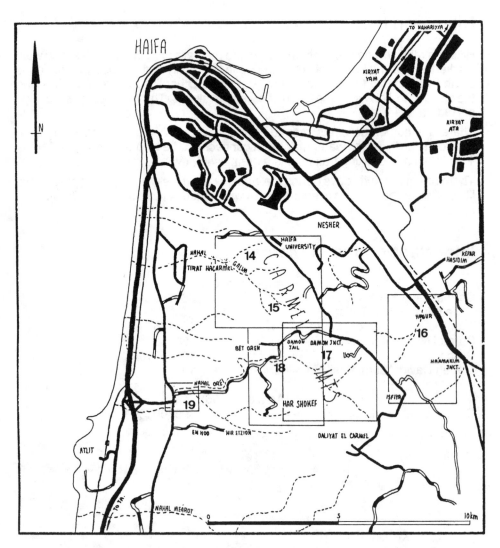

Carmel Mountain range. Numbers represent hike numbers.

Nahal Kelekh-Galim

14

Nahal Neder

Points of interest: Mediterranean forest, spring, prehistoric cave, falls.
Length of hike: 8 km. loop trip.
Hiking time: 5 hours.
Preferred season: All year.
Suitable for: All.
Maps: Carmel marked hiking trail map.
Special preparation: Flashlight.
Starting & ending point: Entrance to the Haifa University.

To begin hike:

By bus: Take bus from the Central Bus Station to Haifa University. Get off at second stop in the campus. Take right. Walk down the entry road to the University. Cross main road onto dirt road (cars may be parked there) and take left. You will see a green-marked trail sign, 'Nahal Galim.' This is your trailhead. (1)

The narcissus blooms in late fall, early winter. See map on page 75

By car: Coming to Haifa University. Turn right south just beyond entrance to University onto wide dirt road and make a left. Park your vehicle by the green-marked trail sign which reads, 'Nahal Galim.' (1)

At the trail head there is a pleasant camp ground with tables and facilities that affords a good view of Nahal Kelekh-Galim on its western aspect. Start down the green-marked trail through pine trees and Mediterranean forest, after a few hundred yards crossing dirt road. Walk alongside fence and enter open gate which leads to Hai-Bar Reserve. The 'Hai-Bar' meaning 'the wildlife' reserve, is a closed-in reserve in the Nahal Galim area of the Carmel Mountains. This reserve, under the auspices of the Nature Reserves Authority, is attempting to rehabilitate the animal population that once inhabited Israel's forest, such as the roedeer, the wild goat and wild rams. These animals have now been imported from abroad and following periods of adaptation each species will be released into the wild.

Walk on through burnt-out forest. Descend along gully until you reach Nahal Galim. (2) Turn right descending into Nahal Galim. *Watch your step on the wet rocks. During the rainy season they are slippery.*

Pass measuring instrument. Note how the green moss is more abundant as the wadi deepens. About one km. down Nahal Galim you reach Nahal Kelekh. (4) Take a right, following blue-marked trail down wadi bed. The kelekh, the giant fennel, is a plant usually growing in the fields of Israel which is ignored by goats and cows. In folklore medicine the seeds serve as a remedy for kidney stones.

One km. down Nahal Kelekh note cliffs on left and right which are dotted with caves. Perhaps you will catch sight of individuals or pairs of raptors. The wadi cuts through the hard rock. Note flint embedded in the stone. From this point, the wadi cuts into a small gorge and afterwards reopens, exiting the rich Mediterranean forest.

Here you will begin to see carob trees, denizens of dryer and warmer climates. Two km. down Nahal Kelekh, Nahal Neder joins it from the north, and you pass through a gate which exits the Hai-Bar Reserve. 150 meters down the trail from the point where the wadis have merged, reach the black-marked trail heading up Nahal Neder. Here, the Israeli iris blooms during early winter. (3) To your left (400 meters south) up the hill is the Ornit Cave. Head up to it through a gate in the fence. The Ornit Cave is a prehistoric karstic cave. Relics from the mid-Paleolithic and Chalcolithic periods have been found here. The cave is very interesting and has many entrances and rooms on two levels.

From the Ornit Cave you return down to the black-marked trail and head up Nahal Neder through groves of ancient olive trees. The trail, at first a dirt road, continuously narrows. One-half km. on the ascent of Nahal Neder you reach En Kedem. To the far right, across and above the wadi is Hirbet Kedem. In the wadi to the right of the trail, right before En Kedem you will see a huge sycamore tree. Here, adjacent to the trail, are remnants of an ancient aqueduct. En Kedem is a layer spring. The tunnels were chiseled out during the Roman period to increase the water flow. The water was conducted via aqueducts downward and westward toward Tirat HaCarmel. Explore the tunnels. On many of the rocks beside the spring you can find fossils. (4)

Continue up trail as it narrows in the wadi, approaching some houses on the left side of the wadi. Leave the wadi bed, ascending to the right and soon you will cross open fields. Leave trail and climb to the top of the ridge, there turn left and eastward into the open area (5) of Hirbet Mikhlol. Hit dirt road and ascend it, until you arrive at dirt road which is parallel to the Haifa-Usifiya Road. Turn right onto it and return to starting point. (1)

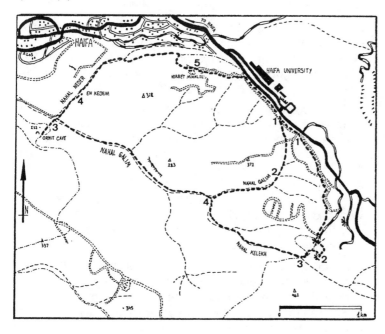

Hike 14, Nahal
Kelekh-Galim and
hike 15, Small
Switzerland

Small Switzerland

15

Points of interest: Burnt forest, thick Mediterranean forest, small falls.
Length of hike: 6 km. loop trip.
Hiking time: 4 hours.
Preferred season: All year.
Suitable for: Experienced hikers.
Maps: Carmel marked hiking trail map.
Special preparation: None.
Starting & ending point: Entrance to Haifa University.

To begin hike:

By bus: Take bus from Haifa Central Bus Station to Haifa University. Get off at second stop in the campus grounds. Take right, walk down to the entry road to the University. Cross main road and head 500 meters down south on the Haifa-Usifiya Road to starting point on black-marked dirt road. (1)

By car: Drive to Haifa University. After the second entrance continue on paved main road for 500 meters. Here there is a small road, and turn-off to the left leading to the Forest of the Forty. Take right to beginning of dirt road with a black trail mark. Here your hike begins. Park here. (1)

Descend down black-marked dirt road which curves around a small wadi and enters burnt-out Aleppo pine forest. The road passes bathroom facilities and continues its curve left. Here the black-marked trail turns off to the right onto a trail crossing gully. When the trail hits road take a left and then an immediate right for 200 meters to a gravel parking lot. Here take unmarked trail to the cliff observation point by turning left, crossing small wadi and heading up to the ridge. On top of ridge, head to your right through open forest and rocky terrain until you reach the cliff observation point. (2)

Here you have a good view of what Israelis have nick-named Small Switzerland and of the Nahal Kelekh region. Return to wadi walking freely down the forest, parallel to your ascent route. You may pass two hewn squares in the rock; this is an ancient wine press. Turn left in wadi and descend a small fall.

Enter gate of Hai-Bar Reserve and take a left at the first path you reach. Follow path to Nahal Kelekh at bridge which you will cross before you descend to Nahal Kelekh along the blue-marked trail. (3) Descend Nahal Kelekh through thick Mediterranean forest made up mostly of oak trees and creepers. Climb down the small falls, *but be careful as on a wet day the rocks*

See map on page 75

are very slippery. The burnt forest is a painful reminder of the great fire that raged in the Carmel in the summer of 1989.

The Madonna Lily, one of the prettiest and largest wildflowers in Israel, grows here. The size of the flower, its color and sweet fragrance make it unique, even among the modern range of cultivated flowers. The large bulbed Madonna Lily reaches a height of $1^1/_2$ meters and its stem can contain up to 20 white flowers which bloom to sizes of 10 centimeters and more. Blooming in April and May, the Madonna Lily's odor is especially powerful at night when the flower opens to be pollinated by moths. In Israel the flower grows in moist regions of Upper Galilee and the Carmel. Today it is one of Israel's most cultivated flowers and its oil is extracted for perfume manufacture. This lily may have been the flower mentioned in the Song of Songs, 2:1, "I am a rose of Sharon and a lily of the valleys; as the lily among thorns, so is my love among the daughters." In Christianity it symbolizes purity, therefore monks living in the Holy Land during the Byzantine period often dug up the bulb so as to ship it home to Europe. Naturally, this practice nearly erased the Madonna Lily from the landscape of Israel.

$1^1/_2$ kilometers down the 'adventure packed' route of Nahal Kelekh, meet green-marked trail entering from Nahal Galim on the right. (4) Take right up Nahal Galim following green-marked trail in wadi. After a bit more than $^1/_2$ km. the green-marked trail leaves the wadi bed (2) ascending to the left, north, and begins the climb back to starting point.

Head up the ravine and then veer up to the right through burnt Mediterranean pine forest. After a km., exit the Hai-Bar Reserve through a gate, cross dirt road and continue up to the green-marked trailhead near camping site with facilities, directly across from the entrance to Haifa University. (1) From here, your starting point is only 500 meters to the right, the black-marked trailhead.

Nahal Yagur

16

Points of interest: Spring, falls, thick forest, wild flowers.
Length of hike: One-way 6 km., loop trip 10 km.
Hiking time: One-way 5 hours, loop trip 8 hours.
Preferred season: All year.
Suitable for: One-way — all; loop trip — experienced hikers.
Maps: Carmel marked hiking trail map.
Special preparation: None.
Starting point (& ending point for loop trip): Usifiya.
Ending point for one-way hike: Kibbutz Yagur.

To begin hike:

By bus: Take bus to Usifiya. Get off at southern end of town near sharp curve on main road. (1) Take steep street up into village.

By car: Near sharp curve in main road at southern end of village; (1) head left into the village up a steep street.

Follow the street until reaching a square with a pole mast in the center. From here take road east toward soccer field and summer camp. Near the last house of the village the road turns into a dirt road. Begin hike here. (2)

Turn left into wide wadi of Nahal Yagur and descend to below the houses of Usifiya. Ancient Usifiya was a Jewish community known as Hussefa which was destroyed by the Crusaders. In 1933, a mosaic synagogue floor was uncovered, embellished with depictions of the menorah, shofar, lulav and etrog as well as other religious symbols and decorations. Today, this mosaic can be viewed at the Rockefeller Museum in East Jerusalem. The mosaic also includes two inscriptions thanking the donators and a third blessing, 'Shalom Al Yisrael,' 'Peace be to Israel.' The Druze settled Usifiya a few hundred years ago. Today, 75 percent of the village is Druze and the remainder includes other minorities.

Half a km. along the wadi you come to En el Balad, (3) 'the spring of the village,' on the Usifiya side of the wide Nahal Yagur. En el Balad is a layer spring and near it Nahal Yagur is a shallow wadi cutting through the soft chalk rock, the topsoil is grey rendzina.

Continue down clear red-marked trail on southern bank and note how ¹/₂ a km. from the spring the earth becomes brown and the wadi deepens into canyon. The rock strata here is hard dolomite and the brown earth is terra rossa, from the Latin: terra — ground; rossa — red. Terra rossa is the typical soil of the mountainous stones of Israel — in Judea and Samaria,

See map on page 80

Carmel and the Galilee — in every region where the predominant sedimentary rocks of Israel, the limestone and dolomite are found.

Nahal Yagur, named after Kibbutz Yagur at the foot of the canyon, flows from the eastern Carmel into the valley below. Kibbutz Yagur takes its name from the Arab village Yajur which used to be in this area. The Carmel Mountain range watershed is unique since both runoffs eventually reach the same spot, the Mediterranean Sea. To the west, the wadis gradually descend and flow through the 1 to 4 kilometer wide strip of the coast to the Mediterranean Sea. On the east, however, the wadis are small and run down the steep inclines into the famous Kishon River which drains the Jezreel Valley, entering the Zevulun Valley north of Haifa, and then into the Mediterranean. Nahal Yagur is one of the larger wadis of the eastern Carmel, dropping 500 meters in less than three aerial kilometers. Many rare plants grow in the Nahal Yagur Nature Reserve, including the famous Madonna Lily, which blooms in the late spring and is found only in the Carmel and Upper Galilee. This area, so rich in wildlife and vegetation, was part of an even larger nature reserve before the establishment of the State of Israel, after the British mandatory government set aside this region as a nature reserve.

The trail crosses a dirt road, suitable for private vehicles, that runs along the eastern Carmel. Continue down Nahal Yagur, descending various falls. *Be careful on wet days*. The trail clings to the wadi; 2 km. from the dirt road and 400 meters below, the wadi comes to Kibbutz Yagur. (4) Right before the kibbutz fence, the blue-marked trail heads southeast along the fence. If you finish your hike at the ending point of the one-way hike, follow the red-marked trail as it climbs north and then descends to Nahal Nahash, the 'wadi of the snake.' The red-marked trail circumvents Kibbutz Yagur arriving at the entrance gate of the kibbutz. (5)

To return to Haifa by bus, head through kibbutz road half a km., by taking right on main road that intersects kibbutz, then left to the Haifa-Jezreel Valley Road to bus stop. (6)

b) For those taking the loop trip, head along the blue-marked trail. The trail, which runs along the fence of Kibbutz Yagur and continues along the base of the Carmel ridge, is not very good. Crossing small wadis, note the redbud tree. The redbud, a beautiful tree belonging to the carob family, grows in the moist forest found mainly in northern Israel and reaches a height of 5 meters, shedding its leaves in the fall and spring. A pinkish red tangle of flowers distinguishes this tree from the other trees of the forest. Today the redbud is also a popular garden tree in Israel. In the spring, mountain tulips and hyacinth squill bloom here.

From a distance, the small wadis crossed by the trail look like small scars on the ridge of the Carmel. The following is an Arab folk tale about the Carmel Mountain and a mountain called Har Gamal — camel mountain — located north of the Carmel ridge: The two mountains fought over the opportunity to give shelter to Mohammed and the Carmel struck a blow on Har Gamal's back leaving it with a camel shaped indentation. Har Gamal on its part got in a few knife slashes at the Carmel, leaving the wadi 'scars' on the northeastern slope of the Carmel.

Four km. from Kibbutz Yagur, the trail begins its ascent. Cross wadi and head up the Carmel through a series of switchbacks. (5) The forest is not overly dense here and you can look back for a nice view of the lower western Galilee. Where the trail meets the same dirt road that crossed Nahal Yagur, continue up the mountain on the same blue-marked trail. The trail finally reaches a new neighborhood of residential homes on the outskirts of Usifiya and heads up dirt road to the curve in the road where your hike began. (2)

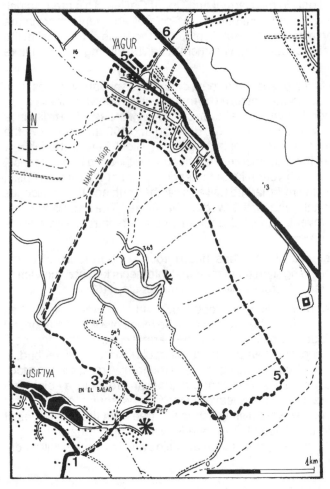

Hike 16, Nahal Yagur

Nahal Heik – Nahal Alon

<table>
<tr><td>

17

</td><td>

Points of interest: Canyon, springs, view, volcanic debris.
Length of hike: 9 or 13 km. loop trip.
Hiking time: 5 hours or 8 hours loop trip.
Preferred season: All year.
Suitable for: All.
Maps: Carmel marked hiking trail map.
Special preparation: None.
Starting & ending point: **By car** — entrance to Nahal Heik before beginning of the Druze town Usifiya on the Haifa-Usifiya Road. **By bus** — Beginning point: from Rom HaCarmel, 1 km. south of Damon Junction on the Haifa-Usifiya Road. Ending point: Damon Junction.

</td></tr>
</table>

To begin hike:

By bus: Get off bus one km. after the Damon Junction near Bedouin community located on the northern outskirts of Usifiya. (1) A road posted with several national park signs heads north from here. Climb the bare hill at the southwest side of the road. This is Rom HaCarmel. Enjoy view. Descend hill parallel to main road, and continue southeast through pine forest until reaching dirt road. Head down a wide wadi, Nahal Heik. Here the hike begins. (2)

Cave tomb at Hirbet Rakit (hike 18). See map on page 85

By car: Take road past Haifa University to Damon Junction. Head 1$\frac{1}{2}$ km. towards Usifiya. Just before entering the town take right on the dirt road by the green-marked yellow sign, 'Nahal Heik.' Park near dirt road. Here your hike begins. (2)

The dirt road descends gradually between forest. The land here is grey rendzina soil made of chalk rock and is some 100 million years old. (Upper Cenomanian period). At one time, the inhabitants of Usifiya grew various crops here. In contrast to 80% of the population in 1958 who raised olives, wheat and farmed honey bees, less than 10% of the Druze today farm the land. Most of the villagers now work outside the village. The Druze of Usifiya have always had friendly relations with the Jews and they serve in the I.D.F.

A dirt road enters the wadi from the east. Rising above the valley of Nahal Heik, continue on green-marked dirt road. Follow green-marked trail as it descends to the groves of fruit trees in the valley and comes to En Heik (3) on the southern bank. In the morning the two and a half meter pool is full to the brim with clear water that has drained in during the night, and is home to many small creatures including salamanders during the winter and spring — a rare amphibian in Israel. En Heik is a layer spring but unlike many layer springs with water-impermeable marl layers at En Heik the volcanic tuffs contain the water that has seeped in through the chalk soil. The spring is ringed with the greenery of fig trees, bramble bush and maidenhair fern.

Continue on clear path past the spring and several hundred meters along the way drop to Nahal Heik. Cross small wadi, continue on dirt road down Nahal Heik. As wadi comes in from the right observe planted grove of cedars of Lebanon. 500 meters from En Heik a dirt road crosses Nahal Heik to the right. Turn right onto dirt road above Nahal Heik walking for 500 meters and passing through pine forest. Where a dirt road breaks off to the left, continue straight for another 250 meters until you reach an open area overlooking the Alon Valley. From excellent view point on your right you can see an interesting deposit of volcanic tuffs — soft stone that is relatively bare of vegetation. (4) Retrace your route to Nahal Heik.

Descend Nahal Heik reaching the famous Makhteshet, (5) (water hollow) of Nahal Heik, which you can choose to either pass from the right or descend. From this water hollow which usually contains small quantities of water all year round, the wadi plunges into a dark moist forest, typified by less common Mediterranean vegetation such as the strawberry tree and the laurel. The laurel is an evergreen tree which grows as high as five meters with a relatively wide trunk, shiny green leaves and whitish-yellow clumps of flowers in the springtime. The laurel grows in the moist areas of Israel's Mediterranean forest on earth created from hard limestone rock, usually terra rossa, and is pollinated by the wind and insects. Growing mainly in the Carmel and Upper Galilee, the laurel is quite rare in the Judean and Samarian Hills. The leaves contain a very useful oil which is used as a condiment for meats and pickled vegetables and can also be added to soups and salads. The leaves can be added to tobacco mixes and dried figs. The Arabs of Israel use the laurel as a curative for many ailments: rheumatism, cuts, hair strengthening, colds, diarrhea and constipation. This was one of the most important trees in ancient Greek culture. The prophetess of Delphi chewed leaves to enhance prophecy. The Greeks and the Romans believed that the laurel was so powerful that it could guard one from different natural disasters such as lightening. They claimed everyone who rested by the shade of the tree would be saved from witches and curses. The Greeks also used the leaves as a cure for bee and wasp bites and to prevent certain illnesses. Israeli Arabs utilize the fragrant leaves for clothes closets and to wash clothes. In Turkey the leaves are packed with figs and other dried fruits. Some say that the oil of the laurel is a good preventative for insect bites.

The 'jungle' comes to a sudden end as the wadi reaches the Alon Valley. During the Lower Cenomanian period, the Carmel range was covered with a sea that deposited dolomite on the sea bed. Volcanic rock broke through this dolomite deposit, cooled quickly and became what we call tuff. With time the sea deepened and deposited dolomite and chalk on top of the tuff. This mass rose and became the Carmel range. External erosion, such as winds and rain, cut through the soft chalk, reaching the sediment of even softer tuff and this created the Alon Valley. Similar valleys developed in the upper regions of the southern Carmel.

The trail crosses the wadi back and forth until reaching Nahal Oren, the draining wadi of the Alon Valley. Take a right on the dirt road along Nahal Oren. When the ridge on your right reaches the dirt road, look for a black-marked trail that breaks off to the left and crosses Nahal Oren, passing a couple of trees leading southwest up the valley.

a) On the short loop hike, continue straight until reaching Nahal Alon coming in from the northeast. Along it is a blue-marked trail which you take (right) to complete this hike.

b) For the longer, more scenic hike, take left onto clear black-marked trail, crossing fields until reaching the ridge. Follow the ridge around the left on black-marked trail. Begin climb up small wadi. Don't forget to look back and enjoy view of the lovely Alon Valley. The trail takes a right as two wadis meet. An assortment of orchids bloom in the spring along this trail.

The trail hits a dirt road where you take a left. Then leave the dirt road to the right, following marked trail, before it curves right. Here you hit the Har Shokef-Daliyat el Carmel dirt road by large pine tree. Cross it and continue on red-marked trail to the flat summit of Har Shokef (6) and enjoy the view.

Descend on red-marked trail 100 meters to the north to a dirt road intersection. Head north onto blue-marked dirt road to Har Arkan passing through pine forest. After one km. the blue-marked trail leaves the dirt road for the last time, passing the scenic peak of Har Arkan. Here you will see many white sage leaved rockrose which bloom in late spring.

The trail takes a steep descent towards Nahal Oren negotiating thick pine and oak forest, then meets with paved road that leads to Givat Wolfson — a small private community of summer homes founded in 1939. After the Carmel became a nature reserve the development of this area was frozen. Turn right, walking on paved road until the blue-marked trail breaks off to the right, descending to Nahal Oren to the pumping station of En Alon (7) where there is a drinking water faucet. Near the trail intersection follow green-marked trail up the small stream to the source of En Alon. En Alon is a layer spring like En Heik. Today the water is pumped up to Kibbutz Bet Oren and the Damon Prison; the latter is one km. to the north and can be heard resounding throughout the upper Carmel each time the Damon loudspeaker blasts forth its announcements.

As told by the oldsters of the local Druze, leopards were spotted in this area around En Alon and En Oren until the beginning of the 20th century.

From the spring, head up Nahal Oren through one of the nicest parts of Nahal Oren. From the end of canyon and above to the left is Hirbet Alon. The as yet unexcavated ruins are not very impressive although the tools, pottery and stones found here indicate that this region has been inhabited from Chalcolithic times on.

Follow green-marked dirt road until Nahal Alon enters from the left. Head up along Nahal Alon. The blue-marked trail on the northern side is not close to the river bed. Here we can see more tuff. The blue-marked trail becomes easier to follow along the wadi and into pine forest. Along the trail on the left there are small cliffs with a line of green color. What you are seeing is the greenery clinging to the surface which has collected seeping moisture that has penetrated the limestone and chalk until the marl layer holds back the seepage. This layer is exposed here and the moisture has moss. The blue-marked trail ascends, leaving Nahal Alon and heading up a small wadi to the north toward the Damon Junction on the Haifa-Usifiya Road by a camp ground. (8)

If you came by car, continue another 100 meters up Nahal Alon where a wide wadi comes in from the right with a long grey wall of limestone on the right. Ascend this wadi (there is no clear trail) heading east toward Rom HaCarmel. Here you walk free for one km. along the left side of this wadi. Many Serapias orchids grow here in the spring.

When you come to the ridge of Rom HaCarmel, take left at top of bare ridge until you are directly above the Haifa-Usifiya Road, near the soccer (football) field. You are now at the highest point of the Carmel ridge — 546 meters above sea level. The Druze call this spot, 'The Hat of the Druze' because of its shape. (1) North of the Haifa-Usifiya Road is an even nicer view, looking north toward the Galilee.

Descend southeast through an open area between pine trees back to dirt road. Take left on it back to the starting point. (2)

Hike 17, Nahal Heik - Nahal Alon

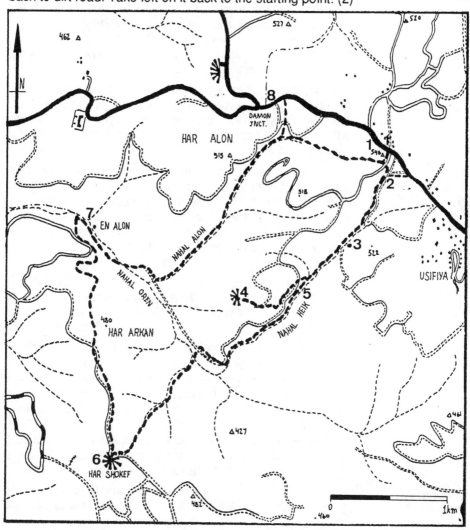

Har Shokef

18

Points of interest: Springs, ruins, views, forest.
Length of hike: 10 km. loop trip.
Hiking time: 6 hours.
Preferred season: All year.
Suitable for: All.
Maps: Carmel marked hiking trails map.
Special preparation: None.
Starting & ending point: Junction near Bet Oren (1) or curve on road below Bet Oren. (2)

To begin hike:

By bus: Take bus from Haifa to the junction near Kibbutz Bet Oren. (1) Take black-marked dirt road south from the junction. Continue on black-marked trail as it branches off the dirt road to the right past the camping ground. Descend and cross wadi to starting point. (2)

By car: Coming from Haifa take Usifiya Road until Damon Junction. Take right toward Bet Oren. At junction by Kibbutz Bet Oren take left 1 km. to the second sharp curve on the road where you will see carved stair shapes in the rock near a parking lot. Park here. (2)

During the Byzantine period there were ancient quarries here, the stone utilized for building sites such as Hirbet Rakit and Hirbet Shalala. At the eastern section of these quarries is a cave-tomb and on the side of the road where the black-marked trail hits the road to the left is an olive oil press basin. Take right southwest onto dirt road to crest of hill where you will reach Hirbet Shalala. These are the Carmel Forests. (2)

People have inhabited this scenic hill from the Chalcolithic period on. During the 18th century, Hirbet Shalala was the site of a Druze village. It was later destroyed along with two other Druze villages on the Carmel Mountain by Arabs from other nearby villages in revenge for mistreating one of their girls.

When the Jewish pioneers settled here in 1935 they named this area the Carmel Forests. Throughout the late 30's the Jews were constantly harassed by Arabs who murdered a number of Jews. The Carmel Forests also served as the secret Hagana army base which suffered Arab attacks. In 1939, a fortress was built here and Kibbutz Bet Oren was founded, later moving to its permanent location. Near the fortress there is a good view of Nahal Oren and its environs.

See map on page 88

Descend again to the ancient quarries and take a right onto green-marked trail down to Nahal Oren. At the wadi bed are some ruins dating from the Crusader period — the only flour mill on the Carmel Mountains. This mill utilized the water of En Alon, the source of which is farther up Nahal Oren, which was brought to the mill by means of a small channel. Take the trail on the right, passing through summer blooming oleander shrubs. Pass some man-made empty pools and you arrive at a virtual Garden of Eden — citrus, varied figs and other trees were planted here about a hundred years ago. When the first settlers arrived to establish Kibbutz Bet Oren, they found these lovely orchards directly beneath their home. Today, the entrapped waters of En Oren and En Alon have caused the garden to diminish in its lush vegetation, however, it remains a beautiful spot. (4)

Continue on red-marked trail under bridge. Take left on dirt road (by bathrooms) and cross gravel parking lot. Head up red-marked trail parallel to wadi that drops into Nahal Oren. The forest thickens as the trail crosses several dirt roads. Toward the top the trail hits a green-marked trail.

Continue on the red-marked trail to the left, shortly reaching Hirbet Rakit. (5) Dating from the Roman period, Hirbet Rakit boasts of an impressive cave-tomb which you can see adjacent to the trail. It is embellished by a Greek inscription and rosette — a petal shaped ornament cut into the rock. A hundred meters to the left on an unmarked trail is an olive press and wine press. Continue up the red-marked trail past green-marked trail intersection and head up through open fields until reaching dirt road. Here you hit the blue-marked dirt road, which you will follow to Har Arkan. But first head up a bit more, following the red-marked trail to the summit of Har Shokef, 497 meters above sea level. (6) Shokef in Hebrew and Arabic means to see, to view, and from here you really have a great view of the Carmel coast; the extent of both the Carmel and the Menashe Mountains, south of the higher Carmel mountain block. From Har Shokef, return back to blue-marked trail on dirt road.

Follow blue-marked trail to Har Arkan thick with Aleppo pine; this is *the* pine tree of Israel. The Aleppo pine grows in a moderate dry climate. This evergreen is a native of Israel and is the tree usually planted by the Jewish National Fund. Though abundant in the Carmel, natural pine forests today are quite rare in the Galilee and Judea. This tree grows to a height of 15 meters and has a short life span of up to 150 years. The edible ornia mushroom grows off the tree's shallow root system, (from the word oren which is Hebrew for the Aleppo pine). The pine needles emit a certain substance which inhibits plant growth, as a result the underbrush of the pine forest is unusually thin.

From the peak of Har Arkan a trail descends toward Nahal Oren through a thick forest of pine and oak. Hit a paved road which leads to Givat Wolfson, founded in 1939. After the Carmel became a nature reserve, development came to a halt. The one-time community of summer homes is now a private community.

Walk down to the right on paved road to blue-marked trail that breaks off to the right and descends to Nahal Oren near the pumping station of En Alon. Here is a faucet with drinking water and a trail intersection; follow green-marked trail up the small stream to the source of En Alon. En Alon is a layer spring.

Head down wadi to the west. Until the 20th century leopards could be found here. Keep a lookout for the water aqueduct that supplied the flour mill on the north of the bank. One km. from En Alon reach flour mill and head back up to starting point (2) by the ancient quarries.

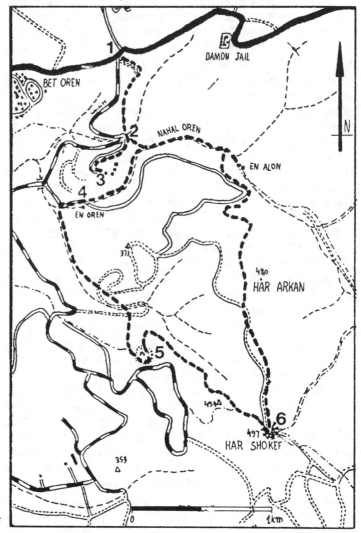

Hike 18, Har Shokef

Etzba Ridge

19

Points of interest: Prehistoric cave, lush vegetation, view.
Length of hike: 2 km. loop trip.
Hiking time: $1\frac{1}{2}$ hours.
Preferred season: All year.
Suitable for: All.
Maps: Carmel marked hiking trail map.
Special preparation: Flashlight.
Starting & ending point: Half a km. east of Oren Junction, at booth.

To begin hike:

By bus: Take bus from Haifa onto old Haifa-Tel Aviv Highway. Get off at Oren Junction. Head $\frac{1}{2}$ km. east on the road to starting point. (1)

By car: Leave Haifa-Tel Aviv Highway at Atlit Interchange to old Haifa-Tel Aviv Road. Take a left $\frac{1}{2}$ km. to Oren Junction and then right $\frac{1}{2}$ km. to starting point. (1)

Begin hike at booth of Nature Reserves Authority. (1) Cross old bridge on Nahal Oren and head up blue-marked trail with built-in stairs to the pill-box — the British guard fort overlooking the road and a quarry where Italian prisoners of war hewed stone during World War II. The trail climbs through Mediterranean forest. The gladioli bloom here in April. Soon you will reach the Etzba Cave. (2) Etzba in Hebrew means finger. Note that across the road, on the northern slope across Nahal Oren, the vegetation is a lot less dense due to the fact that it is exposed most of the day to the sun that moves from the east to the west through the south. The earth on the southern slope of hills dries faster. Due to longer exposure to the sun, variation and density of vegetation is limited. The oak and pistachio grow where you are standing now. Across the way on the southern slope you will find the carob and mastic pistachio which grow in warmer

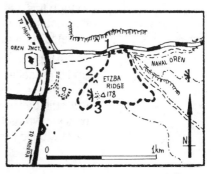

Hike 19, Etzba Ridge

89

climates. Further up on the ridge, vegetation is dominated by the Aleppo pine.

The Etzba Cave is a karstic cave with three rooms. The first room is the oldest, dating back 40,000 years. In 1941 the cave was excavated by the archaeologist, Moshe Shtekilis who divided the finds into four layers. 1) Layer A is 90 centimeters deep, black soil, and consists of more recent remnants. 2) Layer B is from the Natufian period. The simple pottery, flint pieces, basic agricultural tools, and remnants of animals indicate that the inhabitants' diet was based on hunting and fishing. 3) Layer C — here you see flint articles and bones from 35-40,000 years ago. 4) Layer D — 2.35 meters below hits bedrock. Fruit and insect bats live in the third room of the Etzba Cave. The insect bat has tiny eyes and large ears. The echo of sound they make is interpreted like radar, enabling them to sense objects in the dark. The insects they eat are caught in the air. Although bats are mammals, this bat usually sleeps outside and its body temperature adapts accordingly to the temperature of its environment. These bats travel a lot and may even go from continent to continent. Today bats in Israel are an endangered species, due to the many disturbances of their natural habitat and various insecticides sprayed on agricultural fields.

A carob tree grows near the entrance to the cave. Head along trail crossing karstic-formations and head up to top of ridge. During World War II the British prepared Palestine for a German invasion. Special attention was given to fortifying the Haifa area down into Nahal Oren due to its strategic and logistic importance — there was both a port and an air strip, in the Zevulun Valley, north of the Carmel. There was also the nearby industrial area, and of course the Carmel range which is topographically difficult to capture in war.

Today, along the Etzba Ridge we can see trenches and other remainders from this effort which fortunately were not put to use as Rommel was defeated in Egypt before he could arrive at the shores of Palestine. This project, known as the Carmel-Tubruq Plan, was based on similar fortifications in Tubruq, Libya. The Jewish Hagana cooperated with the British although this was very problematic due to the publication of the infamous British White Paper of 1939 which restricted Jewish development and immigration to Palestine.

At the top of the ridge (3) there are large wild Aleppo pine trees and an excellent view of the Carmel coast. Beside the Mediterranean Sea, close to you and to the west, lie the ruins of the Atlit fort built by the Crusaders to control the Haifa-Jaffa Road. It was known as Chastel Pelerin, named after the pilgrims who helped build it.

This trail, made by Haifa high school students, meets a red-marked trail at the summit that leads along pine trees to the artists' village of En Hod.

Continue on black-marked trail down ridge to Nahal Bustan. Take left at bottom on dirt road for a few hundred yards to a large attractive picnic area with facilities. The carob tree grows here, which, growing alongside the mastic pistachio tree, composes a specific type of Mediterranean forest. After being cut, the carob can make a comeback. It seems to be evergreen but actually the leaves last only one year, the young leaves sprouting before the old leaves are shed. The carob has both female and male trees, though some may be bi-sexual. Pollination takes place with the help of the wind and insects. Some researchers maintain that the carob is of tropical origin since the flowers grow directly on the trunk as in tropical trees and it flowers in late summer. The carob is not mentioned in the Bible but is often discussed in the Talmud. Therefore, some assume that the carobs were brought to Israel after the First Temple period. Due to the powerful odor of both flowers and fruit, the Talmud instructed that the carob be planted at least 25 yards outside of town limits. The carob's large fruit is edible and its outer part contains 40-50% sugar. Ashkenazi (European) Jews in the diaspora often included the dried carob fruit — called 'bokser' in Yiddish, in their Tu B'Shvat holiday packets, which symbolized the fruits of the Land of Israel. The Arabs make a honey out of carob, cutting it into pieces and placing them in a large wooden barrel together with water. After 24 hours the water is drained and the residue is a sticky-sweet substance. Today many health-food stores sell different foods based on carob fruit, and our diet-conscious society markets carob syrup and carob ice-cream as substitutes for chocolate related products. The seeds may have once been used for measurements. The scientific name for the carob seeds is kratunia, and some maintain that the standard karat measurement of gold originates from the carob seed. The name in Hebrew possibly comes from the word 'herev' which means sword and is similar to the shape of the fruit or the sharpness of its taste. The Hebrew 'harev' which means barren explains the name as well, since the carob grows in arid regions.

Beyond picnic area reach the starting point (1) to end the hike.

Judea

The area of Judea was the land parcel which the tribe of Judah inherited in Biblical times. Until the destruction of the Second Temple in 70 C.E, Judea, the area around Jerusalem, was the nucleus of the Israelite nation. The city of Jerusalem was at the northeastern corner of this parcel. Many of the events mentioned in the Bible took place here. The origin of the word 'Jew' is Judah; the tribe of Judah was not exiled and dispersed by kings of Assyria in 721 B.C.E. along with the other Israelite tribes.

The Judean Hills are divided into three sub-regions, distinct from each other in morphology, rock formation, soil and climate. In the west are the foothills, in the center are the hills, and in the east is the Judean Desert. Disparities in rainfall characterize each sub-region as well as differences in rock formations. The foothills, usually soft chalk covered by nari — a hard crust formed by evaporating water depositing calcium on the earth's surface — are typified by around 400-500 mm. of rainfall annually. In the hills, mainly limestone and dolomite, rainfall is between 500 and 600 mm. annually. The Judean Desert, mainly chalk, hills and limestone escarpments which drop abruptly to the Dead Sea's level, annual rainfall is between 50 and 200 mm.

The watershed runs alongside the eastern section of the Judean Hills, creating a more gradual decline to the west than the eastern declination to the Dead Sea and Jordan River. The ratio is about 4:1 between the declines.

The geographical borders of Judea are Samaria to the north, the Syrian-African rift to the east (Jordan River, Dead Sea) the northern Negev and Beer Sheba Valley to the south and Mediterranean coast to the west.

The hikes in this book are in the Jerusalem Hills region of the Judean Hills and the Judean Desert.

Judean Hills

The Judean upfold exceeds 1000 meters above sea level. The axis points from south-southwest to north-northeast. The watershed runs alongside the eastern face of the hills.

The Judean Hills are divided into three sub-regions. Bet El Hills in the north, Jerusalem Hills in the center and the Hebron Hills in the south. The crest of the upfold is compact and is higher in the north and south. The Jerusalem Hills run more or less parallel to the Jerusalem Corridor, which is a relatively narrow strip of land extending from Jerusalem westward that the Arab states did not succeed in capturing during the war in 1948.

The Jerusalem Hills

The Jerusalem Hills are 100-200 meters lower than the other sub-regions of the Judean Hills to the north and south, forming a saddle linking them. This explains the development here in antiquity of important towns such as Jerusalem. Here the north-south highway (the 'hill road' of the Bible) crossed the west-east road, taking advantage of the flat upfold crest where the hills were less steep, therefore an easily traversed route. The Dead Sea, just to the southeast, posed no obstacle.

The Jerusalem Hills peak at around 850 meters above sea level, the average altitude around 650 meters. The hills are formed by long branches extending from the watershed crossing Jerusalem, which head westward, and is divided by deep wadis, such as Nahal Kesalon, Nahal Sorek, and Nahal Refaim. The entire area is composed of sedimentary rock, usually limestone and dolomite, with some marl in several locations. The soil is the reddish brown terra rossa, 'red soil,' the outcome of deteriorated limestone and dolomite.

Climate

The Jerusalem Hills enjoy a partially humid Mediterranean climate. The Jerusalem average annual rainfall is 500 mm. The highest amount of precipitation actually falls west of the watershed around Kibbutz Kiryat Anavim which is 650 meters above sea level, where the average is around 600 mm. rainfall annually. Almost all rain falls during Israel's mid and late rainy season which is between October and April.

The number of rainy days in the Jerusalem Hills is around 55. One or two days of snow falls in the Jerusalem Hills around the areas which are 750 meters above sea level and higher. Dewfall averages 150 nights annually. Jerusalem's average annual temperature is 17.1°c. The minimum temperature reaches -1°c, and in the summer 35°c as the daily high is rarely exceeded. The differential between the average temperature in the hottest month and the coolest month is 15°c. Humidity is around 60%.

Vegetation

The vegetation in the Jerusalem Hills is influenced by it location, the southern Mediterranean zone. Perpetual human presence in this area has effected remarkable changes in the flora and fauna as well. The Mediterranean forest of oak and pistachio is less dense here than in the colder and rainier Galilee and there are less creepers. Many plants have infiltrated from the nearby borderline desert zone. For example, some experts maintain that the poterium, a thorny bush growing throughout Israel, is a native of the non-forested area of borderline desert which was introduced into Israel's Mediterranean zone following its massive and long-term deforestation.

Natural Aleppo pine forests which flourish on rendzina soil are found in very few spots. Often adjacent to holy sites, large trees can be found, possibly a remnant of natural forest that used to cover this landscape. In the Book of Joshua, 17;15, we read, "And Joshua answered them, 'If thou be a great people then get thee up to the wood country and cut down for thyself there in the land of the Perizzites and of the giants, if Mount Ephraim be too narrow for thee.' " The 'wood country' in Joshua relates to the Bet El Hills and southern Samaria, both north of the Jerusalem Hills.

Many herbs grow in the fields of the Judean Hills and altogether, around 1000 different plants can be found in the Jerusalem Hills.

Wildlife

After centuries of man's involvement and man's misuse of the environment, wildlife today is relatively limited; these include drastic changes in the natural vegetation, pollution, and over-hunting in addition to the agricultural uses, human settlement and road development.

The Bible offers numerous testimony of the original quantity and variety of wildlife in the region. Samson had no problem in getting 300 foxes, a mammal that still lives in the Judean Hills. King David living in Bethlehem, in the northern Hebron Hills, tells this brave tale, "And David said to Saul, thy servant kept his father's sheep and there came a lion and a bear and took a lamb out of the flock." (Samuel I, 17:34). Lions have not inhabited Hebron's Hills for centuries, although in the 1930's bears were spotted in nearby Transjordan.

The gun was an important factor in the decimation of many species. Thanks to nature preservation, gazelles have made a comeback in the open areas, but wild boars, wolves and striped hyenas, once common here, are now rare. In the early 1960's — before the mass agriculture related poisonings — you could still hear the wilderness sounds of the jackal's call in the outskirts of the then provincial Jerusalem. Along the trails you will most likely find discarded quills of the Indian crested porcupine.

The raptor population has been severely reduced as a result of chemicals which entered the food chain when they were sprayed on crops and then devoured by crop-eating rodents. Only the short-toed eagle which prefers lizards and snakes, is still common. You can usually view it nesting in the pine trees. Kestrels are seen hovering over fields, looking for prey, and even in Jerusalem the high meowing call of the kestrel can be heard ringing out from the antennas of an occasional tall building where these birds like to alight.

There are a number of reptiles which are mostly active during the non-rainy months. The Palestinian viper is the only poisonous snake, and is usually found in the rural settlements, especially moshavs, where there is an abundant supply of rodents. There are no salamanders in Judea and only the green toad, stream frog and lemon tree frog represent amphibian life here.

Human Involvement

Following the Chalcolithic period when the Jerusalem Hills were not inhabited, possibly because of dense forest conditions, Judea became one of the most densely populated areas and remained so throughout history. During the mid-Bronze period, development began, however, on a smaller scale than the cities of the foothills. Jerusalem was first mentioned in the Egyptian execration text, dated 2000 B.C.E. — small clay tablets bearing the names of towns and rulers who were enemies of Egypt. Smashing the tablets symbolized the downfall of the places written on them.

During the Israelite period, Jerusalem was the border between the tribe of Benjamin and Judah to the south. Most of the population farmed the land. Sixty percent of the Jerusalem Hills is terraced and 87 out of the 101 springs in the Jerusalem Hills contain agricultural relics such as pools and water channels. Grapes and olives were main crops, needing no irrigation. On many of these hikes you will come across wine presses hewn out of the natural stone.

The Second Temple era was a peak period in the area. Since Byzantine times the Jerusalem Hills region has slumbered, an outcome of the many conquerors who cared little for its development. Although there has always been a small Jewish presence in the Holy Land, it has been only during the last 100 years, with the mass return of Jews to the Land of Israel, and influx of Arabs from different Arab countries that this area has begun to develop.

In 1948, the small Arab villages of the area were ordered to leave by ambitious Arab leaders who planned to wipe out Jewish settlement in Israel within a few days. Israel withstood an onslaught from seven different Arab nations but most of the Arabs of those villages never returned to their homes and until today have refugee status.

Jewish settlement before 1948, concentrated in settlements north of the old Jerusalem-Tel Aviv Road, was quite sparse in the Jerusalem Hills. Today, three friendly Arab villages and approximately 20 moshavs and kibbutzes are situated along the Jerusalem Corridor.

Three main roads lead east-west: the Tel Aviv-Jerusalem Highway based on the old Jerusalem-Jaffa Road; the Eshtaol Road from the Kastel runs along a ridge between Nahal Kesalon to the north and Nahal Sorek in the south, passing many villages; the Bar Giora Road exits Jerusalem from En Kerem, along the extent of Nahal Sorek. Near Bar Giora the road divides, one route heads toward Bet Shemesh running on top of the southern ridge of Nahal Sorek, while the other follows an ancient road to the Elah Valley.

Water

The Jerusalem Hills contain many layer springs and one karstic spring which is also the largest, En Gihon, the spring of ancient Jerusalem. Most of the springs yield only meager amounts of water. Nearly all of these springs were utilized by man, usually for growing vegetables. Some springs have dried up, leaving only remnants of pools and channels.

A layer spring forms when rainwater seeping down into the earth reaches a water impermeable layer. In the hills of Israel, layer springs flow off of marl which is soft yellowish flint clay mixture; these particles expand when saturated, sealing off passage of the water.

Before reaching the marl, the rainwater usually seeps through the hard limestone and dolomite rocks which are cracked. When erosion exposes the marl layer, the water seeps out of the earth in the form of a spring, known as a layer spring.

The springs usually have a man-made tunnel which improves the water drainage. At the end of the tunnel is a hewn out cave. The tunnel drains the water into a pool and from here small channels or ditches irrigate vegetable gardens.

The large amount of rainfall that the hills absorb is released along the Dead Sea in a series of springs and at a few locations in the west. There are hundreds of water cisterns everywhere dating back to different periods. There are no streams in the Jerusalem Hills that carry water all year round, but at several spots, spring water trickles down the stream bed, such as in Nahal Ktalav and Nahal Matta.

After strong rains, the wadis flow for short periods. Today, Nahal Sorek, the main wadi of the Jerusalem Hills, and its tributary, Nahal Refaim, carry some of Jerusalem's sewage to the Mediterranean Sea. This ecological problem will in time contaminate the underground reservoirs of water.

Hiking in the Jerusalem Hills

Access to trailheads is easy from many directions. The buses which you will need for these hikes start in Jerusalem and lead west to the area's settlements. Considering all the factors, terrain, temperature and animal life, this region is one of the safest to hike in. Also there is no wilderness in the Jerusalem Hills and every few kilometers there is a village.

Two litres of water for a winter day, and 4 litres of water for a summer day per person is sufficient. A helpful hint to remember is that all wadis in this region gradually descend from east to west.

Important telephone numbers:

(Area code 02)

Jerusalem Society for the Protection of Nature office	252357
Mt. Gilo Field Study Center	742586
Ofra Field Study Center	976411
Jerusalem Field Study Center, Helene HaMalka Street 13, city center, Jerusalem	252793
Nature Reserves Authority, Jerusalem	232936
Jerusalem Police	100
Jerusalem Magen David Adom (First Aid)	101; 691144
Bet Shemesh Fire Station	911288
Bet Shemesh Police	914444

Foggy morning in the Nahal Sorek Reserve (hike 22)

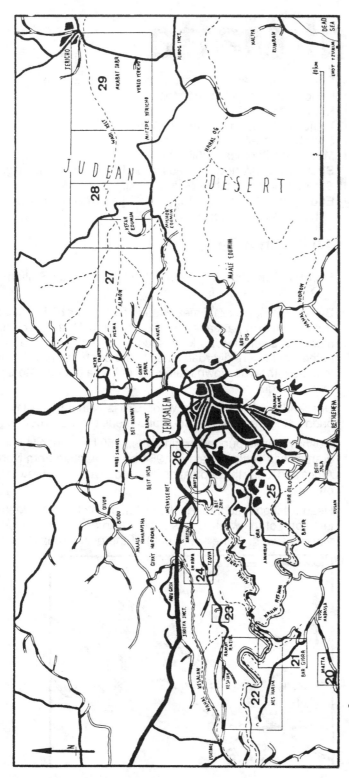

Jerusalem Hills and northern Judean Desert. Numbers represent hike numbers.

Nahal Matta

20

Points of interest: Springs, ruins, mosaics, wildlife.
Length of hike: 5 km. loop trip.
Hiking time: 4 hours.
Preferred season: December-May.
Suitable for: All.
Maps: Bet-Shemesh 1:50,000.
Special preparation: Clothes for walking in water, flashlight.
Starting point: Moshav Matta.
Ending point: Moshav Matta or 1.7 km. west of Moshav on main road by Hirbet Hanot.

To begin hike:

Bu bus: Take bus from Jerusalem Central Bus Station to Moshav Matta. Get off at far end of Moshav.

By car: On Bar Giora-Emek HaElah Road west of Jerusalem (En Kerem exit) park at entrance to Moshav Matta. If you are a party of 2 vehicles, park the second 1.7 km. down the road to the west where dirt road leads to the north and paved road to the south. Walk down main road of Matta through Moshav toward wadi.

Descend north on road to wadi. Cross Nahal Matta (1) on bridge. Fig trees, willow trees and reeds grow on your left.

Moshav Matta, founded originally in 1950 by Yemenite immigrants, was settled again in 1954 by immigrants from North Africa and today the population is mixed. Matta in Hebrew is an orchard.

Head west on road through the last houses of Moshav Matta, just north of the wadi. Cross soccer field (football) and head along the wadi to the south (left) of the plum orchards. One

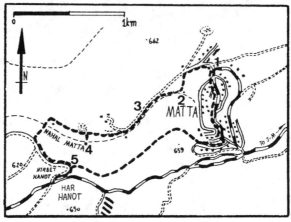

Hike 20, Nahal Matta

hundred meters west of the soccer field, En Matta emerges from a small jungle of trees (2) before two dirt roads meet. Return north to blue-marked dirt road heading west, just north of the uncultivated orchards.

150 meters before the eucalyptus trees in the wadi, just to the right of the dirt road, is a large fig tree and an ancient pool. These are part of a small unused water complex covered by vegetation. (3) Head to eucalyptus trees near large carob and fig trees where a layer spring flows. See how far you can crawl into the small tunnel there.

Just west of the trees, the blue-marked dirt road heads right along the northern part of the wadi and black-marked trail crosses stream heading up to Hirbet Hanot to the southwest. Continue on blue-marked dirt road through lots of fennel bushes. This bush grows to a height of 3 meters, its strong aroma a sure sign of recognition. Clusters of yellow fennel flowers bloom in the off-season between July and November. Fennel (shumar) grows in open fields of the Mediterranean areas of Israel. The leaves, young stems and seeds are edible and taste of 'licorice.' The fresh leaves can be eaten, sucked or added to salads, or try the leaves in soup. Boil leaves 3 minutes and have some fennel tea, good for stomach aches. Melted sugar with fennel seeds or leaves makes a kind of sweet candy. The Moroccan Jews enjoy drinking Arak, an alcoholic beverage tasting of the fennel leaf, which is also used in the wine industry. As you can see, throughout history the plant has been used for just about everything. The Arabs use water that was cooked with fennel seeds to cleanse infected eyes and water boiled with the leaves to help colds, digestion and throat problems, and to supply an energy boost.

To your right along the slope is Hirbet Tanur, a Crusader farm. Head to the large fort, 50 meters north of the dirt road and explore it. Note the thick walls and firing slots. Perhaps this was the farmlord's home.

Just beyond this building and down the dirt road, several well used trails through the fennel lead to a huge fig tree standing in the stream bed. This is the point where (4) En Tanur emerges from a lovely arched tunnel. Take off your shoes and wade into the high tunnel until you arrive at the source in a large cave.

Return to dirt road and continue your hike along it. This whole area is quite isolated and therefore flourishing with wildlife. After a curve to the right the blue-marked trail breaks to the left as indicated by a blue trail mark on a large rock to the right of the dirt road. The trail crosses the valley rampant with the fennel. The trail is unclear here, so look for trail mark across the wadi before you begin your descent.

The trail then heads up the opposite bank through typical Mediterranean forest; oak and Palestine pistachio, rockrose and soft hairy calycotome.

Hit dirt road, taking left and following green-marked trail which heads to Hirbet Hanot just south of the paved road. The pine forest on your side of the road was planted by the Jewish National Fund. Across the paved road is a pine forest planted by the British who even supplied a house for a forest curator.

Alongside the paved road runs an ancient road, that lead from the southern coast and Lachish region towards Jerusalem. The ascent here is gradual and remnants from many periods have been found along the way. Hirbet Hanot, meaning ruins of the inn, dates back to the Roman and Byzantine periods. (5) There are a number of beautiful mosaics here, along with water cisterns and other relics. In the main building you can enjoy a huge mosaic floor that is coated with sand, uncover it carefully with your hands. Just north of the building below some small oak trees are several more mosaics, these covered with leaves. Please re-cover the mosaics before you continue your hike.

Remnants of more than 1000 mosaic floors have been found in Israel, most of them dating from the Byzantine period. Mosaic floors have been found at many locations in the Middle East and Mediterranean area. The Roman historian Pliny the Elder claims that it was the Greeks who first began to decorate their floors with mosaic. The word mosaic is derived from the Latin concept, 'the labor of the muses.' A laborious craft, it is estimated that a skilled worker can set 200 small mosaic stones per hour, and a completed mosaic includes thousands of stones. All the colored stones necessary for crafting such a floor were not always easy to find in all regions, and this is probably a second reason why mosaic floors were crafted only for homes of the wealthy or for community buildings such as synagogues and churches.

To head back to Matta, you can hike 2 km. farther east on paved road or hike on unclear trail that may leave you with scratches but is more interesting.

To hike back, take unclear dirt road which continues parallel to the paved road, 50 meters below it to the east to an abandoned orchard. There the dirt road swings up to the paved road. Continue comfortable walk on terrace with grassy vegetation.

A narrow trail runs along the terrace. Here and there are piles of rocks, trail marks. Stick to terrace all the way until reaching old chicken coop at Moshav Matta. From this trail you can continue the remainder of the hike. Follow road through Moshav Matta to entrance.

Nahal Ktalav

21

Points of interest: Springs, Mediterranean forest, sheikh tomb.
Length of hike: 6 km. loop trip.
Hiking time: 5 hours.
Preferred season: All year.
Suitable for: All.
Maps: Bet Shemesh 1:50,000.
Special preparation: None.
Starting & ending point: 750 meters east of Bar Giora Junction.

To begin hike:

By bus: Take bus to Bar Giora Junction from Jerusalem. Return down road eastward toward Jerusalem for 750 meters to sign saying Nahal Ktalav. (1)

By car: Exit Jerusalem from En Kerem to Bar Giora. 750 meters before Bar Giora Junction, 400 meters after a sharp curve right there is a sign, 'Nahal Ktalav.' (1)

Note marl deposit on eastern side of road. This soft yellowish rock holds the underground water, creating layer springs.

Take clear black-marked trail to En Giora, a layer spring surrounded by bramble. The ruined building once belonged to Arab farmers who lived here until 1948. Continue down trail.

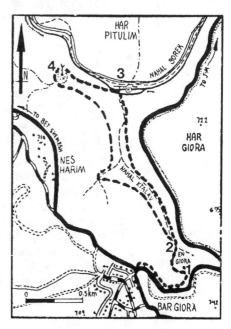

Hike 21, Nahal Ktalav

101

Explore this area rich in lemon, almond and fig trees. The area below En Giora used to be cultivated with waters of the spring, before the irrigation system fell into disrepair.

Fifty meters above Nahal Ktalav the trail breaks left, reaching a black and a blue trail mark intersection. (2) Here you begin the loop intersection. You can go in either direction. The hike will first head out along the blue-marked trail which follows Nahal Ktalav from above.

Looking ahead across a tributary of Nahal Ktalav, you will observe a burned out area. Note the bare terraces which remain intact. The trail crosses the tributary and then descends it. The trail veers left from the wadi.

The trail passes near a lone cypress tree. Below this tree is an ancient wine press. Arrive at intersection with green-marked trail near wooden sign. From here you can take left to Nes Harim or follow the hike of 'Nahal Sorek' — both options are one-way hikes.

Turn right onto green-marked trail in direction of Dar e Sheikh (4), the white dome, a monument and tomb for the famous Sheikh Bader (see Nahal Sorek hike). Follow trail through overgrown terraces to the Bar Giora train station. (3) The wooden sign in Hebrew below train tracks is incorrect; it is actually about 2 km. to En Giora.

The Bar Giora station was once a busy place, but today one train a day makes its round trip, connecting Jerusalem and Tel Aviv via Bet Shemesh. Head up Nahal Ktalav on wide trail. Note willow (arava) trees in the stream bed, evidence of water. The trail crosses the wadi back and forth. Note remnants of water channel on right side of watercourse, which once conducted the waters of En Ktalav. Nahal Ktalav, rich in vegetation, is one of the most popular hiking routes in the Jerusalem Hills.

Ktalav is Hebrew for the strawberry tree. Easily recognized, the leaves glisten brightly and the reddish bark peels off at a touch. Growing in the moist regions of the Mediterranean zone on chalk and marl soil, the ktalav grows from 3 to 10 meters high. It blooms in the spring and the red berries are sweet when ripe and are relished by both man and birds — the latter dispersing the seeds. There are many tales told about this tree, especially connected to the unique bark. Arabs tell of a shepherd and his father who fell in love with the same girl. The shepherd murders his father with his staff and from the blood ridden staff a red barked tree sprouts to immortalize the father. This story is based on the fact that the ktalav berries never shrivel and fall. They are intact all year and only fall off when the new growth (the next generation, i.e., the son) comes on the scene to force them off. This story also explains the Arabic name 'katlib' which means 'killed father.'

Another tradition relates that once the ktalav grew in the streambeds. Becoming jealous of other trees which grew high up on the ridges and had such a good view of the world, the ktalav extracted itself from the wadi and by a tremendous effort made the ascent to the hills; naturally the strain caused it to become a very red color.

After coming to the end of that part of the wadi which always flows with water, head up dry watercourse for 300 meters. Many unmarked trails lead up to the right.

The black-marked trail ascends the western bank to the right through small cliffs passing oak and strawberry trees, to complete the loop trip. (2) Head up the same trail, passing En Giora and returning to starting point. (1)

Bar Giora train station, hike 21, 22. In the background: Dar e Sheikh

Nahal Sorek Reserve

22

Points of interest: Mediterranean forest, different relics, views.
Length of hike: 10 km. one-way plus 2 km. to bus stop.
Hiking time: 6 hours.
Preferred season: All year.
Suitable for: All.
Maps: Bet Shemesh 1:50,000.
Special preparation: Flashlight.
Starting point: Moshav Ramat Raziel.
Ending point: 3 options: 1) Nes Harim; 2) Avshalom Stalactite Cave; 3) Bar Giora Junction.

To begin hike:

By bus: Take bus from Binyanei Hauma, across the road from the Jerusalem Central Bus Station, to Moshav Ramat Raziel. Get off at entrance to the Moshav. Fifty meters before the curve in the road, a green trail mark on a small cement structure leads you south on dirt road past chicken coops. (1)

Moshav Ramat Raziel, like other moshavs in the Jerusalem Hills, raises chickens and cultivates orchards. Ramat Raziel also has a dog kennel. The village, founded in 1948, was named after David Raziel, the first commander of the Irgun Zevai Le'ummi (I.Z.L.), the underground nationalist fighting organization. (David Raziel was killed in Iraq at age of 31 while on a bombing mission for British Army intelligence after the I.Z.L. had joined forces with the British to help defeat the Germans during World War II.)

From the dirt road a nice view is soon revealed ahead; to the right you view the green slopes of the Nahal Sorek Reserve, the Hebron Hills are ahead in the distance and to the left are the outskirts of Jerusalem.

Along the trail many herbs from the labiatae family grow. Labia in Latin is lip, which well describes the shape of the flowers. These flowers, which include marjoram, sage and thyme, usually bloom during the late spring, from April to June.

The dirt road heads toward the two rotund hills ahead, Har Pitulim, meaning 'the twisted mountain,' visible from Mount Herzl in Jerusalem. Just before bee hives on your left is a water hole hewn into the rock. The dirt road passes Har Pitulim on its right. Here you have a nice view of the cone-shaped hill, Hirbet Tura, that you will arrive at later, walking west. In the distance behind it is the Tzora Forest in the Judean foothills, not far from the development town of Bet Shemesh.

See map on page 108

The forest that you pass just on your right (2) is one of the few natural pine forests in the Judean Hills, the majority have been planted by the Jewish National Fund.

From here we can observe the difference between the northern and southern slopes; there is a strong contrast between the southern faced parched slope which is exposed to the sun most of the day and the green, north-faced slope which enjoys the more comfortable conditions of moisture and shade.

Sorek, which means grape vine, is mentioned in Isaiah, 5:1-2, "Now I will sing to my well beloved a song of my beloved touching his vineyard. My well beloved had a vineyard in a very fruitful hill and he fenced it and gathered out the stones thereof and planted it with the choicest vine (sorek) and built a tower in the midst of it and also made a wine press therein and he looked that it should bring forth grapes and it brought forth wild grapes."

Nahal Sorek drains the Jerusalem Hills, beginning north of Jerusalem and joining the Mediterranean Sea near Palmahim Beach. Today, western Jerusalem's sewage flows down this wadi, and it can be seen and smelt beside the dirt road along the Jerusalem train tracks built in 1892.

Continue down along the water pipe toward the Bar Giora train station at the bottom of Nahal Ktalav, by large pine and eucalyptus trees. (3)

At the bottom of descent reach dirt road, and continue on black-marked trail across Nahal Sorek over bridge to the deserted Bar Giora train station.

Crossing over the sewage flow, note the castor tree with its large blue-green palm-like leaves. This bushlike tree, growing up to 4 meters, seems to thrive on organic refuse. Growing throughout central Israel, including the northern Negev, its origins are most likely in East Africa or India. The castor tree offered shade to the Prophet Jonah, 4:6, "And the Lord God prepared a castor and made it come up over Jonah, that it might be a shadow over his head to deliver him from his grief. So Jonah was exceedingly glad of the castor." The castor is a useful plant even though it contains very toxic substances. An oil is extracted from the seeds for medical and industrial uses.

From the train station, pipes lead up Nahal Ktalav; the springs of Nahal Ktalav supplied water to this station during the British mandate. A myrtle is growing near the train station's western wall. Called 'hadas' in Hebrew, the myrtle is usually found only in the environs of Safed in the eastern Galilee and in the Golan Heights. Besides the passage under the train tracks a clear green-marked trail sets out to Dar e Sheikh.

For a shorter option you can head up Nahal Ktalav, following that hike (no. 21) and ending up at Bar Giora Junction.

Head up green-marked trail. Seek out the ancient terraces which line the route of this hike; these are hidden under the brush and can easily go unnoticed. 60% of the Judean Hills is terraced, and dates back to peak settlement period, such as the Second Temple period. In 1948, 50% of the terraces were being utilized by the Arabs living in the area, today that percentage is lower.

The trail passes through almond and olive trees and comes to the white dome of Dar e Sheikh,(4) named after Sheikh Bader who is buried here. He was a holy figure whose name graces several sites in the area. Until 1948 there was a small Arab village here.

Just beyond the domed tomb reach trail divide and signs. Turn right coming to another trail divide straight away. Head west on black-marked trail which holds to more or less the same elevation. One km. the trail rounds a small wadi on your right. Beneath a pistachio tree and nearby to almond tree, you will see a cave that contains a small spring. Check it out!

After another $1/_2$ km. you reach a water cistern and trough carved into the rock. (5) Head up to Hirbet Tura, passing wine presses, water cisterns. On your left, before you begin the ascent, note a columbarium cave clogged up with earth. Many hundreds of these columbarium caves have been found in the

Dar e Sheikh, hikes 21, 22

Judean foothills. The triangular shaped ledge hewn in the rock characterizes this type of construction, which most likely dates between the 3rd century B.C.E. and 1st century C.E.

There are a few possible explanations for these strange niches: perhaps they served as hollows for jugs containing ashes of the deceased, this being both Hellenistic and Roman ritual. The fact that these ledges seem too small and that no ashes or pottery have ever been found here seems to contradict this theory.

The more accepted theory is that pigeons were raised in the niches and their droppings were used for manure. During the Second Temple period, pigeons were a favorite sacrifice, being much more reasonable in cost compared to a cow or sheep. Some say that these caves were part of a Hellenistic worship ritual. Until further research, these hollows will remain shrouded in mystery.

The terraces around Hirbet Tura are truly ancient. Hirbet Tura at the top of the hill is most likely from the First Temple period. From the summit (6) you can enjoy a panoramic view of the Sorek Reserve. To the west you see the Tzora Forest in the Judean plains.

Nahal Sorek below curves around finger-shaped ridges. One of the theories explaining this phenomena is that during an earlier period, before the Syrian-African rift was formed, Nahal Sorek drained part of Transjordan; a large body of water flowed here in a gradual descent. The deepening of the wadi was caused by erosion and other related factors. Another possibility is that Nahal Sorek preceded the present geological forms and during different geological changes this nahal kept on flowing.

Retracing your steps, descend to the trough (5) and continue on trail westward, while keeping level. The trail passes between cliffs and through the thickest, most forested part of the reserve. Here mountain tulips bloom in the spring.

Two km. from Hirbet Tura the trail begins to rise toward Har Ya'alah. On the ridge down to your right is Hirbet a Ras.

The trail reaches intersection (7) with red-marked trail leading to the famous Avshalom Stalactite Cave. (8) You can take it but be advised that there is no public transportation back from the cave.

Continue on black-marked trail. Reach dirt road in pine forest and turn right. One hundred meters ahead, at the curve, follow trail up water pipe to the left. At wide dirt road, turn right at the Samuel Lewis Forest.

Before reaching the paved road there is a fountain on the right and if it is not working, you can use a water cistern to the left.

Reach paved road. Right beyond the road is a series of water cisterns and wine press.

If you have some energy left, head up to Mitzpe Ya'alah, 250 meters to the northwest, where there is a tower plus a grand view of the Sorek Reserve and the Judean foothills all the way to the Mediterranean Sea. This was once the site of an Arab village known as 'dwelling place of the wind.'

Two km. down the paved road and you are at the Avshalom Stalactite Cave. (8) Two km. to the east (left as you arrive) along the paved road above to the right is Moshav Nes Harim. To get there, walk 1 km. on paved road overlooking Nahal Sorek. Reach dirt road leading to the right. (9) Take right and then immediately left onto dirt road heading into Nes Harim. The bus stop is in the center of the Moshav.

Hike 22,
Nahal Sorek
Reserve

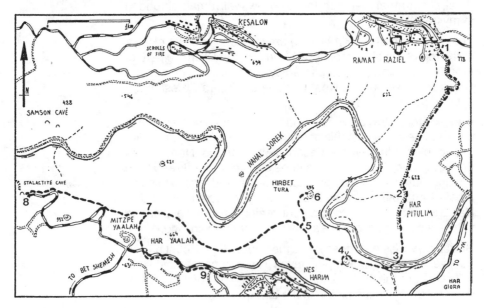

Har HaTayasim

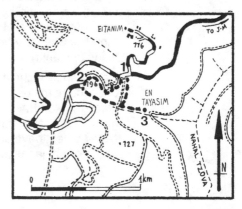

Points of interest: View, monument, spring.
Length of hike: 2 km. loop trip.
Hiking time: 2 hours.
Preferred season: All year.
Suitable for: All.
Maps: Bet Shemesh 1:50,000.
Special preparation: None.
Starting & ending point: Entrance to Eitanim Hospital.

To begin hike:

By bus: Get off at entrance to Eitanim Hospital on road to Ramat Raziel.

By car: Exit Jerusalem via En Kerem or Harel Junction on Jerusalem Highway. Take road to Ramat Raziel. Park by turnoff to the Eitanim Hospital 3 km. after Kibbutz Tzova.

After a curve on the main road, a dirt road by a Hebrew sign (1) announcing a nature reserve heads up in a series of switchbacks. Here your hike begins.

Follow dirt road around the right side of the mountain. Come to another dirt road on the marl where thyme and savory grow. Directly ahead of you is the monument in memory of soldiers who fell throughout the Arab-Israeli conflict.

The engine is of a Norseman plane that crashed in the fog only three days after it had arrived from France to join the young Israeli air force. The site of the crash and a monument is nearby, on the banks of Nahal Kesalon. This plane could carry a load of 750 kg., which included 28 hand-tossed bombs of 20 kg. each, the weight of the pilot and his one-man crew.

The Israel Air Force holds an annual ceremony here in memory of all its fallen. (2) Har HaTayasim means 'mountain

Hike 23, Har HaTayasim

of the pilots' in Hebrew. In Arabic the summit is called Hirbet el Kurd.

The view from the 796 meters high summit is panoramic; the stark, flat Hebron Hills range to the south and the Mediterranean coast to the west. Eastward, you are looking at the Jerusalem Corridor. Large strawberry trees grow here in the summit area, amidst rich Mediterranean forest as well as a large number of rare orchids, such as the Carmel bee orchid, the yellow bee orchid and some others.

A number of trails head around the summit which is also accessible by vehicle. Follow black-marked trail down and southeast. After 400 meters cross dirt road that leads back to starting point. The black-marked trail descends along a small wadi to En Tayasim (3) a layer spring. Below the spring, called in Arabic En Joz, is a small fruit garden with lemon, almond and walnut trees.

The Hebrew word for almond, 'shaked,' is from the root of the word 'diligence.' The almond tree reaches 8 meters. The leaves usually make their appearance after the tree has blossomed in early winter, thereby symbolizing the coming of spring. The lovely pinkish-white flowers which stand out dramatically on the as yet flowerless landscape, emit a honey-like odor. The fruit is covered with a shell and a velvety green envelope, ripening in late summer. The almond tree grows in the hilly regions of Israel and, oddly enough, the occasional tree can be found in the desert. The almond was one of the choice fruits of Israel during Biblical times. Jacob dispatched almonds to the ruler of Egypt, "take of the best fruits of the land . . . a little balm, a little honey . . . and almonds" (Gen. 43:11). Its early blooming signifies a diligence which connects to the Hebrew root referred to above. The almond can be eaten green, soon after the tree blooms or three months later when it is ripe; the outer rind shrivels and the inside layer becomes a hard shell. Almond oil is used for baking and for healing balms. During January and February, Israeli children begin to sing of the 'shekedia' and almond blossom fragrance permeates the brisk air, just in time for the Jewish calendar's New Year of the Trees, 'Tu Be'Shvat,' the 15th day of the Hebrew month of Shevat, when both children and adults go out into the fields to plant new tree-saplings.

Note a small niche in the rock at the side of the trail, possibly once the home of a small idol. Return from spring, ascending black-marked trail back to dirt road. A lot of sage and inula grow here. Take right 400 meters back to starting point. (1) Note cement paved on the dirt road in an attempt to keep the road from being washed out during the rainy season.

Tzuba

24

Points of interest: Springs, Crusader fort.
Length of hike: 6 km. loop trip.
Hiking time: 5 hours.
Preferred season: All year.
Suitable for: All.
Maps: Jerusalem 1:50,000 or Northern Judean Desert marked hiking trail map.
Special preparation: Flashlight, clothes for wading in water.
Starting & ending point: Kibbutz Tzova.

To begin hike:

By bus: Take bus to Kibbutz Tzova from Binyanei Hauma across from the Central Bus Station. Get off at the Kibbutz stop.

By car: Take Tel Aviv-Jerusalem Highway, get off at Harel Interchange. Drive through Maoz Tzion (Kastel) for 3 km. to Kibbutz Tzova. Park in Kibbutz.

If you are coming from Jerusalem, drive through En Kerem and up to Kibbutz Tzova.

Pool at En Limor, hike 24. See map on page 113

Kibbutz Palmahim-Tzova is sited on the watershed between the two main wadis of the Jerusalem Corridor, Nahal Sorek and Nahal Kesalon. The Kibbutz was founded in October 1948 by ex-members of the Palmah. The Palmah brigade was the Haganah's permanently mobilized striking force, founded by an emergency order of the Haganah's national command —

111

which was responsible for defense of the yishuv — in 1941 when the Axis forces were nearing approaches to Palestine. The Palmah was absorbed into the fledgling Israel Defense Forces upon the declaration of the State of Israel, at which time David Ben-Gurion, Israel's first Prime Minister, insisted that all pre-State fighting forces be disbanded.

The word Palmah is an acrostic for 'plugot mahatz' the 'crusher companies.' Kibbutz Tzova today runs a small industry for reinforced vehicle windshields.

Head through Kibbutz (1) on main paved road to the eastern exit right before the windshield factory. Follow dirt road that exits Kibbutz parallel and to the right of paved road, just to the right of the wooden sign in Hebrew describing the battle that took place here in 1948.

Follow clear dirt road for 800 meters through orchards. As dirt road curves sharply, walk down to a couple of buildings in the wadi. This is the spring complex of En Tzuba. (2) One hundred meters up the wadi, within a small peninsula of vegetation in the open fields, a ladder descends to the tunnel and sources of En Tzuba.

Have on your wading clothes and shoes and have your flashlight ready. Descend and follow the 60 meter chiselled out channel till its conclusion. If the exit is locked, crawl up open crevice on the right. En Tzuba is a typical layer spring. The underground chamber was most likely carved out during the Byzantine period and is one of the longest and largest such channel in the Jerusalem Hills.

From En Tzuba head north onto dirt road up wadi into open fields and continue onto clear trail until you reach the paved road leading from Kibbutz Tzova. Head left on this private road and ascend to Har Tzuba. Climb on clear marked trail to the top of Belmont, meaning 'the beautiful mountain,' a Crusader fort. (3) There is a nice view from here of the Jerusalem Corridor. Looking north you can see the Arab villages of En Rafa and En Nekoba along Nahal Kesalon and this is where you are headed.

The Crusader Tzuba was destroyed by Salah a Din in 1191 and an Arab village was established on the Crusader ruins. In 1834 this hill served as a fort for Abu Gosh during the fallahs' (peasants') revolt against the Egyptian Muhammed Ali. The Egyptians destroyed the fortress and the Arab village. The latter was rebuilt some time later and, during the War of Independence in 1948, was a strategic base behind the Kastel from which the Arab fighting forces controlled the Tel Aviv-Jerusalem Road. Egyptian volunteers from the regiment of the Moslem Brothers held Tzuba. On the 12th of July 1948 the village of Tzuba was captured during the Dani operation by a couple of companies from the Harel regiment.

Descend down toward the paved road and before reaching it take left onto small dirt road that circles around the fortress from the east. Note remnants of moat and trenches, examples of varying defense tactics from different periods on the same strategic spot.

From dirt road a green-marked trail descends from the north through terraces. The trail crosses a red-marked trail and dirt road, passing to the left of some orchards. Six hundred meters from Tzuba, as the trail turns sharply to the left by a large carob tree, before descent observe a chiselled out channel in the rock to your right. Leave trail and ascend right 50 meters to the ridge summit, to a large flat chiseled out area, most likely an ancient place of worship. (4) Nearby is a small spring that flows in to a cave.

Return to and descend green-marked trail. Before you reach orchards, veer left and continue on side of wadi toward the village of En Rafa. Reach the main square by bus stop and new mosque. Next to the mosque is one of the pools of the En Rafa spring.

Follow red-marked road that runs west alongside Nahal Kesalon, landscaped by small gardens that are watered by En Rafa. One hundred meters down the road is another pool of the En Rafa spring. (5) One km. from En Rafa, 100 meters after a sharp curve to the left and above to the left of the dirt road, are large boulders and a large fig tree. Ascend to En Limor. Note large ancient pool and smaller, more recent pool; these are fed from two different sources. Explore. (6)

From En Limor backtrack 100 meters to the east and head up clear dirt road to the south, reaching main road near Kibbutz Tzova. Head left 400 meters up road leading to Kibbutz, back to starting point. (1)

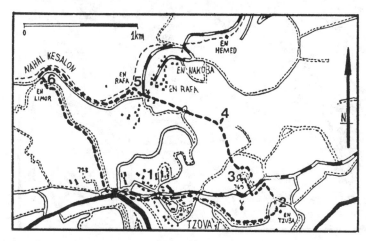

Hike 24, Tzuba

113

Springs around Jerusalem

25

Points of interest: Four layer springs, restored spring complex, Byzantine church, Biblical scenery.

Length of hike: 9 km. one-way; can be loop trip with short bus ride.

Hiking time: 5 hours.

Preferred season: All year.

Suitable for: All.

Maps: Jerusalem 1:50,000 or Northern Judean Desert marked hiking trail map.

Special preparation: Flashlight, clothes for water.

Starting point: Ora Junction.

Ending point: Manahat Stadium.

To begin hike:

By bus: Take buses that head to Hadassah En Kerem Hospital. Get off at Ora Junction, before the road descends to Hadassah Hospital. (1)

By car: Head from entrance to Jerusalem west on the Herzl Blvd. Do not get off Herzl Blvd., continuing toward Hadassah En Kerem Hospital until the Ora Junction. Take left by gas station and park there. (1)

Hike 25, springs around Jerusalem

At entrance to gas station, turn right on a dirt road for 50 meters. Turn right onto dirt road. On your left is a cistern with

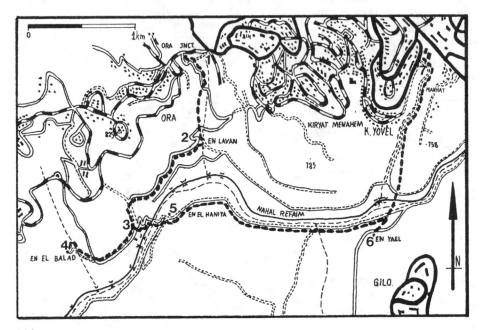

garbage. The dirt road heads around the wadi. A hundred meters along the dirt road on the right slope is a wine press. Continue around wadi, join dirt road coming in from the right and head down it on the right side of the wadi following now the blue-marked trail.

As dirt road crosses wadi beyond the orchards, there is clear marked trail that descends to the right of the wadi near an almond tree. Head onto the trail. Pass planted pine forest. The trail crosses dirt road and continues to descend joining dirt road on right side of the wadi. One hundred yards along this dirt road you come to En Lavan (2) which emerges from a tunnel in the wadi. One terrace layer above the opening of the tunnel is the opening of the hole covered with branches that descends to the source of the spring; at another higher level are some caves. One terrace layer below the spring is a nice pool and the water flows between the pool and spring down an open channel and alongside large walnut trees. These trees appear in the Song of Songs, 6:11, "I wandered down into the garden of nuts to see the fruits of the valley." Fig trees grow below the pool of En Lavan.

The fig tree is one of the seven species of Israel. Reaching four meters high, the many branched tree spreads its large-leaved boughs wide and is a true shade tree, shedding its leaves in winter. The fig fruit ripens in the summer turning from green-yellow to a winey-blue color. An ancient domesticated tree which grows throughout the Mediterranean area, the fig thrives near water sources and other shady moist locations. It grows in the desert oases. Excavations have unearthed figs from the Neolithic period. The fig is mentioned in the Bible 16 times, along with the vine and obviously it was a very important food source during Biblical times. The honey mentioned in the Bible sometimes refers to the fig, though usually to the date. The fig is mentioned in Kings I, 5:5, "Every man under his vine and under his fig," which describes the ideal period under King Solomon's rule when the Kingdom of Israel enjoyed a time of true prosperity and peace. The fig can be eaten raw but only following a very meticulous examination in order to ensure that the fruit is free of worms. Worm infestation is very common in the fig; being that the worms adapt a form identical to the white fibrous flesh of the fresh fruit, the fig must be checked with extra-special care. But the effort is well worth the pleasure of this luscious treat. Fig jam is considered a delicacy and today imported dried figs from Turkey are sold everywhere. The Arab sector of Israel still grows figs. The fig is also a curative. A fig compress cured King Hezekiah (Kings II, 20:7). Very important in Talmudic times, the fig is mentioned over 70 times in Talmudic literature and is thought to have been the forbidden Tree of Knowledge in the Garden of Eden.

From spring head up a few terraces to blue-marked dirt road and head left on it. Below is Nahal Refaim, the main tributary of Nahal Sorek. Refaim was a nation which occupied Canaan in Biblical times. The area west of old Jerusalem, farther up Nahal Refaim was known as Emek Refaim, mentioned in Samuel II, 6:8, "The Philistines also came and spread themselves in the Valley of Refaim."

Nahal Refaim begins at Jerusalem's train station, which is on the watershed of Israel. Along the nahal runs a dirt road and the Jerusalem-Tel Aviv train track, via Bet Shemesh. While the Turks ruled Palestine with a 'backward' hand, in the 19th century Jewish settlement, prompted by certain wealthy benefactors who wished to establish a Jewish economic foothold in the Holy Land, began to expand outside the fortified walls of Jerusalem. At the turn of the century nearly 50,000 people lived in Jerusalem. Joseph Navon initiated the development of the train to Jerusalem and a French company completed the construction in 1892. Currently, the train runs only twice a day and is an unprofitable business, being used mostly for outings as its route is breathtakingly beautiful but very slow and tedious. There is talk of modernizing it.

From the dirt road is a nice view of Har Gilo, known as the 'Everest' of the area as it is 923 meters above sea level and the highest mountain in the Jerusalem environs. On the ridge is the village of Walaje and further down the track is the village of Batir, or in Hebrew Betar where the famous commander

Cave in Nahal
Halilim (hike 26)

Shimon Bar Kokhba fell in the year 135, bringing to an end the last Jewish uprising against the Romans. This Arab village, like many others, has taken its name from the ancient Hebrew site.

One km. after En Lavan, the dirt road curves around a wadi and continues down to Nahal Refaim. (3) Here take right onto dirt road and continue along middle of the ridge. The track becomes a paved road and heads up. Take small dirt road continuing on ridge level, observing large nest on electricity pole. The dirt road soon curves around wadi and reaches En el Balad (4) meaning, 'spring of the village.' The layer spring contains a small tunnel and a small pool.

Below the dirt road the spring enters another pool. Two more layer springs emerge further up the small wadi nearby, in the direction of Moshav Aminadav. Here until 1948 was the village of Walaje, which today is situated on the other side of Nahal Refaim.

Head back to blue-marked dirt road and descend to Nahal Refaim. Take care crossing train tracks and Nahal Refaim. Continue left onto black-marked trail and soon reach En el Haniya, emerging just south of the dirt road. (5) There are Byzantine remnants above the spring and to the side is a large pool. This site is a popular meeting place for the shepherds of Walaje and Batir; 175 cubic meters of water pass through this spring daily. In 1932, remnants of a mosaic of a Byzantine church were found here.

From the spring head east on a smooth dirt road, continuing northeast, and running parallel along Nahal Refaim for 2 km. Here the En Yael complex is noticed easily above the dirt road to the right near a lone cypress tree. Across En Yael, coming in from the north, is Nahal Manahat. Head up to the right on a clear trail to En Yael. (6) A few seasons of archaeological digs were carried out on the forty acre En Yael complex recently, unearthing several levels of remains reaching as far in the past as the Iron Age.

Although there are no ibex in the Jerusalem Hills, the name En Yael, means 'spring of the ibex,' known in Arabic as En Yalu, it is a layer spring like En Lavan. The most spectacular find here is a Roman villa with beautiful mosaic floors and fresco (painted) walls. The house dates back to the 3rd century. Roof tiles bearing the stamp of the 10th Roman Legion and a coin dated to the time of certain Roman procurators were discovered above the floor. Pottery was found from the 7th and 8th century B.C.E. The water system is more recent, from the Arabic period.

There are plans to restore the site, to rebuild the walls, terraces and the water system and create a workshop for illustrating ancient farming methods to tourists and schoolchildren. Today workshops are held at En Yael where children learn how to perform home crafts, such as weaving, pottery making, ancient farming and ancient cooking methods.

Return to dirt road, cross it, pass through orchard, cross Nahal Refaim and start ascent to ridge south of Nahal Manahat. Below electric wire pole and in a small grove of olive trees are remnants from the Israelite period, 1000 B.C.E., including a home and a wine press.

From here head up a bit and take left onto dirt road which runs beneath the ridge, above and parallel to Nahal Manahat, reaching the Manahat Stadium.

Another option is to head up ridge to the top, turn back to enjoy view of the hike, then continue along ridge past cisterns, wine presses and other remnants to the community of Manahat. Manahat, also known as Malha, is mentioned in Chronicles I, 8:6, "These are the sons of Ehud, these are the heads of fathers, houses of the inhabitants of Geba and they were carried captive to Manahat."

Situated southwest of Jerusalem, until the time of Israel's War of Independence, Malha was an Arab village originally built by Moslems who farmed here and worked in Jerusalem. It is believed that the villagers originated in the Caucasus mountains and were brought here during the Middle Ages to build the Monastery of the Cross. The Monastery of the Cross is located in the valley below the Israel Museum in Jerusalem. During the British mandate, the youth of Manahat attacked Jewish settlers and in 1948 the village participated in attacks on Jerusalem communities.

On July 14th, 1948, following a fierce battle, the village was captured by the I.D.F. and the residents ran off. Eighteen Jewish soldiers fell and there is a monument situated near the main road by the bridge. (Derekh Malha) Today Manahat is a comfortable Jewish suburb of Jerusalem, rising 775 meters above sea level.

From Manahat descend down toward the stadium by the intersection where there is a bus stop. (7) Here you can also take bus no.19 back to the Ora Junction to pick up your car. (1)

Mevasseret to Jerusalem

26

Points of interest: Karstic caves, springs.
Length of hike: 7 km. one-way; can be loop trip with short bus ride.
Hiking time: 5 hours.
Preferred season: All year.
Suitable for: All.
Maps: Jerusalem 1:50,000 or Northern Judean Desert marked hiking trail map.
Special preparation: Flashlight.
Starting point: Entrance to Mevasseret.
Ending point: Main entrance to Jerusalem.

To begin hike:

By bus: Take bus from Binyanei Hauma across from Central Bus Station to Mevasseret Tzion.

By car: From entrance to Jerusalem, turn on to Road no. 4 toward Ramot and immediately take left and park car in parking lot. (6) Return to junction by foot and just down the Jerusalem-Tel Aviv road is the Mevasseret bus stop. Take Mevasseret bus.

Get off bus at stop after sharp curve in the road between Mevasseret Tzion and Mevasseret Yerushalayim, (1) the fourth stop after the bus exits the Jerusalem-Tel Aviv Road. Some buses enter Mevasseret Tzion. Mevasseret, founded in 1951 is a developing village, now a suburb of Jerusalem, consisting of 3 communities: Maoz Tzion near the Kastel on the other side of the highway; Mevasseret Tzion — which the bus either passed or entered — part of which is an absorption

Hike 26, Mevasseret to Jerusalem

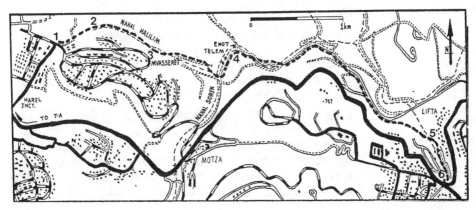

119

center for new immigrants; and Mevasseret Yerushalayim which is a residential community.

Cross road and look 100 meters to the right where there is a brown wooden sign with a green trail mark on it, 'Nahal Halilim.' The sign is also marked with two insignias: the iris of the Society for the Protection of Nature, and the insignia of the Keren Kayemet, which is the Jewish National Fund. Follow dirt road alongside the outer homes of Mevasseret. To your left is Har Ahiram, where the Israel-Jordan border passed until 1967. After 250 meters, the dirt road heads to the left for 100 meters and then right as the road divides. The trail drops to the wadi of Nahal Halilim. A lot of fennel and inula with yellow flowers blooming in the fall grow in the wide dry riverbed.

After 250 meters the trail leaves the wadi to the left and passes a chiseled-out burial tomb-cave, with an almond tree gracing the foreground; it contains several rooms, most likely from the Second Temple period. (2) Tomb-caves usually are typified by catacombs where the dead were first interred in sarcophagi for about a year; following disintegration of the flesh, the bones were transferred to an ossuary, the size of which depended on the extent of the longest bone, the thigh bone. Explore the cave, maybe you will find some skulls.

The trail heads up to the ridge where you will see remnants of an unidentified settlement. The trail crosses a large stone surface that contains water cisterns, caves and a carved out wine press. From here the green-marked trail returns to Nahal Halilim and descends the wadi. Your walk here begins through rock terraces from different periods, but these soon end since Nahal Halilim deepens and the wadi is less suitable for agriculture. Straight ahead on the ridge is the Jerusalem-Tel Aviv Road and above it the Givat Shaul Cemetery, called Har Hamenuhot — the mountain of final rest.

Half a km. down the trail the wadi cuts through hard limestone and on both sides of the wadi, the trail leads you to several karstic caves. (3) Explore. Halilim in Hebrew means flute, or hollows, connected to the belief that the wind, as it blows through the hollows of these caves, plays a unique melody. These caves are of hard limestone typified by the karstic weathering phenomenon; in the winter, drops of water drip down from points in the ceiling and create puddles on the rock. Note the circular basins formed throughout the ages of this continuous trickle.

Rabbi Akiva, the famous Jewish sage from the Second Temple period, who began his Torah learning at the age of forty at the prompting of his beloved wife Rachel, noted this phenomenon as he stood by a well and observed a stone being struck again and again by drops of water. He thought to himself, "If soft water can carve hard rock, then the difficult Torah learning, the study of Jewish wisdom which are as strong as iron, can easily shape my flesh and blood heart."

From caves continue on trail along the wadi toward grove of tall pine trees. From pine trees descend and cross Nahal Sorek and on road take left, following red trail mark. The valley here is called the Valley of the Cedars. Soon on your left, you will note a large patch of bramble (raspberry). From this wadi one of the Telem springs emerges. Half a km. from Nahal Halilim the wadi and the dirt road curve to the right and Nahal Luz comes in from the north. Head to your left to a building across Nahal Sorek. Another spring emerges into a cement lined pool of water. Behind the pool by the building is a huge pool of large stones. (4) To view the dry but impressive reservoir, the adventurous can climb onto the roof of the deserted building.

Many fruit trees and grapes grow around the spring. One hundred and fifty meters up the hill to the north above Nahal Luz is another dry spring, its channel and pool hidden amongst dense brush. Return to dirt road and continue along orchards. The Tel Aviv-Jerusalem Road runs parallel to the dirt road above it to the right. Some wild Syrian pear trees that bloom in clumps of lovely white flowers in March and April grow along the right side of road after the dirt road crosses Nahal Sorek.

The path recrosses Nahal Sorek and enters an open gate. Here the dirt road divides. Take the right option as the dirt road ascends a bit, and you will have a nice view of the Arab village of Beit Iksa and the mosque of Nebi Samuel. Situated on the summit of the highest hill of the region and with some large trees growing nearby, this mosque is visited by Jews as well since tradition holds that the prophet Samuel is buried here. The mosque, standing nearly 900 meters above sea level, is easily sighted from Jerusalem's western neighborhoods, and from the entrance to Jerusalem.

Across Nahal Sorek the large neighboring community of high-rise buildings and split level homes is Ramot. The dirt road passes some planted pine forest and from there begins to descend, toward Nahal Sorek, the main wadi of the Jerusalem Corridor. Sorek means grape vine and grapes were usually grown along Nahal Sorek. As dirt road curves left, a clear trail heads off to the right. Follow it and you soon find yourself at the deserted village of Lifta, or Mei Niftoah. (5)

The trail crosses a small wadi and heads up to the houses. In the first house which the trail reaches, there is an oil press, but only the basin for the crushing of the olives is left. The square depression in the center of the basin once held the axle that was connected to the grinding stone.

From olive press house, explore Lifta, then head up the clear path to the spring, 150 meters up the wadi along the trail from the olive press. A lot of sabra cactus grow around Lifta. Being the only cactus in Israel it is assumed to be an import. The large, prickly bush is usually found on the outskirts of Arab villages; it was used to mark the borderline between properties. Today the fruit of the sabra is sold throughout Israel, the thorns are removed and the skin peeled off to reveal a succulent tropical fruit. The leaves are water saturated and the flesh is also edible, an important water source. The Sabra is also used in herbal medicine to treat cuts and skin diseases and the flowers are used to cure dysentery.

Mei Niftoah is mentioned in Joshua,15:9, where the frontier between the tribe of Judah and Benjamin is described; in 18:15 it is named as the southern border of the tribe of Benjamin. The Arab village of Lifta, situated nearby the Jerusalem-Jaffa Road was mentioned often by various visitors to the Holy Land during the 19th century, described as a small village with vineyards, olive trees and wheat crop.

Lifta was also famous for its citron (etrog) trees, the citrus fruit prescribed for the blessings integral to the fall holiday of Tabernacles, Succot. The Hebrew newspaper, 'Hatzvi,' in 1887 informed its reading public that "2000 etrogs were brought from Lifta."

Lifta had over 50 households in 1854 and in the 1870's it was noted that there were around 300-400 residents there. Around the beginning of the 20th century the Arabs of the village of Lifta, who owned many properties outside their own town limits, sold land to the Jews for the establishment of the communities of Mea Shearim and Sha'arei Hesed. During the Arab riots of 1936 and in the War of Independence in 1948, Lifta's residents disrupted the orderly movement of traffic on the Jaffa-Jerusalem Road. During the War of Independence the people of Lifta deserted their homes.

The village was built high on the slope, freeing the base of the hills and the valley for agricultural use. Note openings in the wall of the hillside which might be burial caves to the left of the springs. The recently restored spring contains 2 tunnels that lead to the source. Explore this tunnel and arrive at the source.

From the spring, head up the very steep paved road which ascends the left side of the wadi. Soon you will pass on your right the remains of a hole, now sealed, which drops to the spring source. Continue up to parking lot (6) below road no. 4 connecting the western and northeastern entrances to Jerusalem. From here it is a five minute walk back up to Central Bus Station.

Judean Desert

Geography

The Judean Desert is in the eastern section of Judea, situated between the Judean Hills to the west and the Syrian-African rift to the east — where we find the Jordan Valley and the Dead Sea. The northern border of the desert is not sharply defined since the Desert narrows very gradually toward its northern extent, however, Wadi Auga which is 10 km. north of Jericho is generally considered the demarcation line between the Judean and the Samarian Deserts. On the south the Judean Desert borders the Negev at Nahal Ashalim, west of the southern point of the Dead Sea.

To the east, the Judean Desert drops to the Dead Sea in sharp escarpments. The western borders are also clearly defined as the extreme differences between the Jerusalem Hills and the Desert are quite obvious. However, due to certain geological factors, there are differences of opinion as to where the exact borders of the Judean Desert are on the north and south. The Judean Desert has no sand or sandstone. In contrast to the Negev, the Judean Desert is a shadow desert, unrelated to the globe's desert zone which is farther south. The Judean Hills are posed like a wall that cuts the wind which blasts off the Mediterranean Sea, bringing in clouds of precipitation. Before the clouds pass over the watershed, the rain falls onto the Judean Hills and, when released of their burden, the clouds rise. From the watershed to the east is a sharp decline in elevation, the clouds lighten and rise heading toward the Syrian-African rift in the east. Thus the Judean Desert is formed in the shadow of the Judean Hills.

Another factor which helped form this Desert is the water impermeable chalk soil on the plateau; most of the precipitation that does fall is washed away to the east into the Dead Sea without having been absorbed in the ground.

Some of the tributaries of the Judean Desert's canyons begin along the watershed and during rainfall in the Judean Hills, the rain falling east of the watershed pours down the Desert canyons in a great deluge of flashflood, while further east down the canyon there is not a cloud in the sky.

Small canyons like Nahal David by En Gedi draw flashflood waters from the Desert plateau, in other words, only when strong rains fall quite close to the escarpments and the canyon vicinity does a flashflood occur. This is why flashfloods in the smaller canyons are rarer. The general direction of the canyons in the Judean Desert is from the northwest to the southeast.

From west to east, the Judean Desert is divided into a few sub-regions. The western part of the Desert, east of the watershed, is actually a 3-5 km. wide divide between the Jerusalem Hills and Judean Desert; rainfall is around 350 mm. and the vegetation is neither typically Mediterranean nor desert. A desert is usually defined as an area where the total rainfall is less than 200 mm. annually.

The predominant area of the Judean Desert is the Desert plateau. This 13-15 km. wide strip drops from 600 meters above sea level to around sea level, the area is made up of small hills which are not more than 100 meters above the average height of the surrounding vicinity. The chalk hills are embedded with flint and the wadis are shallow and wide; the many tributaries merge into a larger wadi which cuts through the escarpments in the east, creating magnificent canyons.

East of the Desert plateau, just above the escarpments, is a narrow strip of level hills, about 1-3 km. wide of limestone and dolomite rock and relict hills; relict hills are remnants of an earlier period when the area was covered with chalk. This is where the canyons begin. The most spectacular sight in the Judean Desert are these canyons and escarpments that drop sharply to the Dead Sea at a 65° angle, sometimes from 600 meters high. They are composed of several rock layers, mainly limestone and dolomite. Along the escarpments and some of the canyons is a more recent layer of marl, a deposit from the larger and more ancient Dead Sea.

These impressive cliffs run along the parallel fault lines which typify the Syrian-African rift. The cliffs hug the Dead Sea shore for 65 km. and near Enot Tzukim (En Fashkha) there is almost a perpendicular drop to the Dead Sea. The hikes off the Dead Sea Road will be along the escarpments and the narrow strip above it.

The Dead Sea is 830 sq. km., of which 100 sq. km. are evaporation ponds, and is divided into two regions, north and south. The northern region is 75% of the Dead Sea area, it contains 95% of the water volume, and the maximum depth is 400 meters. The southern Dead Sea is much shallower — only about 4-5 meters deep. The water has sometimes been so shallow here that caravans were able to cross the Dead Sea in the center of the southern section.

The Dead Sea is the most saline sea on earth, 32% as compared to 3% in the Mediterranean Sea. Forty-three billion tons of minerals are concentrated in the Dead Sea, including magnesium, bromide, chloride, potassium and more.

The shore-line level of the Dead Sea has always been an ever-changing one. Today, due to the fact that the Jordan River, which is the main source of Dead Sea waters, is being heavily utilized by both Israel and Jordan, the Sea is constantly shrinking. The surface is now over 400 meters below sea level.

The combination of the metallic blue sea, the sharp pale escarpments against the blue horizon, the springs and green oases nestled among the cliffs and canyons make the Judean Desert, only a 40 minute drive from Jerusalem, one of the most beautiful places in the country.

Climate

The Judean Desert descends from east of the watershed to the Dead Sea, from 600 meters to -400 meters. The topographical change is echoed by a change in temperature. For every drop of 100 meters in elevation, there is a drop in 0.66°c in the annual average temperature.

Jerusalem, 800 meters above sea level, has an annual average of 17.1°c. Jericho at -260 meters above sea level — 1,060 meters lower than Jerusalem — is warmer by 6.5° with a 23.6° annual average temperature, one of the hottest temperatures in Israel. Average annual rainfall drops from 500 mm. in Jerusalem to 100 mm. along the Dead Sea.

This trend continues as you go further south. At Sedom on the shores of the Dead Sea, the annual rainfall is 47 mm., half of the amount at the northern point of the Dead Sea. The average annual temperature in Sedom is 25°c, in contrast to 23.5°c at the most northern edge of the Dead Sea. Sedom is the hottest spot in Israel and in July the average high there is 40°c.

Winds from the west usually enter the region in the afternoon, heating up as they drop from the watershed, eastward to the Desert. On the eastern side of the Judean Desert morning breezes waft in from the Dead Sea.

Vegetation

Compared to the barren environment of the average desert, the small Judean Desert is rich in vegetation which is often quite dense. For this reason, this area is one of the most unique in Israel. Plants grow where there is water or access to water — at least during certain months of the year. Although desert conditions are more extreme and the vegetation more sparse to the east and south, in the north the hills are covered with shrubbery, mainly seablite. This plant is very noticeable from the Jerusalem-Jericho Road, especially around the sea level sign.

In the southern part of the Desert, plant life is restricted to the wadi beds. Another main problem restricting plant development is the high soil salinity and the chalk and marl deposits which do not allow the earth to absorb large amounts of water. Rainwater naturally containing some sea salt seeps into the top layer of the soil. Since the water cannot penetrate, it evaporates quickly leaving a salt layer. This salt residue process repeats itself and since water never penetrates, a permanent layer of salt is formed close to the surface of the ground.

The proximity of the salt layer to the ground surface is a direct result of low annual rainfall. At Ma'ale Edumim the layer is relatively deep at 1-2 meters. Further east, above En Kelt, the layer is 50 cm. below the surface and near the Dead Sea you can sometimes see salt layers coating the ground. This salt factor causes an osmotic problem for plants.

Many desert plants are typified by 'life-saving' mechanisms to overcome this problem, for instance, a lengthening of root system or the ability to store salt in their leaves and stem. This enables plants to absorb more water.

On the escarpments and in the canyon environs, plant life is richer, as salinity conditions do not occur on hard limestone and dolomite. The shade offered by the cliffs prevents evaporation, especially on the northern slopes (northface) which receive less sun.

Oases can be easily spotted by the green belt of vegetation surrounding them. A number of tropic, Sudanese and African species of plants and trees can be found in the Judean Desert, such as the Persian salvadora.

It is amazing to realize that tiny Israel includes four phytogeographic vegetation zones with the narrow Judean Desert being the only geographic zone in Israel that includes three of the four vegetation zones. The western Judean Desert is typified by vegetation from the Irano-Turanian zone. Vegetation primarily from the Sudanese zone grows along the main plateau of the Judean Desert; on the escarpments and above them are plants typical of the Saharo-Arabian zone.

Wildlife

The Judean Desert is actually the only place in Israel that maintains a full life cycle (of the ecological chain), due to the fact that the leopard has made a comeback and today several thrive along the escarpments, from Kumran south. This species of leopard, one of the smallest of its kind, weighs only 35 kilograms. The ibex (mountain goat) and hyrax should be its main food, but smaller rodents and cats from the few settlements along the Dead Sea are usually easier prey. The capacity of the Judean Desert for mammal life is peaking and hundreds of ibex today live along the escarpments, during the hot and dry summer they are concentrated around the oases. Fewer gazelles live on the plateau and along the Dead Sea shore. Hyenas, foxes, wildcats and the newly discovered Blanford fox are not uncommon.

Common birds in the Judean Desert are Tristram's grackle and the black and white desert wheatear. The black fan-tailed raven is easy to spot, doing acrobatics above the cliff escarpments. For many raptors the Judean Desert is one of the most tranquil habitats in these hectic times, and therefore it is a popular nesting area.

There are fish in the waters of the northern Judean Desert oases, like the cichlid fish, which originates in Africa. The edible frog and green toad are amphibians which also inhabit the more southern bodies of water. The Burton's carpet viper is the predominant poisonous snake found in the Judean Desert. The very rare and venomous black mole viper is also a native of this region.

Interesting invertebrates can be found in the Judean Desert: for instance, a poisonous grasshopper sporting colorful dots on his black body; the black widow spider; and numerous types of scorpions — the most poisonous one being the yellow scorpion whose sting can kill a small child. Scorpions are found under rocks.

The animal life of the Judean Desert originates from the Asian, African, tropical and Mediterranean regions. As you can well imagine, this factor contributes to the many other elements which make the Judean Desert a very special place.

Human Involvement

The proximity of the Judean Desert to central Israel and the fact that, although it has been classified as a desert, it is blessed with abundant water sources, has guaranteed a human presence throughout history. The most documented desert on earth, this Desert was often throughout history a shelter for castaways and rebels from the central government in Judea. King David and Bar Kokhba hid here from their respective foes. Even in this century the Palmah units, practically under the nose of the occupying British, used the Desert for their maneuvers.

Usually the northern Desert was more densely populated than the southern part, due to the more abundant water sources of the Desert north of Masada.

The Judean Desert is packed with historical remnants. Beginning with prehistoric times, hunters occupied caves and canyon notches in the western Judean Desert close to the forests of Judea. The oldest relic found here is from the Stone Age, 100,000 years ago and the first pre-historic find is from the Chalcolithic period. Many caves have been found containing relics of these nomads who lived throughout the area which today is Israel. Many artifacts of worship have been found in the temple at En Gedi as well as 429 bronze pieces in a cave in Nahal Mishmar.

The Judean Desert includes the Biblical sub-regions of the Tekoa Desert, the Zif Desert, the Maon Desert and the En Gedi Desert. From the time of Abraham and throughout the Biblical era, the Judean Desert has played a dominant role in many dramatic episodes: the destruction of Sedom and Gomorrah; the Children of Israel crossing into the promised land north of the Dead Sea; King Saul tracking down the future King David.

Bethlehem, where King David grew up, bordered the Desert. In Psalms, King David, who spent his formative years as a shepherd wandering the hills of Judea and its desert, vividly includes the landscape, flora and fauna of the Judean Desert in his praises of the Almighty.

Uziah, King of Judah, established forts along the Desert, (Chronicles I, 20:10). Solomon in the book of Song of Songs talks of En Gedi's spice industry. King Herod renovated the palaces and water systems that were established by the Hasmoneans, the most famous of course being Masada. The Essenes lived their communal life in caves of the Judean Desert. The rebels of the Bar Kokhba revolt lived in the caves of the canyons that dropped to the Dead Sea.

Ninety sites were established during the Byzantine period — including a large network of monasteries, situated mainly in the north of the Judean Desert, a number of them by the famous Haritun. Following the Arab conquest of 636, the Desert was ignored, except for the city of Jericho.

The European Crusaders viewed the Desert as hostile, by and large preferring to leave the area alone. Only two sites from this period have been found. From the 13th century on, Bedouin nomads have made use of the Desert to graze their flocks of sheep and goats. The fact that these domestic animals demolish the ecosystems where they graze has served to further decimate an already sensitive environmental region.

In 1930, the Dead Sea Works were established on the northern part of the Dead Sea. Kibbutz Bet HaArava was established nearby in 1939. In 1948, during the War of Independence, Jordan gained control of the northern Judean Desert, destroying Bet HaArava and the northern Dead Sea Works. Fortunately, the latter had already re-established their main factory on the southern part of the Dead Sea by Sedom in the early 1930's.

During the 19 year period of Jordanian rule, the border between Israel and Jordan ran from En Gedi to the southwest. In order to reach En Gedi and Masada from Jerusalem at that time, one had to travel many hours on a roundabout route to the bottom of the Dead Sea on the Eilat Road and then swing back and arc to the north. In 1953, Kibbutz En Gedi was established on the land between Nahal Arugot and Nahal David, and here the first field study center of the Society for the Protection of Nature was established. Today there are nearly ten settlements along the Dead Sea. The escarpments and canyons are nature reserves. Much of the Judean Desert, mainly the plateau, serves as firing zones for the I.D.F.

The sharp cliffs dropping to the Dead Sea have always been an obstacle for man. Today a paved road runs along the Dead Sea and one paved road heads up the escarpments to Metzokei Deragot. The road to Metzokei Deragot, based on an ancient road, leads on to Tekoa near Bethlehem.

There is a dirt road heading along the top of the escarpments going north-south just to the west of all the canyon heads. Many man-made trails, known in Hebrew as 'ma'ale,' head up the escarpments. Some of these trails have series of switchbacks to enable domesticated animals to negotiate the steep heights. Rock heaps alongside the trail, meant to mark the way, are called Rujum in Arabic.

Water

The underground geologic watershed of Judea is farther west than the topographic watershed. Thus rainfall falling west of Jerusalem, west of the watershed, flows into the wadis leading to the Mediterranean Sea. But water seepage reaches the oases along the Syrian-African rift to the east. In the narrow canyons, in certain locations water hollows hold the water all year round. On the plateau the soft chalk is easily chiseled away and being impermeable to water, it is ideal for water cisterns and water holes.

The springs of the Judean Desert release around 100 million cubic meters of water yearly, nearly all flowing at sites from En Gedi northward. The further the springs are from the area of water concentration, the longer the water is exposed underground to the earth and rock, becoming more saline. Springs like En Gedi that flow on the slopes off the escarpments are layer springs while fault springs emerge along the shores of the Dead Sea and are more saline. The strips of vegetation which line the shores of the Dead Sea, usually north of En Gedi, are sure signs of springs.

Mineral springs are characterized by high salinity, a variety of mineral content, radioactivity and high temperatures. In Israel these springs are situated only along the fault lines in the Syrian-African rift, the waters originating deep in the earth. There are a number of these springs along the Dead Sea. Around the southern base of the Dead Sea, the Dead Sea Works have drilled several wells for industrial use.

Flashfloods are relatively common in the Judean Desert since several of the larger wadis originate along the watershed of the Judean Hills rather than in the Desert. These flashfloods collect water in the non-desert part of the wadi and the torrent is carried down swiftly to the Judean Desert.

Hiking in the Judean Desert

The Judean Desert is an ideal place for hiking. During the winter the temperatures are comfortable. You have a desert, less than one hour away from Jerusalem, blessed with awesome canyons; in late winter if rain has fallen, the northern region is covered with gorgeous carpets of colorful wildflowers. On nearly every hike along the cliffs you may meet some ibex and if you are lucky — a leopard. If so, keep your distance and give him some respect. In Israel there have been no cases of man being attacked by leopards. You also have many opportunities to take a swim in the Judean Desert, more so than on a Judean Hills hike.

Though all the trails are marked, many trails are not always clear. Maps are a must for hiking in the Judean Desert. Even in the winter, sun can be quite strong — hats are *always* a must and suntan lotion can be quite helpful, especially if you have a light complexion.

Looking from above, beware of the occasional illusion that descent is easy. Follow the marked trails only. If darkness falls and you find yourself in the area of canyons and cliffs, stay where you are and wait until daylight. *Do not attempt to negotiate in the dark at all. Staying put is the very safest alternative.* Take care also not to settle down before checking that your resting place is clear of sundry, uncalled for, and unwelcome small visitors.

Before leaving on a hike check with someone, such as the field study center, making sure that there are no current problems along your planned route. Leave your route details either with your family, friends, or the district field study center.

Flashfloods are especially dangerous. While rain is falling in the hills, the sun may be brightly shining and the skies clear as a bell in the Desert. Persons hiking in the Desert on such a day have absolutely no warning of what is to come. Therefore, during the winter make sure to listen to the weather forecast for the entire Judean Hills region before hiking in the Desert canyons. Witnessing a flashflood from a safe vantage point is a thrilling experience. *If you come on a flashflood that has overtaken the road, enjoy it but don't try to negotiate it. Many attempts to cross a flashflood with a private vehicle or truck have ended in disaster.*

During the winter take care not to hike in the wadis on days that rain is expected in the country. After bathing in the Dead Sea make sure to wash your body with fresh water. Three litres of drinking water per person should be sufficient in winter, while *in the summer 1 litre of water for every estimated hiking hour is a must.* Evaporation is rapid and unnoticed in the dry desert climate. Drink constantly.

Important phone numbers:

(Area code 057)

En Gedi Field Study Center	84288	
En Gedi Nature Reserve	84285	
Neve Zohar Police	84112	*Ibex on Metzokei*
First Aid En Gedi	84348	*Deragot Road*
First Aid Neve Zohar	84181	*overlooking the Dead*
at night:	84191	*Sea*

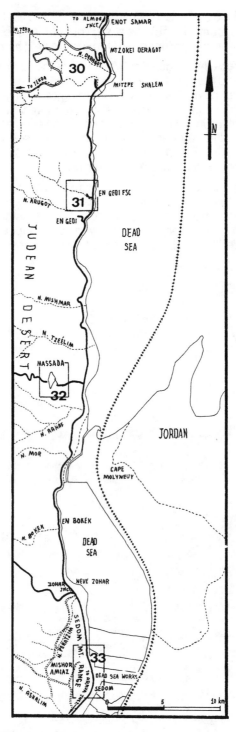

Eastern Judean Desert along the Dead Sea. Numbers represent hike numbers.
For hikes numbered 27-29, see page 97.

Upper Wadi Kelt

27

From Neve Ya'akov to Kefar Edumim

Points of interest: Canyon, waterscape, hike into Desert.
Length of hike: 12 km. one-way.
Hiking time: 8 hours.
Preferred season: All year.
Suitable for: Experienced hikers.
Maps: Northern Judea marked hiking trail map.
Special preparation: Clothes suitable for walking through water, flashlight.
Starting point: Neve Ya'akov.
Ending point: Kefar Edumim.

To begin hike:

By bus: Take bus to Neve Ya'akov, a northern suburb of Jerusalem on the Jerusalem-Ramallah Road. At second stop after the bus turns right into Neve Ya'akov get off the bus at Moshe Dayan Blvd. and Neve Ya'akov Street. (1) Neve Ya'akov, one of Jerusalem's largest suburbs, was founded in 1924 as a farming village of the Jewish Colonization Organization. In the War of Independence in 1948, Israel lost control of Neve Ya'akov and nearby Atarot for nineteen years, until the Six Day War. Since 1967, Neve Ya'akov has been rebuilt and is now a large community which is part of the greater Jerusalem area. Many new immigrants from all over the globe live in Neve Ya'akov.

Head south on Moshe Dayan Blvd., leading to the new suburb of Pisgat Ze'ev straight ahead of you. The high hill, 1½ km. to the south, is Tel Ful or in Hebrew Givat Shaul, Saul's Hill. The building near the top was meant to be one of the palaces of

Reeds grow at the oases in the Judean Desert. See map on page 135

Jordan's King Hussein. Construction began in 1965 but was cut short due to the Six Day War.

This hill is directly above the main road connecting Jerusalem to the north and situated between the rich agricultural fields to the west and the grazing area reaching into the semi-desert to the east. It made Givat Shaul a very important spot in Biblical times. It is identified as a city of Givah, belonging to the tribe of Benjamin. King Saul grew up here and later named the hill after himself, apparently a common practice among kings, "And Saul went to his house, to Givah" Samuel I, 10;26; "And Saul went up to his house to Givat Shaul," Samuel I, 15;24. During Biblical times the tribe of Benjamin was situated here and was quite densely populated. Throughout the hike, you will see numerous remnants dating from this and other periods.

The hike passes through three geographical zones. Beginning in Neve Ya'akov, just east of Israel's watershed 760 meters above sea level, you start off in the typical mountainous zone of Israel where the vegetation is Mediterranean. As you head east and descend, the hike gradually enters the Judean Desert region, passing through a narrow region of semi-desert. The increasing aridity of the Desert is well illustrated by the gradual decrease in vegetation throughout the hike. Neve Ya'akov's annual rainfall is about 500 mm. At Kefar Edumim, it is about 300 mm., a drop of almost 50% in nine km. Every 100 meters descent in altitude there is a 0.66°c drop in temperature. Therefore, if the annual average at Neve Ya'akov at 760 meters is 17.1°c, Wadi Kelt below Kefar Edumim at 120 meters above sea level is considerably warmer, around 21 degrees as the annual average temperature.

Two hundred and fifty meters along Moshe Dayan Blvd., descend freely to the wadi to your left (east). (2) This is the beginning of Wadi Kelt which flows into the Jordan River east of Jericho 28 km. from here, after having drained 178 square km. The trees here have been planted. Head down dirt road along the wadi, passing beneath Neve Ya'akov. Two km. from Moshe Dayan Blvd. a dirt road drops to your dirt road and there is a building to your left. Ten meters to the left of the dirt road is a waterhole covered by concrete next to an open pool. The whole region covered by this hike is a large Bedouin and Arab grazing range — as there are many villages in the area.

Continue another km. down the wadi where a semi-paved road crosses the wadi on a bridge. The road leads from the village of Hizma which is right above you to the south to the ancient village of Geba (Gaba'ah). Hizma is known to be Azmaveth, which appears together with the nearby Anatot in Chronicles I, 12:3. Hizma and Anatot were cities of the tribe of Benjamin during King David's reign. Hizma is also Bet Hizma, mentioned in the Book of Ezra, and also as a Levite town, "And the sons of the singers gathered themselves together . . . out of the field of Geba and Azmaveth," (Nehemia 12:28-29). In the 19th century the Jews of Jerusalem used to bake special unleavened bread, matzoh, before the holiday of Pesach from wheat that was grown in Hizma.

Head 400 meters (north) left on the road past the small olive grove on your right. Head to your right where you will see a large ancient rectangular structure made of large stones. (3) In the nearby vicinity are four similar structures. The Arabs call these structures 'kubr bnei Israel,' 'the graves of the Children of Israel.' They are most likely structures connected to worship from the Megalithic period — mega meaning huge and lithos meaning stone. This period has left a legacy of huge stone monuments throughout the world. There are also many dolmens — burial sites — from this period on the Golan Heights. Dolmens from the southern Golan Heights have also been identified as 'graves of the Children of Israel,' most likely by Moslems who came to the Golan in the 6th and 7th centuries.

Some researchers claim that Rachel is buried here — not on the highway to Hebron — and this fits in well with several Biblical descriptions, near Rama or Aram, which are just north of Neve Ya'akov. Saul returns from Rama to his home in Givah and is told by Samuel, "Thou shalt find two men by Rachel's tomb on the border of Benjamin." (Samuel I, 10:2)

Return to Wadi Kelt; 500 meters along your way the dry river bed becomes canyonlike, cutting into hard limestone and dolomite with many small falls and water hollows that fill up in the winter. Two km. from the Megalithic site, Wadi Sunam merges into Wadi Kelt from the south, sometimes carrying sewage from Anata. Open sewage in Israel is still a common sight, flowing down a large number of wadis. Unfortunately, this serious ecological problem has not yet been tackled by Israel.

The trail here is difficult and not clear. Walk down to the river bed from Wadi Sunam. As the wadi heads south there are a few falls. It is possible to walk on the western bank about 75 meters above and descend down a sharp curve to the east in the canyon. (4) Here a comfortable goat's path heads along the southern bank, which generally runs about 15 meters above the river bed, and below the cliffs.

After a bit of a walk, you will reach En Fara. (5) The ruins of a Greek Orthodox monastery stand on the southern bank; the first monastery built by the famous monk Haritun who lived in the 3rd century. This Byzantine monastery was destroyed along with many others by the Persians in 614. In the 19th century it was rebuilt with the help of the Czar of Russia.

Haritun was kidnapped by robbers on the road to Jerusalem and led him to their cave above En Fara. That night all the robbers miraculously died and Haritun inherited the cave along with all the belongings of his dead captors. Haritun then used the cave for prayer and solitude. His followers joined him and formed places of worship in nearby caves. After a while, Haritun built a monastery here.

The spring which releases 1100 cubic meters of water per hour emerges from the wadi. Nearby you will see a series of pumps which the British mandate constructed in 1927 to bring water to Jerusalem. The waters of other springs farther down Wadi Kelt, En Fawar, and En Kelt, also led to En Fara and pumped the water from here up to Jerusalem via the French Hill.

From the spring continue on to trail along wadi, pass old pumping station and head along eucalyptus trees planted by the British. A dirt road heads up to the new village of Almon directly above the En Fara canyon on the southern bank. Follow red-marked trail along stream bed; 250 meters from the eucalyptus trees along the trail, note remnants of an aqueduct which channeled water to the Jericho Valley. Note supporting walls. A lot of mint and nettle plants grow here along the wadi.

The nettle is known for its short-term stinging effect. The upper part of the leaf is covered with tiny hairs and the tips break on contact with the skin surface, becoming embedded and thereby releasing a small amount of poison which causes a light sting. Mentioned in the book of Isaiah, the nettle grows in the northern Judean Desert and throughout Israel's Mediterranean zone, favoring garbage environs and ground littered with dung. The nettle leaves, when folded inward, can be eaten raw and both leaves and seeds can be eaten raw or dried with sugar or added to breads. The nettle is an important plant in herbal medicine. The seeds are reputed to strengthen the reproductive system and the leaves help fortify the body. The nettle is also used for many other ailments, such as hair loss and body chill and was widely used by the Roman soldiers to keep themselves warm. Today the nettle is used to make certain natural medications for blood problems and to fortify the kidney. The small green plant contains high concentrations of calcium, iron and potassium. Bedouins utilize the nettles to make tea for nursing mothers, to augment their milk production. In England, nettles are used as a condiment for soups. Since the nettle is found in northern climates it is believed that this plant is not natural to Israel and suggests that the seeds were carried here by migrating birds.

Mint is a common plant usually found around water in Israel. The leaves are good for tea and can be added to salads or pitta bread. In herbal medicine mint is used to alleviate stomach aches, gas and digestive problems and for strengthening the gums. Some believe that mint strengthens the libido.

Two km. from En Fara, after a wadi runs in from the right, a spring, which flows quite strongly in winter, emerges from the northern bank. From En Fara onward you are walking in the Judean Desert. The rock is a light-colored chalk and the hills less rocky. The vegetation above the wadi is also less dense. Small cliffs of hard limestone rise above the wadi. Three km. from En Fara the wadi bends sharply to the south. One half km. later a gully drops (6) from the south. Kefar Edumim is right above you.

Ascend freely up the steep slope, straight to Kefar Edumim. You should emerge in the western section of Kefar Edumim where the first settlers lived. Before entering the village to complete your hike, turn around and enjoy the view to the north and west. Off to the west you will see Neve Ya'akov, Almon and the cliffs of En Fara and directly below you, Wadi Kelt. From here walk to the village entrance to the bus stop where you complete this hike. (7)

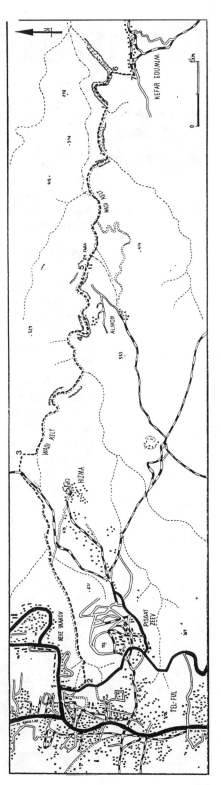

Hike 27, Upper Wadi Kelt

Central Wadi Kelt

From Kefar Edumim to En Kelt

28

Points of interest: Views, canyon, oasis, waterscape.
Length of hike: 10 km. one-way.
Hiking time: 7 hours.
Preferred season: All year. Beware of flashfloods.
Suitable for: All.
Maps: Northern Judean Desert marked hiking trail map.
Special preparation: Clothes for walking in water.
Starting point: Kefar Edumim.
Ending point: Mitzpe Yericho Junction.

To begin hike:

By bus: Take bus from Binyanei Hauma across the road from the Jerusalem Central Bus Station to Kefar Edumim. The bus route passes through downtown Jerusalem, the city of Maale Edumim, the industrial zone of Mishor Edumim before reaching Kefar Edumim. Get off at entrance to village. (1) Here begin hike.

Take left on paved road going through the west side of the village near a basketball court and head on to nearby dirt road. On your right are caravans, the temporary housing set up when the village was first established. On the other side — the east — is the more established part of Kefar Edumim with its spacious homes. Reach the end of the village and enjoy breathtaking view. Looking to the left you can see the village of Almon in the west. Further off on the horizon note Neve Ya'akov, the northern suburb of Jerusalem. Directly below and to the north is the canyon of Wadi Kelt; 3 km. northwest are the cliffs of Nahal Mikhmash. Far off to the north you will see one

En Fawar.
See map on
page 139

of the villages on Derekh Alon. Behind you to the south is the Mishor Edumim industrial zone.

Head east for 150 meters going parallel and just beneath the caravans. You will come to an unmarked trail that comes from the village. Join trail and head toward embedments of flint in the middle of the slope ahead. From the double layer of flint, the trail drops a bit, continuing toward a cone shaped bare hill along the line of the ridge. The trail passes to the left of this coned hill, continues on top of the chalk stone ridge for one more km., and descends down to Wadi Kelt where Derekh Alon crosses the wadi. There is usually a Bedouin encampment here.

Derekh Alon, meaning the 'Way of Alon' running south-north, starts just east of Kefar Edumim and runs parallel to the main road in the Jordan Valley. (2) The scenic road is named after the late Yigal Alon who proposed a political solution in 1972 for Judea and Samaria. The area to the west of the road is mountainous northern Judea and Samaria, heavily populated by Arabs. To the east of the road lies the northern Judean Desert and the narrow Samarian Desert. Yigal Alon's idea was that the area east of the road, or the so-called 'line,' be settled by Israelis to help secure Israel's eastern border, while to the west Alon proposed the area should be left to the large populations of Arabs living there. In 1974, this topographically illogical road was built — illogical since the wadis run from west to east, from the hills of Judea and Samaria to the Jordan Valley, while the road was constructed to run south-north.

During the years after the 1967 Six Day War, this section of Derekh Alon was often the scene of I.D.F. chases after terrorist infiltrators who crossed the Jordan River to attack Israelis and smuggle arms to terror activists in the Arab villages; that is why it is called the, 'Infiltrators Road.' Its construction was originally kept under wraps until a *New York Times* article unveiled it to the world, thus giving the road another name, 'The New York Times Road.'

Cross Derekh Alon and join the red-marked trail which heads down Wadi Kelt in a small canyon. Above you to the right is Derekh Alon. One km. down the wadi reach En Fawar, sur- rounded by eucalyptus and pine trees. (3) En Fawar is a karstic spring, water is collected from various underground tunnels and streams that slowly eroded the limestone. The water collects into a pool connected to the outside by a V-shaped tunnel which directs upward in the middle, at the bend in the V. The water level in the pool has to reach the level of bend in the tunnel so it can be released. This is an illustration of the well known laws of physics, the Law of Connecting Vessels. This off- and-on spring, flowing for short periods until the pool nearly empties out, is known as the 'crazy spring.' Some maintain that the mystery is the outcome of a battle between a good and bad ghost. When the good ghost has the upper hand he opens the faucets, when the bad ghost is in control, the water is restrained from flowing. Usually the spring flows at 20 minute intervals, filling the pool. In the winter, the spring may have a steady flow. En Gihon, the main spring of Jerusalem and En Po'em in the Nahal Ammud Nature Reserve in the upper eastern Galilee work along similar lines.

The building near the spring was in use until 1967, pumping water to En Fara in upper Wadi Kelt and from there to Jerusalem. An aqueduct runs from En Fawar on the southern brink of the wadi to En Kelt where it drops into the wadi in a lovely waterfall.

From En Kelt the aqueduct passes the St. George Monastery and extends to Jericho. The aqueduct from En Fara is built and based on an ancient Second Temple period aqueduct which led water to Kiprus just south of Wadi Kelt overlooking Jericho. Kiprus was built by the Hasmonean kings and later restored by King Herod. It is named after Herod's mother. Another hiking alternative to En Kelt is alongside this aqueduct.

From En Fawar continue on red-marked trail down Wadi Kelt, starting alongside the aqueduct. After about a km. you may see a fabulous set of waterfalls dropping from the aqueduct down to the wadi in late winter. The canyon opens up farther down and again becomes a canyon. This canyon section of the wadi is usually flowing with water in the winter. Three km. from En Fawar the red-marked trail climbs onto the northern bank (4) and bypasses the En Kelt gorge, returning to the wadi at the opening of the gorge. It is also possible to take the wadi route. Your hike inside the gorge can be quite exciting, but note: *for swimmers only!*

The red-marked trail offers a great view of the gorge and the waterfall which drop from the aqueduct down through the gorge. The trail also passes by a 'bow' cave, remnant of a cave with a collapsed interior. At gorge exit near bridge note carob tree growing by the aqueduct. Those who took the trail should walk up the gorge to the refreshing artificial En Kelt waterfall. (5) En Kelt emerges just beyond the waterfall. From here you have two options.

1) Continue to Jericho following 'Lower Wadi Kelt hike', or 2) cross bridge, head down on wide marked trail on southern bank for 500 meters. Cross small wadi known as Wadi Abu a Tzaba where you can see magnificent remnants of a huge bridge that once carried an aqueduct. Climb stairs passing old pump buildings of En Kelt to your left. When reaching dirt road, head up it.

On top where pavement begins, step off to the left for a last view of the lower Wadi Kelt area. (6) Follow the wadi and look out at the water channel alongside the northern brink. Wadi Kelt enters the Jordan Valley farther east to your right. Note the green oasis and, farther to your right, the flat topped hill Kiprus, which was one of the destinations of these ancient aqueducts.

Looking sharply to your left you see Kefar Edumim, your starting point and Neve Ya'akov off to the distance by the horizon. Continue on road upward. On your left is red lime-stone, which has given the general area the name in Hebrew meaning red, Edumim. One hundred meters along reach parking lot.

To get to bus stop head south 1 km., passing white buildings. To your right is a burnt-out Patton tank, left here from the Six Day War. The white buildings you see here are planned as a local visitor's center.

Hike 28, Central Wadi Kelt

Reach main road by Mitzpe Jericho Junction (7) and return on bus to Jerusalem.

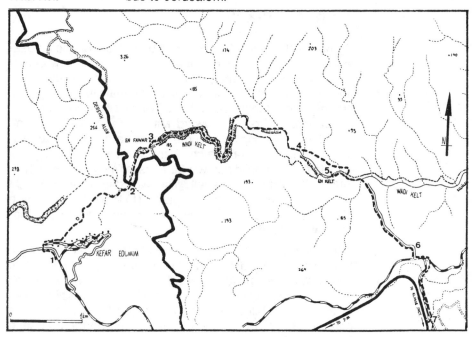

Lower Wadi Kelt

29

From En Kelt to Jericho

Points of interest: Canyon, oasis, monastery, waterscape.
Length of hike: 12 km. one-way.
Hiking time: 7 hours.
Preferred season: All year. Beware of flashfloods.
Suitable for: All.
Maps: Northern Judean Desert marked hiking trail map.
Special preparation: Clothes for walking in water, modest clothes for visit to monastery.
Starting point: Mitzpe Yericho Junction on Jerusalem-Jericho Road.
Ending point: Jericho.

To begin hike:

By bus: Take bus to Mitzpe Yericho, a village on the Jerusalem-Jericho Road. Mitzpe Yericho, meaning the view of Jericho, overlooks the sharp descent to Jericho and the lower Jordan Valley. At the intersection on the main road there is an orange sign, 'Nahal Perat'; this is Wadi Kelt's Hebrew name. (1) Instead of heading toward Mitzpe Yericho take left on paved road heading north, more or less parallel to the Jerusalem-Jericho Road for one km. Pass small white buildings on your left; these buildings will be a visitor's center. Reach T-intersection and take a left. The paved road to the right descends south to Jericho and parallel to Wadi Kelt, a modern narrow scenic road built onto the ancient Roman Jericho-Jerusalem Road.

After 100 meters turn right onto a poorly paved road, and begin the descent to Wadi Kelt. (2) Head down this road. Where it curves to the left, head straight ahead to a small hill and climb it for a nice view of Lower Wadi Kelt and the fortress of Kiprus on a prominent hill just south of the canyon to your east. From here you have a good perspective of the northern Judean Desert.

Continue down the unpaved road which leads to the En Kelt pumping station. To add some color to your hike, drop down to the left to a small wadi where you take right, heading parallel to road above you. In the fall a lot of squills bloom here in clusters of white-yellow flowers. Here and there in the wadi are petroleum-based black bitumen rocks. These rocks release heat that turns the white limestone red. It is this reddish rock which has given the Jerusalem-Jericho Road its name — Ma'ale Edumim — meaning the 'red ascent.'

See map on page 145

Ma'ale Edumim is mentioned in the Book of Joshua, 15:7 in the matter of the tribe of Judah's border, "And the border went up toward Debir from the Valley of Achor and northward looking toward Gilgal. This is before the going up to Edumim which is on the south side of the river." The river, most likely Wadi Kelt, is a clear geographical landmark.

As you might guess from this text, in Biblical times water was generally more plentiful and springs more common than today. Of course water was not pumped and there were no drills searching out underground reservoirs. Climb down some dry falls and soon you will come to where the waters of the wadi have traversed a natural tunnel which emerges directly into Wadi Abu a Tzaba, meaning in Arabic the Wadi of the Father of the Hyena. Researchers consider this wadi to be the Valley of Tzeboim mentioned in Samuel I,13:18 which tells of the Philistine attempt to destroy Israelite property, "And another company turned to the way of the border that headeth to the Valley of Tzeboim toward the wilderness."

Striped hyenas inhabit the Judean Desert as well as in other parts of Israel, feeding generally on animal carcasses and sometimes hunting small animals. They do not attack man though Arabs give them a wide berth.

Take right in Wadi Abu a Tzaba, passing beneath a very impressive bridge which supports an unused water aqueduct leading from En Fawar to a Herodian fortress called Kiprus — which you previously saw overlooking Jericho. Directly ahead is Wadi Kelt. Before the wadi to your left on a clear path is a wooden sign. Take path 400 meters to your left. Take bridge crossing wadi until you come to the mouth of the En Kelt canyon. Take off your shoes and wade up the wadi through the narrow canyon to the waterfall. Although man-made, this waterfall which transports water along the aqueduct from En Fawar, is quite beautiful.

Just beyond the fall, En Kelt flows from the rock. By the bridge is the beginning point of a more recent aqueduct built on the remnants of an ancient Second Temple aqueduct which led water to the Jericho palaces at the mouth of Wadi Kelt. The modern aqueduct was built by the famous El Husseini family in 1919. On the southern side of the wadi is a small built-in sign in Arabic on the cliff declaring, "In the name of Allah, the merciful, hundreds of years have passed and this wadi's water have been lost, until an inspiration came from God for the working man and genius Sir M'chaii a Din Mustapha Hilili el Husseini in 1297 to the Hejera. He built the dam and established the mill and restored the gardens in 1332 to the Hejera, he built the aqueduct that carries water to the fields of Akabat Jabar that is south of the city of Jericho."

Follow red-marked trail on the aqueduct. To your right live the Bedouins of the Ka'abneh tribe. Originally brought here to take care of the pumps that led the water to Jerusalem from here during the British mandate, today they attend to this site. The building just to the right of the aqueduct is a flour mill. Please refrain from climbing onto the building as it is a private home.

The aqueduct crosses a small wadi on a bridge. Cross the wadi from below; 100 meters on there is a small pool just to the side of the aqueduct — ideal for a dip on a hot day.

St. George Monastery in Lower Wadi Kelt

The aqueduct passes large jujube and rare Egyptian balanite trees. Belonging to the been caper family, the thorny-branched balanite grows up to 6 meters high. The greenish flowers, blooming throughout spring, are 1 cm. long and grow in clusters of 3 and 5. The seeds of the edible hard blue-colored fruit are distributed by animals. The Egyptian balanite grows in a few spots along the Syrian-African rift, usually near an oasis.

The most northern growth location is in the northern Jordan Valley, near the town of Bet Shean. The fruit of the balanite, known in Arabic as the 'slave date' has the taste of a bitter date. In India, the fruit and leaves are used to cure worms and as a laxative. In Africa, fishermen use the fruit to poison fish, since it is not toxic to man and animals. In Uganda it is considered a remedy for sleeping sickness. Here in Israel, Arabs extract an oil, which makes up 50% of the fruit. To heal aches in bones and joints, the sore area is massaged with this oil at night after a bath. In ancient Egypt this tree symbolized eternity.

About $1\frac{1}{2}$ km. from En Kelt the red-marked trail cuts away from the aqueduct and drops down to the wadi right after crossing over a small tributary on a natural bridge. (4) Immediately before entering Wadi Kelt the trail bypasses a huge jujube tree with mistletoe clusters — these bright red flowers bloom between December and August.

Turn left down wadi which soon becomes canyonlike. One km. into the canyon, after wadi has curved right, on the southern bank, there is a small sign in Hebrew on a low cliff. In a cave above the sign, officer Tzvika Ofer was killed in a terrorist chase on December 10, 1968. The terrorists crossed the Jordan River through Wadi Kelt and were heading toward the center of the country. During the late 60's, chases after infiltrating terrorists were a daily routine and many soldiers fell during these pursuits.

Two km. down the wadi the aqueduct crosses it to the southern bank, amidst water-loving vegetation. Around the curve of the wadi you will see the St. George Monastery on the northern cliff. Soon you will find yourself surrounded by crosses of all kinds. Ascend to the Greek Orthodox monastery (5) which is usually open to visitors. *Please wear modest clothes.*

Monks have lived along the remote cliffs of Wadi Kelt since the 5th century. The founder of this monastery was St. Johannan of Kosiba who came from Egypt in the mid-5th century. He settled in Wadi Kelt in the year 480, became a bishop of Ceasarea in 516 and returned later to Wadi Kelt where he lived until 520 to 530. Some years following his death the monastery was named after him.

From the end of the 5th century, Wadi Kelt was a very popular site for hermit monks seeking solitary lives. Their routine included community worship once a week and holy ritual on Saturday nights. During the rest of the week, each monk secluded himself among the caves and crevices of Wadi Kelt. Throughout the years, the monastery experienced many ups and downs. After the Crusaders renovated it, it was again deserted. In 1878, the Greek monk Kalinikos started to build a complex here. By 1901 most of the buildings you see intact today were completed; the bell tower was built by Timothy the First in 1952. The monastery was built in three levels; the lower level includes the graves of five monks and an ancient church with a mosaic; the second level holds the main buildings and two churches named after Johannan of Kusiba and the Holy Virgin; on the top level there is the Church of the Cave, named after the prophet Elijah where the monks believe Elijah was fed by the ravens.

From the monastery, known in Arabic as Dir Mar Griss, continue on the northern bank of Wadi Kelt, on the clear red-marked trail. The wadi cuts into a deep and narrow canyon. Two km. along the trail, Kiprus is a distance of less than 1 km. to your south. The trail crosses to the southern bank of the wadi as you reach the outskirts of the Jericho Valley and onto a narrow paved road that connects with the Jerusalem-Tiberias Highway. Take a left onto the narrow road. (Taking a right would lead you back up to Mitzpe Yericho.)

Along the way note just to your left Tel Abu el Alaik. Here, on both sides of Wadi Kelt, are remnants of the Hasmonean and King Herod's winter palaces. (6) Continue along the road until you reach the Jerusalem-Tiberias Road. Take right for 200 meters where you reach bus stop near an army base and hike's end. (7) If you have time explore Jericho.

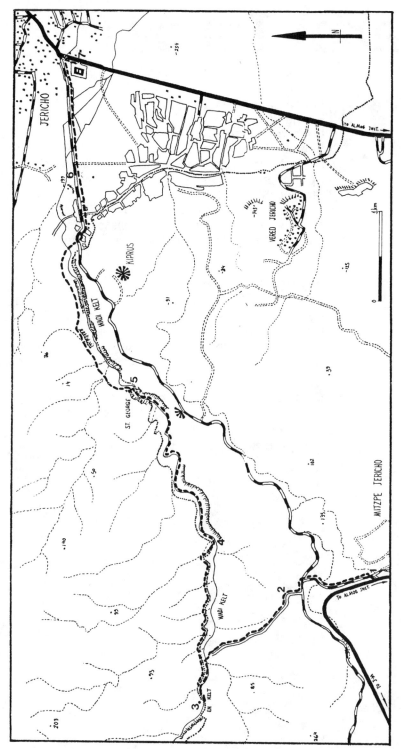

Hike 29, Lower Wadi Kelt

Nahal Tekoa

30

Points of interest: Spectacular view, canyon, Bar Kokhba Caves.

Length of hike: 14 km. loop trip.

Hiking time: 9 hours.

Preferred season: November to May.

Suitable for: All.

Maps: Northern Judean Desert marked hiking trail map.

Special preparation: None.

Starting & ending point: 2 km. west of Metzokei Deragot Climbing School above the Dead Sea Road.

Note: Between (3) and (5) the trail passes through I.D.F. firing zones! This part of hike can be taken only on Saturdays and holidays.

To begin hike:

By bus: Take bus on Dead Sea Road, get off at turn-off to Metzokei Deragot. From here either walk 45 minutes to 1 hour or hitchhike up to the top, to Metzokei Deragot. From Metzokei Deragot continue on road which becomes a good dirt road for about 2 km.

By car: On Dead Sea Road north of En Gedi head up to Metzokei Deragot Climbing School and continue on clear dirt road for 2 additional km.

Gorge in Nahal Tekoa.
See map on page 149

There is a small parking lot here on the right and two signs just to the left of the road, the trailhead of a black-marked trail that descends to Nahal Deragot. Your hike begins here. (1)

Head down on black-marked trail southward towards Nahal Deragot on the right and parallel to a small wadi which drops sharply from the trail. A few hundred meters ahead the trail passes above Nahal Deragot, takes a right and heads west parallel to and above Nahal Deragot.

Look for the Arabian box-thorn, reaching up to $1^1/_2$ meters high, which usually grows near wadis. Like most desert plants, its green leaves are a bit fleshy. Blooming during early winter before the onset of the rains, a scattering of pinkish-purple flowers offer small spots of color throughout the year. In spring and summer the edible red fruits appear, the seeds of which are distributed by birds. The Arabian box-thorn grows only in the desert and in the northern Negev. Like the sabra, it often serves as a property hedge. The box-thorn is also well-known from Yotam's fable in Judges 9, which talks of the plant's usefulness. "Then said all the trees unto the box-thorn, 'come thou and reign over us,' and the box-thorn said unto the trees, 'if in truth ye anoint me king over you, then come and put your trust in my shadow and if not fire come out from the bramble and devour the cedars of Lebanon.'"

You will observe a small trail, set with low stakes to make the ascent easier, which leads you to the right and to the Muraba'at Caves. (2) Ascend to the Muraba'at Caves, so named for their square shape. The four caves are on the northern bank of Nahal Deragot, known here as Wadi Muraba'at. These caves were in constant use from the Chalcolithic period until the early Arabic period.

Many relics of the Bar Kokhba fighters who occupied these caves during the years 132-135 have been found here; the most well-known of these are the letters signed by Shimon ben Kosiba, whom researchers believe to have been Bar Kokhba, the guerrilla leader of the second revolt against Hadrian of Rome. Several letters were written in Aramaic, others in Greek and Hebrew, and one reads, "From Shimon Ben Kosiba to Joshua ben Galgulla and the people of Habaruk. Greetings, I call heaven to witness against me that if any one of the Galileans who are with you are ill treated, I will put fetters on your feet as I did to Beny Aflul. Shimon Ben Kosiba."

These findings transmit the image of a powerful leader, who held his men in very tight reign and felt no qualms at harsh punishment. When the Romans began to successfully suppress the Bar Kokhba revolt, rebel leaders fled with their families to the Judean Desert, hiding in the caves, in the hope that the Desert's geographical pitfalls would save them from the Romans, but to no avail. Phylacteries and mezuza fragments were also found along with other remnants in this cave. Note the remnants of a plastered basin near the cave opening to the right.

Return to trail, continuing down to the Nahal Tekoa-Nahal Deragot intersection. Both these wadis drain the Bethlehem and Herodian area, converging here for the series of descents — known in Hebrew as deragot — which end at the Dead Sea. Nahal Tekoa is named after the village of Tekoa, by its beginning point, not far from the well known palace of King Herod, Herodian. Nahal Deragot drains a total of 380 square km. and is the largest wadi in the Judean Desert.

Cross wadi and take red-marked trail southeast on the southern bank of Nahal Deragot. The trail soon switchbacks up the 180 meter high cliff. Enjoy view of Nahal Deragot and Muraba'at Caves across the way. When you come to the top, take a left, circling a small hill along Nahal Deragot cliffs. After 500 meters, the trail leaves the cliff and ascends a small wadi. Heading southeast, the trail now gradually ascends, crossing a few small wadis and heading toward a hill hosting a small antenna, Mitzpe Mikhvar.

Two hundred meters above sea level, Mitzpe Mikhvar offers a panoramic view of most of the northern Judean Desert, a large section of the Hebron Hills, the eastern approach to Jerusalem and, in the north, the scarps which drop to the Dead Sea. Mikhvar, which is above the eastern edge of the Dead Sea, was one of the last fortresses to fall to the Romans along with Masada and Herodian.

From here, an ancient trail heads down to the Dead Sea, bypassing Kibbutz Mitzpe Shalem. The trail is called Nakb el Hamar in Arabic, meaning 'steep trail of the donkey,' but actually it starts out near Tekoa, and is possibly one of the roads constructed by the Romans on their way to Masada, which is 35 km. south of here.

Head along cliff south to a lookout spot above Nahal Hazezon. On this site the Nature Reserves Authority set up a couple of open huts to offer hikers some rest, relaxation and, most important, shade. (3) To the south of you is Nahal Hazezon, called Wadi Hazáze in Arabic, which drops to the Dead Sea in a series of five falls, the highest fall is a 118 meter drop. From this lookout point a good blue-marked dirt road heads west, take it for 2 km. *Here you enter an I.D.F. firing zone, open on Saturdays and holidays only!* The dirt road meets Nahal Hazezon, here a wide wadi. Pass to the right of a lone acacia tree and as the wadi curves to the left, drop to the eastern bank. Here you find Harabet Mankushia, (4) an ancient rest-stop, used by both the Romans and Byzantines, that serviced the Tekoa-Nakb el Hamar road and the north-south trail above the scarps of the Dead Sea. Harabeh, meaning water reservoir, refers specifically to a large open reservoir on the side of a wadi, usually underground. Mankushia means 'hewn in the rock.' In the Judean Desert this type of water reservoir is rare while in the Negev many Nabatean waterholes can be found. Note the hole on southwestern side to bring up the water and the channel remnants which lead Nahal Hazezon's flashflood waters into the reservoir. At one time the depth reached 5 meters, but today the reservoir has been clogged up by earth. The hollow was cut into the soft chalk which is the prevalent rock here on the plateau of the Judean Desert.

Cross wadi, head north to an intersection of two dirt roads near a Nature Reserves Authority sign in English and Hebrew. Head on smooth dirt road north-northwest for 3 km., gradually descending to Nahal Tekoa. Turn right into Nahal Tekoa (5); 300 meters along your way the wadi swerves south and becomes quite canyonlike.

Throughout Nahal Tekoa you will see large varieties of desert vegetation. The canyon deepens with the wadi's descent and 2 km. off the dirt road Nahal Tekoa heads through several gorges, passing flashflood water hollows. About two and three quarter km. from the dirt road Nahal Tekoa converges with Nahal Deragot. Head up to the left, on the bank of Nahal Deragot, following the same black-marked trail you took earlier past the Muraba'at Caves until you reach your starting point. (1)

Hike 30, Nahal Tekoa

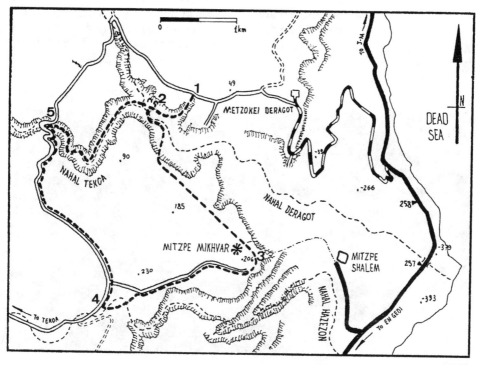

En Gedi - Dry Canyon

31

Two options

Points of interest: Waterscape, oasis, wildlife.
Length of hike: 6 km. loop trip, 7 km. one-way.
Hiking time: 6 hours.
Preferred season: November to May. Beware of flashfloods.
Suitable for: All.
Maps: Judean Desert marked hiking trail map, En Gedi 1:50,000.
Special preparation: Clothes for wading in water.
Starting point: En Gedi Field Study Center.
Ending point: Nahal David parking lot loop trip; bridge over Nahal Arugot one-way.

To begin hike:

By bus: Get off at En Gedi-Nahal David stop.

By car: Begin hike at En Gedi by Nahal David parking lot. Above and to your north is the En Gedi Field Study Center of the Society for the Protection of Nature in Israel.

Do not enter Nahal David Nature Reserve through main gate. Head up to the En Gedi Field Study Center on paved road, passing the youth hostel. This entire complex is built on marl rock sedimentary, remnants of a larger Dead Sea that once reached Lake Kinneret in the north and Hazeva in the northern Arava in the south. Enter the Field Study Center through gate. Where road curves to the left, take left into parking lot.

Water hollow at the Window Fall after a flashflood. See map on page 154

At the Field Study Center you can visit the small but interesting museum of En Gedi and its environs. Use this opportunity to

150

get some advice from Field Study Center guides about the Judean Desert and the En Gedi vicinity. From the museum's lawn you have a good view of En Gedi and Nahal David, named after King David who fled here from King Saul.

From the museum return to road, take left and head up to road's end. Climb up amphitheater and exit Field Study Center through open fence gate. You have a nice view of Nahal David from here as well. Start up black-marked trail that bypasses reconstructed agricultural terraces. Throughout history, approximately 1000 dunams of land around En Gedi has been used for agriculture. Twenty of these 1000 dunams, were north of Nahal David, where you are now. The agricultural plots were watered from two small springs situated 1 km. north of you. Throughout the En Gedi region, certain perfume spices and plants were grown here, as mentioned in the Song of Songs, 1:14. "My beloved is unto me as a cluster of camphire in the vineyard of En Gedi." Unfortunately these plants are unknown to us today.

One half km. along the trail reaches an intersection to the right; a trail ascends to Har Yishai — until 1967 the border between Israel and Jordan. The hike to Har Yishai takes at least one hour. Continue straight on red-marked trail. Climb up small cliff and follow trail on northern bank of Nahal David. Looking down, you can see the lush region between the David Falls and Window Fall. The trail continues above the dry canyon.

The red-marked trail descends to the dry canyon on through a small gully. Take left down Nahal David which is a dry canyon here, (2) the springs of Nahal David emerging further down. The canyon deepens and grows narrower, cutting through hard limestone and dropping down a small fall. Make use of the prepared stakes to pass the fall on the southern side. (3) Toward the end of the canyon are several water hollows which fill up in winter and spring, necessitating shoes and clothing suitable for water if you wish to negotiate them.

The canyon ends at the Window Fall, overlooking the lush Nahal David. The large water hollow near these falls rarely dries up and especially following a flashflood is a great place for a swim. Retrace your steps and reach falls where stakes are posted on (3) the southern brink. Here climb up small ravine to the south. After 100 meters you hit a trail running parallel to the dry canyon. Take a left onto this green-marked trail which runs southeast above Nahal David, offering a nice view of the Window Fall. As trail nears intersection, take right up small hill ahead of you. From here, you have a good view of the En Gedi complex and the Chalcolithic temple directly below you. Descend to it on trail to your right. Except for this temple — where items of brown pottery, burnt bones, ash and animal horns were found — no other remnants of the Chalcolithic period have been discovered in En Gedi. (4) Since there were no findings of residential quarters, archaeologists assume that these Chal-coliths were shepherds and nomads. Head 250 meters to the right to a large clump of vegetation. This is the En Gedi spring. (5) Friendly hyrax live in the reeds surrounding the spring. Large numbers of these small animals live here. They are mentioned in Psalms along with the ibex, also abundant here, "The high hills are refuge for the ibex and the rocks for the rabbits (hyrax)" (Psalms 104:18).

This layer spring yields between 36 to 72 cubic meters an hour. Here in the vicinity of the springs, if you keep still for a while, a lot of wildlife and birds will collect around you, especially in the early morning and late afternoon.

The loud territorial 'yipping' call of the hyrax male and its echo can be clearly heard ricochetting off the canyon walls at different hours of the day. En Gedi is also the habitat of the endemic Tristram's grackle. Blackbird-sized and colored, this lovely bird also sports a conspicuous chestnut patch on each wing which flashes beautifully in flight. The bird pairs dash out simultaneously from the tops of the palm trees and the cliffs, calling out their melancholy song as they fly off.

From En Gedi spring you can either: a) return to Nahal David and complete the loop trip, after stopping by upper Nahal David and the Shulamit Cave, or, omitting the detour, drop to lower Nahal David and Shulamit Cave; or, b) continue down through Tel Goren and ancient synagogue, finishing off one km. south of starting point (with or without a stop at upper Nahal David and the Shulamit Cave.) To reach upper Nahal David, head north from En Gedi on the wide path. Pass underneath the ledge with the Chalcolithic temples.

Meet the trail intersection 350 meters ahead. Head straight down Nahal David's southern bank to Nahal David on a clear trail. The Nahal David spring which emerges, from the nearby reeds, is the sometimes-habitat of a leopard. Note the Window Fall overhang. Take path to the right across the stream and head down it until you reach a large boulder at the top of David Falls. Climb down the safe ladder to the wonderful Shulamit Cave, also called the Dudaim Cave. (6) Return to trail intersection from Shulamit Cave.

a) For loop trip, take left on a well-trodden footpath and begin descent until you pass through En Shulamit. A small amount of water from this trapped spring is released which keeps the vegetation thriving and alive.

The trail switchbacks to the left and reaches David Falls. (7) This is the well known part of En Gedi. From here a clear trail leads you out of the reserve to the Nahal David parking lot, (8) passing through rare tropic vegetation, you cross the stream several times and pass a few waterfalls. b) For the one-way alternative, return to En Gedi spring from trail intersection. Pass through tunnel-like reed overhang. Stop to examine the Crusader flour mill, which was reactivated by the Rashadia Bedouin tribe using water channeled in from En Gedi to turn the grinds. From the mill descend southeast on trail marked by yellow arrows painted onto wooden stumps. Cross dirt road and continue the descent. When you reach another dirt road, take a right and exit through the gate. On your left inside a circular yard you will see a monument in memory of 8 Hashomer Hatzair members who were killed here by a grenade explosion. (7)

The tel (hill) above the monument is Tel Goren, the remnants here have been dated to periods extending from the Israelite to the 5th century. The dirt road now continues until it comes to a paved road that connects the Dead Sea Road to the access to Nahal Arugot. Turn left, passing Tel Goren and the original site of the Field Study Center and Kibbutz En Gedi.

At intersection take left and enter gate; after 100 meters the road curves left. Descend road to the right and walk ahead 100 meters, then cross fence to ancient En Gedi synagogue. (8) During the Bar Kokhba revolt, 132-135, En Gedi was a regional center and a supply base. Boats laden with food embarked for Bar Kokhba's camps arrived at the port of En Gedi from the eastern side of the Dead Sea. After the suppression of the Bar Kokhba revolt, En Gedi was destroyed and its inhabitants dispersed throughout the country. Soon after the remnants of En Gedi's Israelite community began to rehabilitate itself. At the beginning of the 4th century, En Gedi was a large and important center of Hebrew life.

During the archaeological digs of 1970-72, remains of En Gedi's 3rd century synagogue were unearthed. During the Byzantine period the Israelite community of En Gedi continued to flourish and homes were established in the vicinity of the synagogue. Note its direction, exactly facing Jerusalem. Some time later, during the middle of the 5th century a large fire destroyed En Gedi's Israelite community and subsequently En Gedi has been settled on a very small-scale.

A couple of interesting mosaics have been found at the synagogue and taken for display to museums. The very interesting mosaic that you can still see on your visit here is a typical example of the genre.

From the synagogue return to intersection, heading out on paved road that extends between Nahal Arugot on the right and palm groves on the left.

The date palm is mentioned often in the Bible and Talmud. The date is the honey included in the 'seven kinds of cereals and fruit of the Land of Israel.' "A land of olive trees and honey," (Deuteronomy 8:9). The date palm grows up to 15 meters. It blooms in springtime, starting from the age of 5 to 10 years. The fruit dates ripen toward the end of summer. The date palm is a domesticated fruit tree that grows throughout Israel. It is grown commercially in the Syrian-African rift region, both for export and domestic consumption. In several locations the palm grows wild, usually in the deserts in oases such as En Anava in Nahal Tze'elim south of En Gedi. The date palm, which can live up to 100 years, is a very useful and versatile plant. The lulav, the outer leaf growing from the heart of the trunk, is important for Jewish ritual related to the holiday of Tabernacles (Succot). The Bedouins make honey and also an alcoholic beverage out of dates. The high sugar content makes the date a good lightweight high-energy food, used when travelling by Bedouins. The Bedouins of Sinai make huts out of the palms and use the trunk for scrolls and fibres, the branches to extract oils and the leaves to weave into mats. The Bedouins even use the pits as donkey contraceptives! The date palm, rising so high and standing erect, has often been used to symbolize the finest characteristics of man. "The righteous shall flourish like the palm," (Psalms 92:13). "Thy stature is like to a palm tree," (Song of Songs 7:8).

Hit main Dead Sea Road. From here, it is one km. back to the Nahal David parking lot. (1) Just to the right over the bridge of Nahal Arugot, across from the gas station and the large En Gedi camping ground, is the bus stop to end your hike. (9)

Hike 31, En Gedi — Dry Canyon

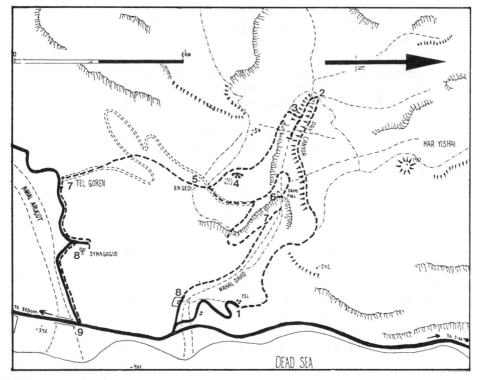

Around Masada

32

Points of interest: Uncommon views of Masada, water hollows, falls.
Length of hike: 5 km. loop trip.
Hiking time: 5 hours.
Preferred season: November to May.
Suitable for: Experienced hikers.
Maps: Southern Judean Desert marked hiking trail map.
Special preparation: None.
Starting & ending point: The eastern side of Masada parking lot off Dead Sea Road.

To begin hike:

Since this hike encompasses Masada, you can choose to begin hike on either side; there are two entrances. This hike begins on the eastern side, at the parking lot, at the point where the trail connecting with the snake trail begins. This was the site of the Roman's Camp A during the siege of Masada. (1) Head down trail to Nahal Mtzada, but rather than continue onto the snake trail, cross wadi heading north and follow red-marked trail which heads up the northern bank. Continue north along the eastern foot of Masada. The wide trail passes west of Camp C and runs parallel to the Roman siege wall dyke. This dyke, which surrounds Masada, was to ensure that no one attempted escape. The occasional large piles of rocks alongside the dyke were most likely guard towers.

This trail leads to the Nahal Tze'elim canyon, 4 km. north of Masada. En Anava, a small spring not far from the canyon opening, served as the Roman's main water supply. Today the spring is practically dry.

One and a half km. from parking lot, the trail crosses a small wadi which extends between the northern section of Masada and the scarps of the Judean Desert. This is known as the Palace Wadi, since it runs below Herod's palace on Masada's northern ledge.

You may notice the white-broom, (rotem) growing in the wadis around Masada. For part of the year the leafless bush hides from the limelight, its modest grey branches performing unobtrusive photosynthesis. But in winter months the rotem comes into its own. Between January and April small leaves appear, the small white peaked flowers blooming and their sweet scent perfuming the desert air. Growing to heights of up to 3 meters, the white-broom grows in sand dunes along the coastline, throughout the desert wadis of Israel, and along the climb of

See map on
page 157

155

the Syrian-African rift to the Golan Heights. Mentioned in the Bible and Talmudic literature, the white-broom was known for its charcoal, which maintains heat for long periods of time. It is said that if one leaves broom charcoal burning during Sukkot (in the fall), one will find it still burning at Pesach time (spring). Psalms 120:4 says, "Sharp arrows of the mighty with charcoal of the white-broom." Elijah, on the way to Mount Sinai, spent the night under the white-broom bush.

Right after crossing the wadi, reach Roman Camp D. (2) Here leave the red-marked trail and head west (left) passing Camp D and turning onto the Messengers Trail. The clear unmarked trail heads up a white chalk deposit, passing a cave which Bedouins used for manufacturing primitive gunpowder, known to them as the sulphur cave. The switchbacking trail twists through the limestone scarps. Note the stone walls along the way, a sign that the trail is an ancient one; this trail was used by Roman messengers for delivering messages between the upper and lower Roman camps. As part of his siege strategy, Flavius Silva built 8 camps around the base of Masada; 4 on the west, E to H, and 4 to the east, A to D. His own headquarters were in Camp F to the northwest of Masada.

Look down between the trail and northern Masada. Note the siege wall heading up the scarp from Camp D. Gazing up at Masada you see the three palaces of Herod, the water holes on the slope below and to the right, and the trail leading to them entering from the southwest. These waterholes served to collect water from flashfloods in Nahal Mtzada and the Palace Wadi. Each waterhole had a capacity of around 4000 cubic meters of water; the 12 could hold a total of approximately 40,000 cubic meters.

When reaching top of escarpment head left toward the assault ramp. (3) Pass by Camp E and F on your way. Note remnants of small dams in the wadis you cross planned to channel the water to the waterholes which you saw on Masada's northwestern slope. When reaching the other access to the climb to Masada there are bathroom facilities, shade, and water nearby. (3) Here you will see the battering ram used for the TV production 'Masada' several years ago. From here, you have a few options. Either: (a) climb up ramp trail to Masada and descend to starting point by snake path or cable car after touring Masada; or (b) hike up Masada and return down same ramp trail to continue hike; or (c) continue hike. From the base of the ramp, head south into Nahal Mtzada. Follow red-marked trail.

At this point Nahal Mtzada runs parallel to the southwestern slopes of Masada. Six hundred meters down the wadi, reach the dry 100 meter high fall. Preceding it are some water hollows. (4) Years ago, hikers used to rely on this water source. Look across Nahal Mtzada to the southeast and note the precipice of Har Elazar, one of the highest and most vertical cliffs in the Judean Desert, and its sheer drop.

Continue on trail southward, running west of the canyon. The trail climbs a gully. At the top, take left onto black-marked trail and reach Har Elazar. (5) Named after Elazar Ben Yair, Masada's zealot leader, Har Elazar, is the only spot in the area which overlooks part of Masada. To the northwest are remnants of Camp H where 500 Roman soldiers were camped. This strategic lookout point over southern Masada was vital to the Romans since descent from Masada was possible along the southern slope. This Roman outpost prevented that. From here you can also see part of the siege wall. Enjoy the view of Masada, only 500 meters away, and the fall of Nahal Mtzada in the direction from which you came. To the south, you can see large parts of the southern Judean Desert. From here descend on black-marked trail to the east, back to your starting point. This steep trail follows the approximate line of the siege wall. When you complete your descent, you pass youth hostel and a small museum just to south of the parking lot, returning to the starting point. (1)

Hike 32, Around Masada

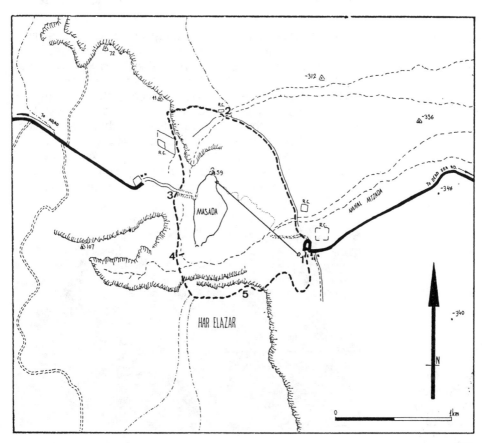

Mount Sedom

33

Points of interest: View, geology, chimney caves.
Length of hike: 7 km. (can be loop trip).
Hiking time: 4 hours.
Preferred season: November to May.
Suitable for: All.
Maps: Southern Judean Desert marked hiking trails map.
Special preparation: Flashlight.
Starting point: On Dead Sea Road near Sedom workers' camp, $4^1/_2$ km. north of Dead Sea Works.
Ending point: On Dead Sea Road, 2 km. north of starting point at blue-marked trailhead.

To begin hike:

By car: Drive $4^1/_2$ km. north of the Dead Sea Works. On the Dead Sea Road between km. 196 and 197, there is a black-marked trail which heads steeply up the mountain on wooden stairs right off the road's edge. (Across the road is a deserted building.) (1)

Head up the steep trail and be careful not to slip. After a climb of a few meters there is a remnant of a pulley once in use here, most likely by the first workers of the Dead Sea Works in Sedom. The Mount Sedom Range is 11 km. long but only 2 km. wide. The highest peak rises to 240 meters above the level of the Dead Sea — this is still beneath the global sea level. Two million years ago the ancient Dead Sea, which was very saline, began to deposit about a 3 cm. thick layer of salt annually. This accumulative salt deposit today covers about 400 sq. km. in the southern Dead Sea basin and is up to 5 or 6 m. deep. Throughout the years, sedimentary rocks accumulated on the

Atop Mount Sedom (3). See map on page 160

158

surface of the salt deposit. The exerted pressure fractured parts of the tougher sedimentary rock above. Certain plastic salt layers gave way, rising to form Mount Sedom and in the process shifting the harder layers of sedimentary rock to its summit. The measured depth of the salt rock layer of Mount Sedom is 2750 meters.

During the last 20,000 years, the mountain has risen 3.5 mm. annually. The harder rock layering Mount Sedom and so prominent on the horizon, seems like a gallery of towers and statues. But these towers and statues are gradually losing their grip on the landscape since the lower, supporting layers are in a state of perpetual erosion. One of these statues may indeed be the pillar of Lot's wife, Genesis 15:30. "His wife looked back from behind him and she became a pillar of salt."

Rainfall in the mountain area is meagre, about 50 mm. annually. Rainwater leaks down fissures between the tough rock and the salt rock; the latter dissolves, creating vertical chimney formations. The water reaches the layer of impermeable rock lower down and seeps out laterally, forming caves and tunnels which afford access to the chimney floors. Hundreds of these caves and chimney hollows dot Mount Sedom including Israel's longest cave. The small amount of precipitation and the geology of Mount Sedom have created one of the most barren regions of Israel here.

After reaching a plateau, pass several buildings (2) and head north on a dirt road. Soon, the marked trail leads toward one of the peaks of Mount Sedom, 164 meters below sea level. (3) Take the trail. Enjoy a view of the Dead Sea Works and evaporation ponds to the east. West are the Amiaz Plains, breached by Nahal Pratzim. Five km. to the west are the steep scarps that follow the entire length of the Dead Sea. This area is the borderline between the northern Negev and the southern Judean Desert.

Head north on dirt road passing several peaks, until you come to another dirt road going east-west. Turn right onto it, heading east for about 300 meters. Leave dirt road before it curves to the right and south. Head north, keeping to same elevation while walking through the small hills. A steep-sloped white hill protrudes 800 meters ahead of you to the north. Head directly there; don't look for specific trail. Climb to the top of this great vantage point, 194 meters below sea level. (4)

The salt of Sedom has been used throughout history. In Zefania 2:9, "Surely Moab shall be as Sedom and the children of Ammon as Gomorrah even the breeding of nettles and salt pits and a desolation for ever." Even during the early 20th century salt was hewn and shipped north of the Dead Sea and on to Jerusalem.

Head down the small hill, retracing your steps, and link onto the blue-marked trail which passes beneath the hill to the south, descending to the northeast. This steep path takes you down through unique chimney formations. *Take care not to get too close to the edge of the chimneys.* Directly above the Dead Sea Road the trail descends north on a dirt road down to it. Head south along the base of Mount Sedom, parallel to the Dead Sea Road to complete this loop trip hike. Note the evaporation pools of the Dead Sea Works and the picturesque salt formations.

Along the base of Mount Sedom there are many caves, *do not explore these as several are not safe.* Three hundred meters south of the trail end you pass the Sedom Cave, (5) once a rest spot for the Dead Sea workers. Along the road, just before returning to your starting point (1) is the Colonel Cave; today inaccessible, it was once used as a movie theater for the Dead Sea Works workers. It is named after a British colonel who was one of the founders of the Dead Sea Works. Directly opposite are a few buildings still standing from the early days of the southern Dead Sea Works. The southern works were set up in 1934 at Sedom, four years after the original works were founded on the northern shores of the Dead Sea. Today the Dead Sea Works is one of the most profitable industries in Israel, manufacturing several important minerals and chemicals for varied domestic uses and for export throughout the world.

Hike 33, Mount Sedom

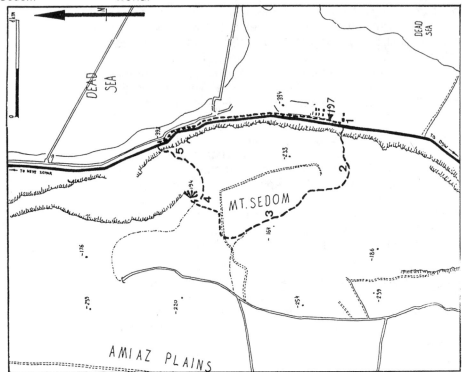

Eilat Mountains

Geography

The Eilat Mountains are in the southern part of the Negev Desert. This Desert's name originates in the Hebrew verb 'nagev' which means to dry. The Negev covers almost half of the area of the State of Israel, some 9800 sq. km. Measured from the geographical points of Beer Sheba to the southern city of Eilat its length is 190 km. At its widest point the Negev is 80 km., the widest extent of Israel. Belonging to the global desert zone — which includes the Sahara — rainfall varies from 200 mm. annually in the northern Negev to 25 mm. in the Gulf of Eilat region.

The Negev is divided into several regions which have different geological, geographical and historical characteristics. The Eilat Mountains are a separate geological entity. They include the three borders of the Negev: Israel-Egypt (Sinai) in the west, the Gulf of Eilat in the south, and the Arava Valley in the east. The latter is part of the Syrian-African rift that runs from Ethiopia in the south northward through Lebanon towards Turkey.

Under ancient Israeli control the Negev area only reached Mitzpe Ramon, in the mid-Negev. During the First Temple period, the kingdoms of David and Solomon and certain periods of the kingdom of Judea, Israel's kingdom, stretched to the Gulf of Eilat.

The Eilat Mountains and the Gulf of Eilat are a unique geographical zone in Israel as only here have magmatic rocks been exposed. Magmatic rock is created from magma within the earth. The Eilat Mountains are divided into 5 different zones: Eilat, Roded, Moon Valley, Amram and Timna, all composed of magmatic rocks. Most magmatic rock is hard, creating a rough and jagged landscape which is typified by very steep cliffs and declines. The Eilat Mountain range begins its decline along Israel's border with Egypt, from an altitude of over 800 meters in the west it drops to 150 and 0 meters sea level in the east — the Arava and the Gulf of Eilat. The five magmatic rock sub-regions are separated by several areas composed of sedimentary rock. The hikes in this book traverse all the sub-regions, except for Timna.

Climate

Generally, in Israel the further south and east you travel, the hotter and dryer it becomes; east is governed by the Syrian-African rift climate and the south by the climate of the global desert zone. Eilat is the southern most point of Israel. The average temperature here is approximately 25°c and in August, the hottest month of the year, the average temperature varies between 28°c in the western part of the Eilat Mountains and 34°c in the eastern parts. The average temperature high in the summer surpasses 40°c at noon.

The average amount of rainfall in the Eilat Mountain region is 25 mm. annually. This amount of precipitation can vary drastically throughout the years; some years without a drop of rain and others with a lot more than the precipitation average which

161

might fall on only one or two days! The average amount of rainy days in the Eilat area is 5. Humidity is around 35% and for this reason the evaporation rate is high. Dew falls in the mountainous area, but to the east, along the Syrian-African rift, dew is quite rare. The magmatic rock formations are another reason for the typically high temperature in the Eilat Mountains; when the sun rays bounce off the dark magmatic rock, they cause the temperature to rise even higher throughout the region.

Vegetation

Due to the climatic factors described, very little vegetation grows in the Eilat Mountains which belongs to the Sahara-Arabian vegetation zone, except during rainy years, when the slopes will be partially covered with vegetation. In an average year, a number of plants do grow in the smaller wadis, such as the box-thorn, millet, fagonia, hammada; in the larger wadis you will usually find several species of the acacia tree.

Wildlife

Although there are a large variety of reptiles and mammals in this region, a direct effect of the scarcity of vegetation is that there are not large numbers of individual species roaming the Eilat Mountains. At the foot of the mountains there are gazelles and several hundred ibex live amongst the Eilat Mountain range. They succeed in reproducing themselves quite well because there is no regional predator to hunt them down. This includes man who, for the past few decades has been subject to a nature preservation law which forbids hunting here.

Quite a few raptors can be found nesting in the Eilat Mountains, among them the rarest and largest raptor of Israel, the Negev (lappet faced) vulture. This is the 'nesher' referred to in the Bible, "ve'esa etkhem al kanfei nesharim," a phrase which experts today consider has been mistranslated into English as "I bore you on the wings of eagles," Ex 19:4. Since the Negev vulture has the greatest wingspan of all the region's raptors and flies the highest, researchers believe that it is only the vulture which transports its young on top of its wings safely, as no natural enemy flies above it.

During fall and spring, hundreds of thousands of migrating birds can be spotted heading between Europe and Africa along the Syrian-African rift above Eilat. Hyrax, foxes, wolves and even packs of wild dogs can also be seen in the Eilat region. Leopards have not yet extended their habitat to the Eilat Mountains, although they do live in the Judean Desert and central Negev.

Due to the small amount of water there are no amphibians in the Eilat Mountains but reptiles are common, including several venomous snakes such as the Burtons carpet viper.

Human Involvement

Due to its harsh climate, the Eilat region was never highly developed. Remnants dating back to the Chalcolithic period have turned up in the Eilat region. Different peoples have passed through the area since the Chalcolithic period. North of the

Eilat Gulf, copper was mined intensively by the Egyptians between the 12th and 14th century B.C.E. Since that time copper has been sporadically mined in the region. Throughout recorded history, Eilat was both an important gateway to the Red Sea and a link between the Red Sea and the Mediterranean Sea. Also the fact that Eilat and Aqaba, the Jordanian port city just east of Eilat, are situated on the route which leads from Egypt to the holy Moslem city of Mecca, ensured that Eilat would always have human involvement.

There was never a high Bedouin concentration in the Eilat region because of the very hot climate and the limited sources of water. In 1948, the Golani brigade seized control of Um Rash Rash, which is Eilat, enabling modern Eilat to adapt a vital role as Israel's gate to the Red Sea. Today Eilat is not only an important southern cargo port but it is one of Israel's main tourist cities and is in a state of constant development.

The three main Eilat routes in use today are: to the south, the highway to Taba which hugs the eastern coast of the Sinai peninsula until Sharm el Sheikh; to the north, the highway leaving Eilat that cuts through the Arava — both these roads are recent; and the ancient Ma'ale Eilat Road that heads from Eilat northwest toward the Netafim Junction. This latter road divides, one roadway continuing into the Moon Valley which is now part of Egypt, and the other extending north along the Egyptian-Israeli border. Further north this road divides again, one roadway extending along the border and the other heading towards the Uvda Valley. Other less used routes to Eilat Mountains are ancient trails, cutting across the Eilat Mountains from west to east, once traversed by Egyptian caravans en route to the copper mines. You will be hiking along some of these trails.

Water

As indicated above, water is very scarce in the Eilat region due to the small amount of precipitation and the geological composition of the mountains. There is only one small spring, En Netafim in Nahal Netafim, yielding about one cubic meter of water daily. The water is quite sweet containing only 183 mg. of chlorine per litre. The spring En Evrona and several series of wells which are fed by underground water are located in the Arava Valley, east of the Eilat Mountains. Another water source in the Eilat Mountains are flashflood waters which are sometimes dammed in the wadis. There is also the thamila. These are trenches dug, usually in the loose gravel of a wadi bed, which tap reservoirs of underground water which most likely seeped down and collected after a flashflood. Thamilas are generally situated at the bottom of falls in certain wadis where the underlying rock is impermeable. The water is contained by the gravel layer which also prevents its evaporation.

In several Eilat Mountain locations natural external water hollows have been formed in the narrow canyons by flashfloods; the high canyon walls serve to guard the collected water from the sun's rays and thus evaporation is very slow.

Hiking in Eilat

Although considered mainly a tourist spot with water sports and sunbathing as its main attractions, Eilat actually has much to offer the hiker in the realm of its unique environmental characteristics.

The hikes in this book describe several exciting and interesting places in the Eilat Mountains, most of them on tracks leading through several unique regions of magmatic rock which are an extension of the Sinai Mountain ranges.

The ideal way to reach the trailhead of the loop trip hikes is by car. The Ma'ale-Eilat bus will do for the one-way hikes. Though there are no official stops near the trailheads, bus drivers will usually stop if kindly requested to do so. Ask for the exact spot I have indicated in the hike you are taking. Most of the buses travel from Eilat to the center of the country on the Arava Road, heading straight north out of Eilat. Also starting out from the Eilat Central Bus Station, buses run from Eilat to Beer Sheba and Tel Aviv through the Ma'ale-Eilat (Eilat-Uvda) Road. There is also a bus from Eilat to the Taba border crossing.

Due to Eilat's extreme heat, it is very important to take large quantities of water on all hikes: at least three litres of water per person per day during the winter and during the hot months *one litre of water should be taken per person for every estimated hiking hour.*

Hiking in the Eilat Mountains is not recommended during the summer months or late spring and early fall. Even during the months of November-December, April and May hiking can be quite uncomfortable. However, it is possible to hike during these months if one starts out before daylight, returning by 10 a.m. Likewise it is possible to conduct short hikes after 4 p.m. until dark. *Hats are a must and suntan cream is also of vital importance.*

The best map for these hikes is the Hebrew language Eilat marked hiking trail map. All of the hikes pass through the Eilat Mountains Nature Reserve.

Important phone numbers:

(Area code 059)

Eilat Field Study Center, P.O.B. 204, Eilat 88101	72021
Almog Beach, P.O.B. 667, Eilat 88101	73988
Eilat Police	100 or 72444/5
Magen David Adom (first aid Eilat)	101- or 72333
Yoseftal Hospital, Eilat	73151/2

Layers of sedimentary rock by the En Netafim Junction

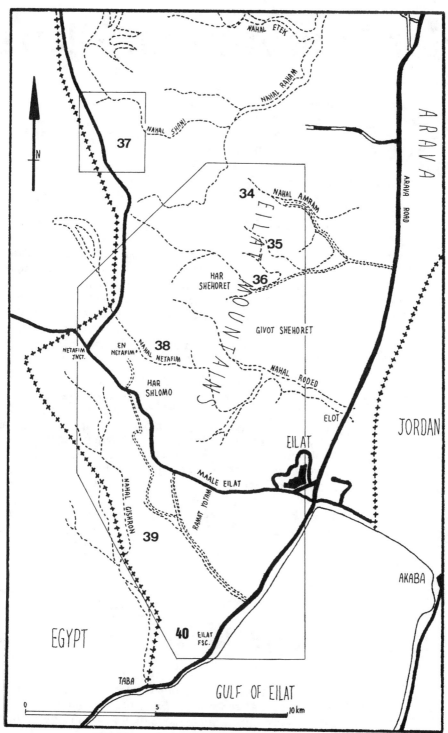

Eilat Mountains. Numbers represent hike numbers.

Har Amir/Amram Pillars

34

Points of interest: Sandstone formations, copper mines.
Length of hike: 4 km. loop trip.
Hiking time: 3 hours.
Preferred season: November to May.
Suitable for: All.
Maps: Eilat marked hiking trail map.
Special preparation: None.
Starting & ending point: Amram Pillars parking lot.

To begin hike:

By car only. Turn into dirt road to Amram Pillars off Arava Road just north of km. stone 20, 8 km. north of Eilat. Take dirt road through the Arava for 2¹/₂ km. and turn right at fork in dirt road. Cross the Eilat-Ashkelon gas pipe line. The smooth dirt road runs alongside Nahal Amram beneath the eastern and northern slopes of Har Amir, through the Amram crater, reaching the Amram Pillars parking lot where you leave your car. Here your hike begins. (1)

Just before the parking lot on the dirt road near a white sign, you will see the trailhead. The blue-marked trail to Mitzpe Amram which has an unobstructed view of the entire Amram Crater. Immediately after the beginning of the blue-marked trail you turn on to a red-marked trail heading south. Cross a wadi with red sandstone banks. After 500 meters, the trail curves to the right (east) and heads up a small wadi at the base of a very impressive sandstone cliff. (5) The steep trail climbs up the wadi as on your right there is sedimentary rock, limestone and on your left is sandstone. The trail climbs up a steep slope, comes to the point where the sandstone first

See map on page 171

166

becomes visible and takes a left, crossing a small ravine. Step off the trail a minute to your left, into the ravine at the top of the fall. This is called a joint; the stream has cut through a natural fissure in the rock. Similar joints have caused the famous Amram Pillars which you will reach at the end of the hike.

Follow the red-marked trail to a small valley; this is the watershed between Nahal Shehoret and Nahal Amram. Here (4) take left onto green-marked trail which heads up a small wadi, first traverse a section of multi-colored sandstone and soon afterwards hits a white sandstone layer, which has become twisted into various forms and shapes. Three hundred meters along the green-marked trail reach trail intersection (3) where a blue-marked trail enters from the south, from Nahal Amir. At blue and green-marked trail intersection on sandstone plateau, turn left and continue on green-marked trail heading southeast over the northwest ridge of Har Amir. You can see Har Amir towering high above with a crown of limestone cliffs encircling the summit.

At the ridge pass, enjoy view to the north of Amram Crater, the Amram Mountains volcanic range and Givat Yokheved, prominent at the foot of the ridge where you stand. To the southwest is the volcanic Har Shlomo ridge and to the south, Eilat and Aqaba. In the west, the whole range of mountains, along the Egyptian border drops sharply to the east.

Descend trail passing ancient copper mines which begin from the sandstone cliffs along the ridge and the slope. Near the holes note foot indentations for climbing and traces of rope marks along the rim of one of the holes. You can find bits of green sandstone near some pits from which the copper was extracted. The trail descends through white sandstone 'art galleries,' carved by water and wind, and curves in an arch in the direction of Givat Yokheved. Note the vegetation here. The trail reaches the lower red sandstone level and heads north along sandy and green foliaged wadi to a point west of Givat Yokheved. Two hundred meters along the wadi near an acacia tree there is a bend in the trail. Head left (west) toward a Roman-Byzantine copper mining camp. (2) One wonders what was the miners' water source, other than the damming of wadis which could offer flashflood water only about once a year. Remnants from the periods of copper mining have been found in the proximity of the few wells of the Arava Valley; these include a fort which probably was positioned there to guard the valuable water source. One of the wells is Bir el Kah near Israel's border with Jordan. Directly east of the Amram Crater is a farm and a series of wells from the Omayyad (early Arabic) period. These wells are possibly more ancient in origin.

From the camp, move on north 150 meters to the gravel road and follow it left back to the starting point. Here follow short clear trail past parking lot west to the Amram Pillars which are 'etched' into the muti-colored sandstone. These 15 meter high columns were formed in a manner much like the famous Solomon's Pillars — water seeping through crevices in the sandstone gradually deepened the cracks. The Pillars are not named after Amram, the father of Moses. The Arabic name for Nahal Amram is Wadi Amrani, and this became Amram in Hebrew. The Amram Pillars are situated at the foot of Amram Cliffs, rising 350 meters above you. Nearby are more remnants of Roman copper mines. Return to parking lot. (1)

Sandstone formations in Nahal Amir (hike 35)

Nahal Amir

35

Points of interest: View, sandstone formations, copper mines.
Length of hike: 7 km. loop trip, with two alternatives of extending hike.
Hiking time: 4 hours.
Preferred season: November to May.
Suitable for: All.
Maps: Eilat marked hiking trail map.
Special preparation: None.
Starting & ending point: $4^1/_2$ km. from Arava Road on green-marked dirt road, at blue and red-marked trail intersection.

To begin hike:

By bus: Take bus from Eilat north. Eight km. north of Eilat on Arava road ask driver to let you off at the yellow sign, 'Amram Pillars.' Follow dirt road.

By car: Turn off Arava Road just north of km. stone 20, 8 km. north of Eilat, into dirt road that will take you to Amram Pillars.

Follow dirt road through Arava for $2^1/_2$ km. and take left at fork in dirt road for another 2 km. By a hill on your right the dirt road curves left. Straight ahead of you on a dirt road a red-marked trail and a blue-marked trail begins heading north. There should be a sign here. Here your hike begins. (1)

Take blue-marked trail (which is a bit indistinct) north in direction of Har Amir ahead, crossing plains strewn with many kinds of rock. After 600 meters, the trail drops to Nahal Amir just to the right of a hill. (2) Take left up Nahal Amir which cuts through white sandstone. Follow blue-marked trail up canyon, passing falls and unique sandstone formations.

The canyon here cuts through red sandstone, the bottom layer of the three sandstone strata deposited in the Eilat region. Sandstone is a sedimentary rock which consists of grains of quartz welded together by a limestone solution and by iron oxide, which paints the rock different hues. After a 200 meter climb in elevation the trail reaches an elevated scenic plateau of white sandstone. Here (3) you intersect with the green-marked trail which you take to the right, onto the ridge where you have a view of the volcanic Har Amram and Amram Crater to the north. Scattered around you and a bit below the ridge are many small holes and tunnels, relics of the copper mining which thrived here 3000 years ago.

Descend a short distance to explore the copper mines. Near the holes, look for greenish sandstone fragments. This sandstone is cemented together by a copper solution which was

See map on page 171

extracted in a few phases: 1 — grinding the rock into powder; 2 — ground charcoal and ground oxides of iron and manganese were added to the powder; 3 — The mix was heated in a special oven hollowed out of the ground. The fire was heated up to 1300°c by means of a bellow. During the melting process additional mix was added, until the oven was again full. The result of the chemical reaction triggered was clear copper layer at the base of the oven while the remainder floated on top. This layer was then drained off through a special opening. A bar was placed into the copper and it was yanked out after the copper cooled, yielding approximately a 50 kilogram piece. This refining process was performed at the camps below. Similar to the mine at Timna, the raw copper from these mines was sold and was not used for local purposes and tool manufacture.

If you prefer to extend hike 3 km., continue on green-marked trail to join the Har Amir — Amram Pillars hike.

Head back over ridge to blue-marked and green-marked trail intersection. (3) Continue down green-marked trail northwest. The trail cuts through interesting white sandstone formations and soon arrives at multi-colored sandstone. At the foot of trail, join the black-marked trail and take left, heading south. But first enjoy the view of volcanic Har Shlomo ridge in the distance and Har Shehoret in front and a bit to the right of Har Shlomo. The trail passes to the right of two large falls. Near the second fall, a large rock juts out — a great spot for a rest and some lunch, especially on a cloudy day. (4)

The trail heads along the wadi to the south along the base of Har Amir. Here again you will see many sandstone formations and columns along the way; these are caused by gradual water erosion down the sandstone fissures. As the trail reaches the end of the Har Amir cliffs, look southeast 1 km. and try to locate your starting point. The black-marked trail continues south 800 meters from the end of Har Amir cliff to a wide wadi, a tributary of Nahal Shehoret. Here in the southern part of the wadi look for red-marked trail which continues to the top of the Nahal Shehoret Canyon to the west (right). Here you can join the Nahal Shehoret hike which lengthens your hike by $4\frac{1}{2}$ km. Take left (5) on wide red-marked trail along wadi directly east for 1 km. back to starting point. (1)

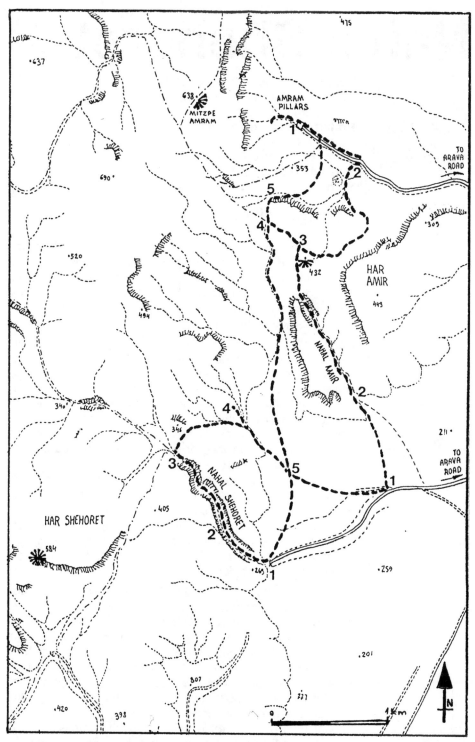

Hike 34, Har Amir/Amram Pillars; hike 35, Nahal Amir; hike 36, Nahal Shehoret

Nahal Shehoret

36

Points of interest: View, canyon.
Length of hike: 4 km. loop trip.
Hiking time: 2 hours.
Preferred season: All year.
Suitable for: All.
Maps: Eilat marked hiking trail map.
Special preparation: None.
Starting & ending point: Entrance to Shehoret Canyon.

To begin hike:

By car: On Arava Road 8 km. north of Eilat, just north of km. stone 20, turn off onto dirt road toward Amram Pillars. By fork in dirt road, take left. After 2 km. you pass Nahal Amir hike trailhead, and $3^1/_2$ km. from fork in dirt road reach the road's end near approach to Nahal Shehoret. Shehoret in Hebrew means black. (1) Begin your hike here.

Head north on black-marked trail ascending small ridge above Nahal Shehoret. The trail crosses a wadi and after 1 km. you come to another wadi. Here take left on red-marked trail (5) walking through a wide but progressively narrowing wadi punctuated with acacia trees, several covered with mistletoe. Noticeable from afar, the mistletoe is a partially parasitic shrub which feeds on the water and minerals of the acacia tree and can often be seen growing on the upper section of this tree, especially in the Eilat region. The mistletoe performs its own photosynthesis; its bright red flower that blooms mainly in spring and early summer do not contain pollen (the green flowers do). The fruit of the mistletoe contains one seed; distributed by birds, the seed adheres itself to an acacia branch where it develops roots which penetrate the water vessels. The flowers are a favorite of the tiny Palestinian Sunbird which is endemic to this region.

As the trail heads up west, just north of the trail is a small wadi that cuts into magmatic rock. The 'baby Shehoret' is a cute canyon to explore and 'catch some shade.' (4) Continue up the red-marked trail. This was once an ancient Egyptian caravan trail along Nahal Shehoret, bypassing the canyon which is unpassable to camels. At the top of the ridge enjoy view of Har Amir. Continue on trail above the baby Shehoret and soon pass watershed dropping directly into Nahal Shehoret. Take left into the Nahal Shehoret Canyon. (3) This nahal cuts through tough metamorphic rock creating this narrow canyon. Along the wadi there is conglomerate evidence of the stream's

See map on page 171

172

different levels, most likely from the Paliestecone period. A few small falls drop down along the canyon. (2)

Continue to descend canyon. Note the variety of vegetation. At exit of canyon return to starting point. (1)

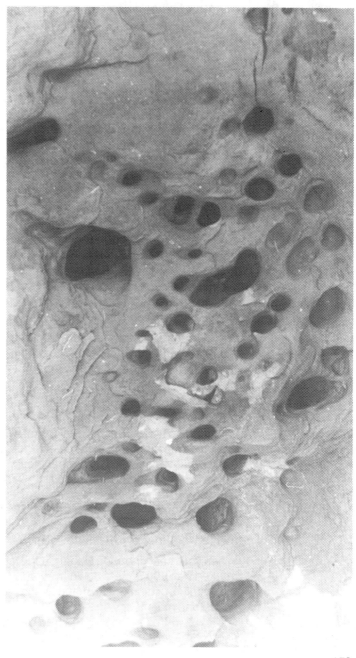

Rock formation
below Har Amir

Red Canyon

Three hikes

Points of interest: Colorful gorge, sandstone formations, canyons, view.

Length of hike: Hike #1 — $\frac{1}{2}$ km. loop trip; Hike #2 — 4 km. loop trip; Hike #3 — 8 km. one-way.

Hiking time: Hike #1 — $1\frac{1}{2}$ hrs; Hike #2 — 3 hrs; Hike #3 — 4 hrs.

Preferred season: Hike #1 & 2 — all year; Hike #3 — November to May.

Suitable for: Hike #1 & 2 — families; Hike # 3 — all.

Maps: Eilat marked hiking trail map.

Special preparation: None.

Starting point: Red Canyon parking lot.

Ending point: Hike # 3 — Har Uziyahu Junction on Eilat-Uvda Road. (8)

To begin hike:

By bus: Take Eilat-Beer Sheba bus toward Mitzpe Ramon and get off 10 km. north of the Netafim Junction at orange colored Red Canyon sign of the Nature Reserves Authority. (1)

By car: On Eilat-Uvda Road, 10 km. north of the Netafim Junction, take right onto dirt road by the orange colored Red Canyon sign of the Nature Reserves Authority. (1)

Go northeast on unpaved road. Note the volcanic Har Neshef mountain range to the south. After 1 km. the road forks. Take the right fork onto green-marked dirt road. After a red-marked trail comes in from the right from lower Nahal Shani, reach garbage cans; nearby is a parking lot. Here your hike begins. (2)

Continue on trail down to Nahal Shani along the wadi. As you descend note the conglomerates — rocks composed of rounded fragments, varying from small pebbles to large boulders, in a cement of hardened clay or the like. Conglomerates help us learn about the water levels during previous historical periods, from 1 million to $4\frac{1}{2}$ million years ago, when the Syrian-African rift was increasing its depth. These rounded stones are cemented together by limestone solutions.

When you reach the wide Nahal Shani, take right following the marked trail 250 meters down the wadi. A large tributary joins the wadi on the right (3) and Nahal Shani hits the hard sandstone that makes up the Red Canyon, which you come to in a few hundred meters. At the Red Canyon, a trail follows the short gorge on the right side. Either take the trail or descend the

See map on page 176

canyon using the installed ladders. Make sure that the ladders are firmly attached when you use them. Either choice is exciting. If you have time, take both.

Note how with time the water has eroded and widened the base of the gorge, giving it a bell-shape. At the opening of the canyon note the caperbush, the salt bush and tamarisk, this is a sure indication of high underground water. (4) The salt bush is very common in the southern part of Israel, and is also seen near many roads. It is one to two meters high, with whitish silvery leaves which give the plant its name and extract excess salt from the plant. The salt bush is perfectly comfortable in salty regions, growing especially in small wadis and marl dominated wadis in the Dead Sea environs. A very useful plant, camels, goats and humans all enjoy the taste. A condiment for salads, fresh or fried, a fried saltbush leaf omelette is considered a treat. Salt bush has been well known since Biblical times, mentioned in Job 30:4 along with the white-broom, "Who cut up saltbush by the bushes and white-broom roots for their meat."

As you exit the Red Canyon and head down the wadi, note how the rock changes to white sandstone. The green rocks along the banks are rock shards.

For Hike #1 — Re-ascend the Red Canyon taking the other route. Continue back up the wadi, retracing your steps until you come to a wide wadi entering in from the left. (3) Head up this wadi passing some acacia trees. After about 600 meters join dirt road and head right, returning you to parking lot. (2)

For Hike #2 & #3 — Continue down Nahal Shani. After about 1 km. from the Red Canyon, southern Nahal Shani merges from the right by a black trail mark on the wall and on a boulder near a tamarisk tree. (5) Head up southern Nahal Shani through canyon of colorful 'iron oxide' sandstone. The wadi bed is peppered with a rock mix — sandstone, sedimentary rock and debris from the volcanic Neshef Mountains. When you reach a 35 meter waterfall, follow trail that takes the fall from the left. Hard limestone makes up the upper $1/_3$ of the fall. The bottom $2/_3$ part consists of multi-colored sandstone. At the top of the fall is a large acacia tree.

After the fall, the wadi soon cuts through a small canyon, made out of the same rock forming Har Neshef. At the end of the short canyon, reach a trail split. (6)

For Hike # 2 — Take right at red-marked trail heading up the northern tributary of southern Nahal Shani. The trail curves north, passes above several wadis along the Shaham Plain and returns you back to the parking lot near the garbage cans. (2)

For Hike # 3 — Take left and follow black-marked trail up the southern branch of southern Nahal Shani, (its southern bank is the base of the Har Neshef ridge). After 400 meters, reach a row of 6 acacia trees. One of the trees on the southern bank hosts a nest of the Negev (lappet faced) vulture, the largest and rarest raptor in Israel. Alongside this tree, (7) a clear unmarked trail heads up steeply to the south along a small wadi and to the summit of eastern Har Neshef which is the eastern end of a mountainous range, mostly under Egyptian control. Take the trail. It consists of black volcanic rock from the pre-Cambrian period. A similar range in the Eilat Mountains is Har Shlomo, farther south and lower — 705 meters as compared to an altitude of 863 meters above sea level here. The rock on Har Neshef is not very tough and is not able to withstand erosion which prevails here. The mountain is steep but with few cliffs which are typical of rock which is not resistant to erosion. Neshef in Hebrew means dark, mentioned in Jeremiah 13:16, "Give glory to the Lord your God before he cause darkness and before your feet stumble upon the dark mountains." There is a spectacular view from Har Neshef.

Head down clear trail to the southwest to the paved road (south). The trail below becomes less clear. Head over to the paved road and follow it to the right along southern Nahal Shani for about 1 km., right to the bus stop on the main Eilat-Uvda Road at Har Uziyahu Junction. End your hike here, just 300 meters east from the Egyptian border. (8)

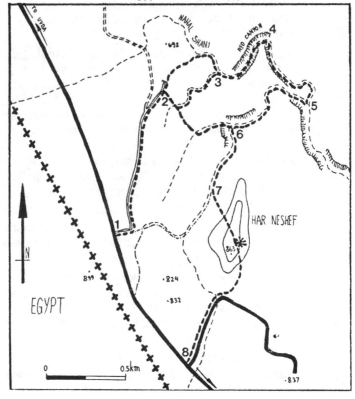

Hike 37, Red Canyon

Har Yehoahaz/Nahal Ha-Mapalim/Har Shlomo

38

Points of interest: Egyptian border, views, ancient city, climbing.
Length of hike: 13 km. one-way.
Hiking time: 8 hours.
Preferred season: November to May.
Suitable for: Experienced hikers only.
Maps: Eilat marked hiking trail map.
Special preparation: Binoculars.
Starting point: Har Yehoahaz, 2 km. north of Netafim Junction on Eilat-Uvda Road, just beyond km. stone 12.
Ending point: Eilat-Uvda Road, near army road block.

To begin hike:

By bus: Take Eilat-Beer Sheba bus toward Mitzpe Ramon. There is no bus stop at starting point. Politely ask driver to let you off at top of Ma'ale-Eilat, 2 km. north of Netafim Junction at Har Yehoahaz, after km. stone 12. Here hike begins.

Cross road to the west to the old and new border stone 83 overlooking upper Nahal Netafim, now under Egyptian control. (1) *Take care not to cross border !* Nahal Netafim below you has a 20 meter fall, and beneath the fall is a thamila. A thamila is a water source situated in wadis covered by gravel. To the left of Thamilat Roded 70 meters down the wadi on the cliff wall is an ancient Egyptian inscription of Ramses III from the 12th century B.C.E. When the Egyptians controlled the copper mines located at a point farther down the mountains to the east, this thamila was used by the caravans that passed by from Egypt to the Arava.

The current Egyptian-Israeli border is not based on a geographical line. In 1906 an agreement was signed between Great Britain and Turkey establishing the border between them at a point from eastern El Arish on the Mediterranean coast down to Taba on the Gulf of Aqaba. There was strong pressure brought to bear by the British on the Turks to sign this agreement. In 1923, when Egypt declared its independence this line was not defined as a border. Upon the establishment of the State of Israel in 1948 the line became the cease-fire border. Only in 1979, following the Israeli-Egyptian Camp David Peace Treaty, did this first become an official border.

From the border, head north on dirt road for 150 meters until you see a black-marked dirt road heading east from the main road. Cross and head onto dirt road, which was once the patrol

See map on page 180

177

road along the Egyptian-Israeli border, the dirt road curves to the left. After about 150 meters on both sides of the road are the remains of a guard station or a camping site for Egyptian caravans. Egyptian ceramics, similar to those found near the Timna Valley copper mines, dating back to the 12th and 14th century B.C.E. were unearthed here. (2)

Return to blue-marked trail that departs from dirt road at a point where the dirt road curves to the left. The trail heads straight east, just north of Har Yehoahaz's summit. After 1 km., the trail turns south, heading on through sedimentary rock; 500 meters later it reaches the top of Ma'ale Bodeda. Veer right toward the rock piles at the corner of the ridge where you will enjoy a wonderful view of the Har Shlomo Range, the Arava, Har Shehoret and more. (3) Descend on blue-marked trail. The switchbacks hint at the trail's age and use; it was prepared especially for the domestic animals which carried the copper from the mines in the Arava and Timna areas to Egypt. After a 2 km. descent, just before the bottom, you reach the Lost City, known as Hirbet Roded or Hirbet Bodedah, situated on the trail above the Boded Valley. Between the ruined buildings are piles of debris which are assumed to be the remains of six structures which housed limestone quarry workers. In one of the structures facing the east there is a cross in the stone. Most likely this room was a small prayer chapel for the men. Finds of pottery, crosses and Greek inscriptions indicate that this is a Byzantine quarry, although finds of use of this quarry rock have not been discovered. Bodeda in Hebrew means lonely, a good description of this desolate area.

Continue down to the bottom of trail. (4) Here follow sign leading you right (south) to black-marked trail. Soon you come to watershed with a great view south to Har Shlomo. Continue down into very interesting wadi running into Nahal Netafim, cutting along a fault line. On your right there are sedimentary rocks and on your left magmatic rocks; the wadi cuts between them down to the sandstone layer.

The wadi emerges into Nahal Netafim, one of the largest wadis in the Eilat region, it begins northwest of Har Yehoahaz in the Moon Valley, now under Egyptian control. Further up Nahal Netafim from where you are standing is En Netafim, the only spring in the region. Take green trail mark left into the Nahal Netafim canyon, cutting through the granite of Har Shlomo and Har Yedidiya. Note the colorful dykes which are magmatic seepages. After rain, this part of the wadi flows with some water. The canyon opens up after several hundred meters and you will see conglomerates adhering to the magmatic stones overhead. Continue in wadi along dirt road for another km. Here, near the signs with trail marks and acacia tree on the right is the beginning of Nahal HaMapalim. (5) Take right following blue-marked trail into Nahal HaMapalim, 'wadi of the falls,' which you now ascend. Climb the first fall of the total of 18 falls from the right side. The wadi widens for 500 meters and you reach a steep canyon. Nahal HaMapalim cascades from the peak of Har Shlomo, from a height of 705 meters to Nahal Netafim at 270 meters; a drop of 430 meters in less than 2 aerial km.

A steep gully cuts through Har Shlomo's ancient rock — consisting of brown granite which is mainly composed of quartz and mica. This entire range is rich with dykes (magmatic seepages), some more and some less resistant to erosion than the granite. Nahal HaMapalim runs through negative dykes that are less resistant to erosion than granite, and are easily washed away, leaving the harder edged igneous rock granite as a compact wall. The negative dykes usually consist of green and black diabase. The falls at Nahal HaMapalim are red, positive dykes, more resistant to erosion than the granite. Some of the falls are hard granite. All of the falls are climbable, *just take your time and watch your step*. The blue-marked trail breaks off to the left before reaching the head of the wadi up from Nahal HaMapalim and continues its steep climb to Har Shlomo.

The vegetation in magmatic rock regions is sparse due to the small amount of precipitation and strong level of sun radiation reflecting off the dark stone. Nevertheless, the ibex like to graze on the Har Shlomo peaks. At the summit take left to the western flank of Har Shlomo, then re-descend and head up to the eastern flank on blue-marked trail.

The pointed peaks are a result of red porphyry. Its strong resistance to erosion creates these jagged points on top of Har Shlomo. (6) After enjoying a really breathtaking view, continue down blue-marked trail to the north, on the watershed between Nahal Shlomo and Nahal HaMapalim. Head west along a tributary of Nahal Shlomo, landscaped with colorful dykes. At the bottom veer left into main wadi where after a few hundred meters a dirt road begins. Again, you are walking between magmatic and sedimentary rocks — this is a geological fault line. Here we see two different types of rock on the same level, but their ages are millions of years apart due to movement of the earth's crust.

Note bushes with long straight green branches, probably leafless and with small yellow flowers. This is the desert ochradenus. Growing up to 2 meters, the simple and long leaves sprout only after the rains. The green branches photosynthesize throughout the year. The $\frac{1}{2}$ cm. yellow flowers bloom during winter and spring, but sometimes last into summer. The white and yellow berries are edible and a favorite of many birds who distribute their seeds. The ochradenus grows in all desert wadis of Israel which have less than 100 mms. annual rainfall.

On your right, is the ascent of the old Ma'ale-Eilat Road which was paved in the forties by the British. Reach the new Uvda-Ma'ale-Eilat Road built in the 1970's, near the army roadblock. (7) There is no bus stop here. Take left on road 1 km. toward Eilat and reach bus stop at army base to end your hike.

Hike 38, Har Yehoahaz

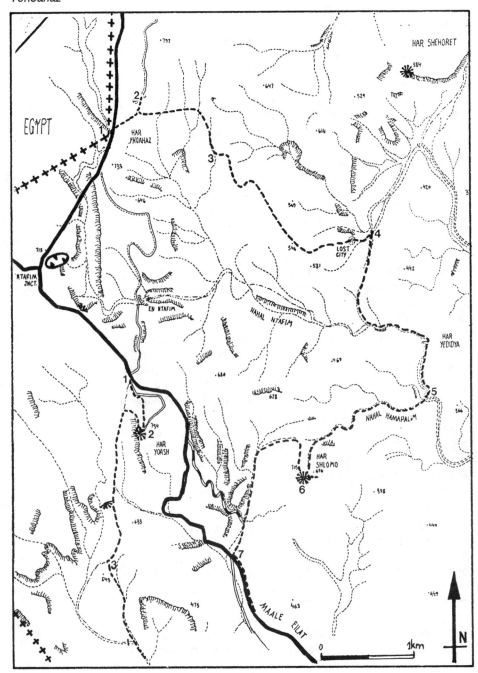

Har Yoash to the Red Sea

39

Points of interest: View, canyons, geological formations.
Length of hike: 13 km. one-way.
Hiking time: 8 hours.
Preferred season: November to May.
Suitable for: Experienced hikers.
Maps: Eilat marked hiking trail map.
Special preparation: None.
Starting point: Har Yoash off Ma'ale-Eilat Road.
Ending point: Eilat Field Study Center.

To begin hike:

View of Maale Eilat (foreground), Har Yehoshafat, Red Sea (background). See map on page 185

At top of Ma'ale Eilat before sign to En Netafim, get off at the curve to the right on the road just before km. stone 9. To the south of the road is a sign in Hebrew with a blue trail mark announcing Nahal Gishron. There is no bus stop here, but Egged drivers usually oblige if kindly approached. Here your hike begins.

At sign, (1) head left on a dirt road that runs east, parallel to main road. You will join the blue-marked trail later on. After 200 meters, along the dirt road, break right toward the ridge, passing wire and fenced-in remnants. The summit can be climbed via the road as well.

Atop ridge stop at old building. In the 8th century, the Egyptian Ebn Tulon constructed a road to Mecca from Suez via the Sinai Desert and Aqaba to supplement the heavily travelled Moslem pilgrimage route to Mecca; called Darb el Hadj, meaning 'road of the celebrators.' Since that time, the existing routes have been improved. What you are looking at now was most likely a small restaurant-cafe along the way, probably built during the Mameluke period. (2)

Head up the ridge to the scenic Har Yoash, 734 meters above sea level. At the mountain top are 4 patios with a view map. Looking southeast you can observe the hike route; the deep Nahal Gishron canyon, volcanic Har Yehoshafat, and to its right the top of white Givat Rehavam 5 km. from where you stand.

In the distance, suspended over the Red Sea, observe Har Tzefahot. To the east the magmatic ranges of Har Shlomo are prominent. Har Yoash is also known as Mitzpe Eilat as it overlooks Eilat and Ma'ale Eilat. It is no wonder the mountain was fortified, until 1967 it was adjacent to the border with Egypt. On its flat table-top are more surprises. Descend to the north between the two northern viewpoints on clear ridge trail which drops to the left 50 meters before a small hut. Take trail, heading beneath the western cliff of Har Yoash on down to the blue-marked trail where you take a left. The ground here is soft marl. The trail soon hits multi-colored sandstone. One km. along the trail a black-marked trail veers to the left into the sandy wadi. The dry riverbed breaks into interesting limestone 'hogbacks' south of Har Yoash. Veer off to the right here for a great view of Nahal Gishron, which cuts a narrow canyon through magmatic rock.

Continue on trail above Nahal Gishron for another km. until reaching a trail split. (3) Take black-marked trail to the left. The blue-marked trail dropping to Nahal Gishron to the right touches the border with Egypt. The trail drops sharply through magmatic rock, cascading several mini-falls along the way. Five hundred meters on, this trail wadi drops a 5 meter fall. Head back a few meters and continue down between the wadi and another narrow wadi on your left. As the wadi widens before Nahal Gishron, observe the many bean caper plants lining the trail. The Latin name for the bean caper is zygophyllum, in Hebrew Zugan. Zygo means two in Latin and describes the thick leaves that grow in pairs along the stem of this long-lived common desert plant.

One km. from the trail intersection, you reach Nahal Gishron at a fault line between granite and sandstone; here a 20 meter high fall embellishes the wadi. Take left. One-half km. down Nahal Gishron near several acacia trees the wadi slightly narrows, cutting a small canyon through the sandstone and curving sharply to the right. Here during long periods of the day parts of the wadi are in shade and it is an ideal spot to stop and rest. On the flat face of the stone are ancient etchings of a boat, camels standing, a party of men and an ibex. (4) Farther down the wadi where it widens there is a sign indicating a green-marked trail which heads up to the east. Follow trail into the exquisite shady gorge in the sandstone called Ma'avar Safra, the Safra Passage. (5) Return to Nahal Gishron and continue on down the trail.

Four hundred meters along the trail the wadi cuts through magmatic rock, forming a cute canyon. After this canyon, the wadi widens and a blue-marked trail heads up to the left toward Tzukei Gishron, the Gishron cliffs. Take left onto Ma'ale Gishron and 50 meters after the beginning of the trail there is a sign in Hebrew, **STOP BORDER, NO PASSAGE**. If you continue along the wadi you enter Egyptian territory. (6)

Follow blue-marked trial to the top of the ridge where you take a right, south onto black-marked trail along the Gishron cliffs. The Gishron cliffs are limestone and chalk and on the top of the cliff there are thick flint embedments. From this trail you have a nice view of northeastern Sinai and the protruding white hill of Givat Rehavam. Givat Rehavam is a relict hill of chalk and marl. Topped with limestone and potato stones (bulbuses) out of flint,. it stands an imposing 60 meters above the surrounding landscape. At one time the whole area was covered with similar limestone and marls, but erosion washed them away. Since Givat Rehavam is situated in a structural trap within the Nahal Rehavam sincline it did not undergo much erosion and this interesting cone shaped hill has survived.

About a half a km. down the trail you reach trail intersection. The black-marked trail continues southward, rising to Mitzpe Tzukei Gishron which is now on the Egyptian border. Take red-marked trail left down wadi into another wadi which you cross. After one km. you reach the 'knife trail,' walking along a magnificent cliff which makes a steep drop to the east. On your left is also a vertical drop. It is as though you were walking along the edge of a knife's blade. (7) This 100 meter high cliff at a 70-80° tilt, is called a 'hogback.' From here there is a nice view in the direction of the magmatic Har Tzefahot range and the Edom Mountains beyond the Red Sea. As you make your way down the trail, note limestone bulbuses, both loose and embedded in the stone, in the wadi to your right and near the intersection with the black-marked trail that climbs up from the wadi. Take left on black-marked trail as setting to the right on Ma'ale Bulbusim takes you of course to . . . the Egyptian border.

The trail leaves the sedimentary rock of the Gishron Fault and hits granite, heading southeast and arriving at Nahal Tzefahot, keeping just right of the wadi. Two km. from Ma'ale Bulbusim, it drops into a wadi where a green-marked trail merges from the left. Continue on green-marked trail straight up wadi. The trail heads south, climbing a small ravine where 1 km. from the trail intersection you reach the panoramic Har Tzefahot. (See hike Har Tzefahot). (8)

The upper part of Har Tzefahot is of grey shist containing shiny particles of mica. This soft metamorphic rock consists of thin adhering layers. Shist is tzefaha in Hebrew, thus the name, Tzefahot, of this scenic hill 278 meters above the Red Sea. (8) The ideal time to be at the top of Har Tzefahot is late afternoon when the sun's rays bathe the Edom Mountains across the Red Sea in a unique reddish light.

Look northeast in the direction of Eilat and Aqaba. Between these geographical points is Tel el Halifa, which is believed to have been Etzion Gaber, the ancient kingdom of Israel's link to the Red Sea during the First Temple period. Eilat mentioned in Kings II,16:6 is most likely where Aqaba is today. "At the time Retzin, King of Syria returned Eilat to Syria and he deprived the Jews from Eilat and Edomites came to Eilat and settled there until this day."

From here you can see the three countries which border Israel: Jordan to the east; Saudi Arabia to the southeast; and to the south and west the Sinai Peninsula under Egyptian control.

From Har Tzefahot there are two trails leading down. 1) Either take the blue-marked trail northwest which reaches the Club Inn Hotel (9) (This is the longest); or, 2) follow green-marked trail down the ridge just to the south of Har Tzefahot, running south of Nahal Garinit to the Eilat Field Study Center. (10)

The $1\frac{1}{2}$ km. trail descends to the Eilat Field Study Center passing it to the north and joining Eilat Taba Road. Across from the Eilat Field Study Center is the Coral Beach Nature Reserve, where your hike ends. If you have time, take a dip. Between the Field Study Center and the entrance to the Nature Reserve is a bus stop. (10) From here buses run from Taba heading to Eilat.

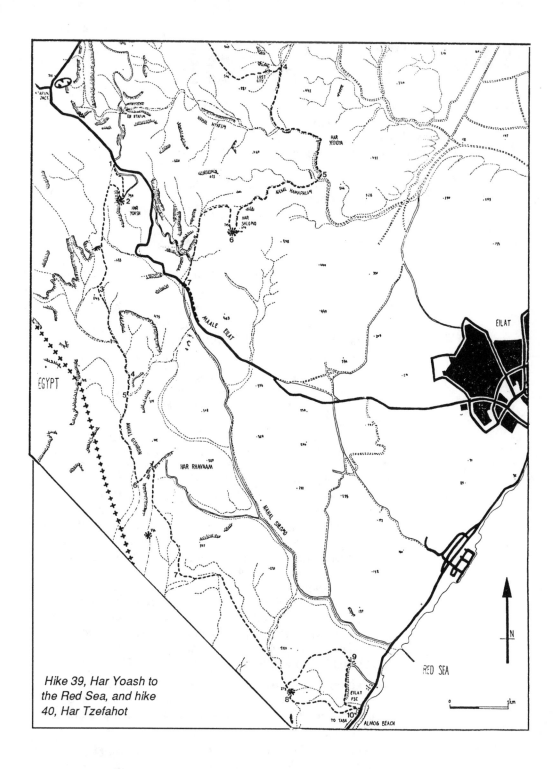

Hike 39, Har Yoash to the Red Sea, and hike 40, Har Tzefahot

EGYPT

EILAT

RED SEA

ALMOG BEACH

N

0 _____ km

Har Tzefahot

40

Points of interest: Panoramic view of Red Sea and Eilat.
Length of hike: 4 km. loop trip.
Hiking time: 3 hours.
Preferred season: All year.
Suitable for: All.
Maps: Eilat marked hiking trail map.
Special preparation: None.
Starting & ending point: Eilat Field Study Center.

To begin hike:

By bus: Take Eilat-Taba bus and get off at Eilat Field Study Center.

By car: Drive south from Eilat on route to Taba. About 6 km. south of the city, across from the Coral Beach Reserve is the Eilat Field Study Center. Here your hike begins.

Before beginning hike, step into the Field Study Center to get up-to-date information about hiking in the Eilat region. The guides will be happy to help you. The hike starts out on green-marked trail beginning north of the Field Study Center, just beyond the fence. (10) The trail then passes behind the Field Study Center and crosses Nahal Garinit to a low ridge just to the south. After a few hundred meters begin to climb up to Har Tzefahot. (8) Enjoy view at summit. From here you can see four different countries. Israel to the north, Jordan to the east, Saudia Arabia to the southeast, and Egypt, (Sinai) to the south and the west. Note the coral reefs in the clear waters of the Red Sea. Tzefaha in Hebrew is the name for a geological form of metamorphic rock called schist, a kind of sandstone or sedimentary rock which undergoes change under the tremendous heat and pressure beneath the earth's surface and many layers of sedimentary rock. The schist deposits, which are easily effected by erosion, are found as small thin layers of greyish rock which are used for floor tiles or sidewalks and to cover roofs. Within the schist deposits of Har Tzefahot you can observe shiny mica which reflects the light. Small amounts of quartz and feldspar can also be found around Har Tzefahot.

The geological nature of this area — typified by metamorphic rock — causes the small amounts of water that fall here to be absorbed quickly in the cracks which limits the amount of vegetation here.

See map on page 185

From Har Tzefahot join blue-marked trail which heads northwest along the ridge. The area is full of red porphyry dykes (magmatic seepages). Nahal Shlomo runs several km. north of Har Tzefahot. Williams, a British geologist, lived alone at the bottom of Nahal Shlomo until Israel gained control of Eilat in 1948. Williams surveyed the Eilat region and mined a small feldspar mine during World War II. Bedouins and Arabs from Aqaba worked the mines here in the Har Tzefahot vicinity. You can observe the remains of these mines and the large number of worker trails in the area.

After one km., the trail drops to a wadi. Take a right in the wadi. Wild watermelons grow here. In Arabic these are called 'snake watermelons.' The fruit is very bitter and inedible. Herbal medicine makes use of the wild watermelon to bring on diarrhea. The seeds are edible but must first be washed and roasted. The flesh of the fruit can be used as a poultice to ease rheumatic pain and when soaked in milk it is given as a purgative, a cure for jaundice and also to bring on abortion. The oil of the seeds is used to create a flame out of a spark of two flintstones. The oil is mentioned in the Mishnah (Oral Law), Shabbat 2:2 as an oil used for lamps.

The wadi reaches the Club Inn Hotel (9) near some acacia trees. Fifty meters down the paved road, a clear trail heads up to the right. Take it as you head right, south, back toward the Field Study Center. Williams excavated quite a bit along this trail.

Before Field Study Center take trail on ridge to the left and descend to Nahal Garinit back to the starting point. (10)

A Layer Spring

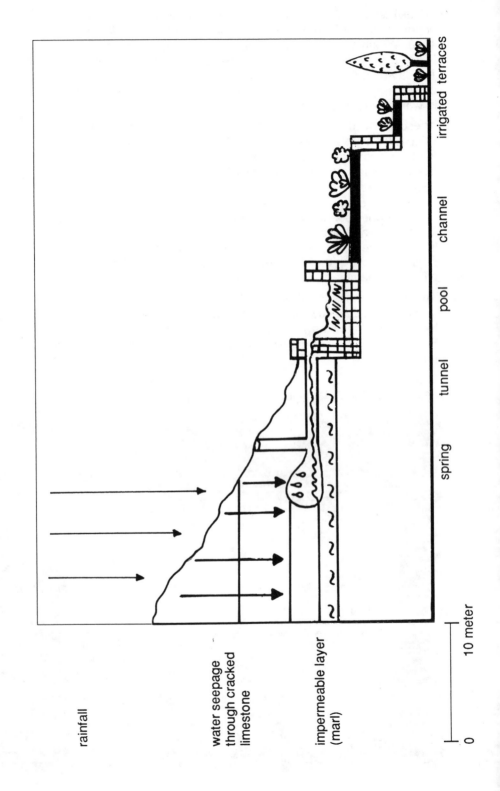

rainfall

water seepage
through cracked
limestone

impermeable layer
(marl)

spring   tunnel   pool   channel   irrigated terraces

0   10 meter

Notes

Notes